IMPERATORES VICTI

IMPERATORES VICTI

MILITARY DEFEAT AND ARISTOCRATIC COMPETITION IN THE MIDDLE AND LATE REPUBLIC

Nathan Rosenstein

University of California Press
Berkeley · Los Angeles · Oxford

University of California Press
Berkeley and Los Angeles, California

University of California Press, Ltd.
Oxford, England

© 1990 by
Nathan Rosenstein

Library of Congress Cataloging-in-Publication Data

Rosenstein, Nathan Stewart.
  Imperatores victi : military defeat and aristocratic
competition in the middle and late Republic / Nathan
Rosenstein.
       p.   cm.
  Includes bibliographical references.
    ISBN 0-520-06939-0
  1. Imperator (Roman title)—Political activity.   2.
Rome—Nobility—Political activity.   3. Rome—Politics
and government—265–30 B.C.   I. Title.
DG83.5.I6R67 1990
321'.14'0937—dc20   89-20653
                                                   CIP

1 2 3 4 5 6 7 8 9

For Mom and Dad, and Anne

Hardly a pure science, history is closer to animal husbandry than it is to mathematics in that it involves selective breeding of facts.

>   Tom Robbins, *Another Roadside Attraction*

Contents

Acknowledgments	xi
Introduction: The Problem of Limits on Aristocratic Competition	1
1. Military Failure, Political Success	9
2. Defeat and the *Pax Deorum*	54
3. Defeat and the *Virtus Militum*	92
4. The Aristocratic Ethos and the Preservation of Status	114
5. Conclusions and Implications	153
Appendix I. The *Imperatores Victi*	179
Appendix II. Powers of Promagistrates	205
Appendix III. Defeats against Hannibal	207
Bibliography	209
Index	217

Acknowledgments

Although this is a short book, many debts have been accumulated in the process of writing it, and I take great pleasure in acknowledging them here. I owe the largest to Erich Gruen. The problem of how the Roman Republic limited aristocratic competition, which has occupied me for nearly the past decade, was first conceived in conversation with him on a warm spring afternoon in 1980. This particular study grew out of his response to a footnote in a rambling and inchoate paper I wrote in 1984. He has contributed to its subsequent growth at every step of the way, always responding to my requests for his comments with unfailing generosity and kindness despite a crowded schedule, always offering in return acute, challenging, and salutary criticisms. What merit there may be in the book stems in no small measure from his efforts to improve it; its many imperfections are probably due to my refusal to take more of his advice.

Others have also been generous with their time and wisdom. Carlin Barton, Richard Billows, John North, and R.E.A. Palmer all read and commented on the manuscript in whole or in part and improved it considerably. I am particularly indebted also to Jerzy Linderski for sharing the enormous wealth of his erudition and especially for guiding a novice through the maze of the *res divina* at Rome. Few scholars could hope to be more fortunate than I have been in my colleagues—Jack Balcer, Timothy Gregory, John Guilmartin, Joseph Lynch, and Stephen Tracy. They as well as Richard Rothaus all read the manuscript in its entirety and greatly enhanced its quality. Needless to say, none of them is to blame for the shortcomings that remain. I am also grateful to Douglas O'Roark for compiling the bibliography. The Department of History and the College of Humanities at The Ohio State University as well as Franklin and Marshall College all generously provided support.

Above all, I owe a far greater debt to my wife, Anne Jewel, than I can possibly hope to express or repay for all the love and encouragement she has provided along the way, together with her good-natured toleration of the whole enterprise.

October 27, 1989
Columbus, Ohio

Introduction:
The Problem of Limits on
Aristocratic Competition

The government that led Rome's rise to world power in the middle and late Republic was founded on aristocratic competition. What drew men to the struggle was the prospect of personal honor and political authority.[1] Entry into the highest stratum of Roman society came with victory at the polls: for most of the history of the Republic those who won a curule magistracy could expect enrollment in the senate at the next census, but even before that date they enjoyed a senator's prerogatives. They perhaps also earned a place among the *nobilitas* and passed this distinction on to their sons.[2] Furthermore, winning public office was inseparably bound up with the moral imperatives of aristocratic status. *Virtus, gloria, dignitas*, and a constellation of associated ideals represented the highest aspirations of aristocratic endeavor, and although in the abstract the qualities these words defined were capable of various manifestations, only rarely and awkwardly in fact could they be revealed apart from service to the state. Hence the vital importance of winning public office and thereby gaining the chance to display them: the moral superiority that their possession implied, quite as much as membership in the senate or noble birth, enabled individuals to

---

1. E.g. Syme, *Roman Revolution*, 11; Taylor, *Party Politics*, 7; Scullard, *Roman Politics*, 1–4; Earl, *Moral and Political Tradition of Rome*, 16; Crawford, *Roman Republic*, 31; Beard and Crawford, *Rome in the Late Republic*, 53–55.

2. On enrollment and prerogatives, see Willems, *Le sénat*, 1:134. After Sulla's reforms membership became automatic following service as a quaestor; electoral victory thus remained the essential prerequisite for senatorial status. Brunt, *JRS* 72 (1982): 1–17; Mommsen, *Römisches Staatsrecht* (henceforth *StR*), 3^2: 462–63; and Afzelius, *Class. et Med.* 7 (1945): 150–200, all argue that election to any curule office bestowed *nobilitas* on the holder and his descendants; contra however, cf. Gelzer, *Roman Nobility*, 27–53, who sees *nobilitas* as the fruit of winning the consulate alone.

stake their claims to privileged status and define themselves as part of the ruling elite.³

But sometimes victory brought spoils more immediate and lucrative. Custom allowed the consuls who conquered the enemies of Rome to keep much of the booty they obtained, and their claims to use what remained in ways designed to benefit themselves were strong. Public monuments memorialized their conquests and gave concrete expression to the glory of their achievements for many years to come. In the short term lavish donatives to the soldiers achieved a similar result and might also ensure that if a commander sought further office, his men would remember his generosity at the polls.⁴ During the late Republic wealth grew even more entangled in the struggle for power and prominence. Candidates at times spent vast sums to win the offices that would lead to provincial assignments, where cash could be extorted to pay off debts, make fortunes, and furnish a basis for further ambition.⁵ Even apart from the opportunities for wealth, however, the *dignitas* of office and the *gloria* of a man's accomplishments in it opened the door to *auctoritas* at Rome. The nexus between achievement and influence was fundamental. Deliberations in the senate and assembly as well as the outcomes of elections were invariably swayed by the men who had held the chief magistracies of the Republic and conferred on it the greatest services. But opportunities to hold public office were strictly limited, particularly those offices that bestowed the highest status and offered scope for the greatest glory or plunder; once there, a man in most cases had only a year to distinguish himself. The result was fierce rivalry within the aristocracy, first to win the chance to manage the *res publica*, then to do so impressively and soon.⁶

Yet if the aristocrats looked on the *res publica* primarily as an arena in which to compete for personal advantage, the other side of the coin deserves equal emphasis: the Republic itself depended

---

3. Earl, *Sallust*, 18–27; idem, *Moral and Political Tradition of Rome*, 20–35; on *virtus* in Republican usage generally, see Eisenhut, *Virtus Romana*, 14–76.
4. Shatzman, *Historia* 21 (1972): 177–205; idem, *Senatorial Wealth*; on the scale of donatives in the first half of the second century, see Brunt, *Italian Manpower*, 393–94.
5. Badian, *Roman Imperialism*, 76–92; Shatzman, *Senatorial Wealth*.
6. The competitiveness of the aristocracy is well brought out by Wiseman, *Roman Political Life*, 3–16.

on this same competitive urge to survive and flourish. No professional bureaucracy directed public affairs at Rome; no monetary payment attached to any public office. Instead, the struggles of individuals for prominence were harnessed to accomplish the variety of mundane tasks essential to the smooth operation and welfare of the state. The senate, the courts, and all magistracies were staffed by interested aristocratic volunteers who competed eagerly for the privilege of serving the state. Without them the gods of the city would not have been honored, its legislation neither debated nor enforced, or its foreign policy fashioned and carried out. The whole diverse mass of public business would have simply ground to a halt and the Republic ceased to function. More important, the driving force behind the city's most spectacular accomplishments came from the same source. Rome's highest offices were by and large military, and triumphant warfare represented the pinnacle of personal glory. The men who trained and led the armies of the Republic and with them conquered its empire did so largely in the hopes of the personal and political rewards that came with success. The interdependence between the two was absolute: apart from the *res publica* there could be no aristocratic competition and no victory, but without that competition and the pressures that drove it the Republic itself was unthinkable.

Yet this linkage entailed a fundamental tension. The competitive drives indispensable to Roman public life could also create serious problems if taken to extremes or allowed to focus on the wrong objects. Hence ambition had to be reined in when it seemed to be going too far. Conducting wars made an important contribution to the safety and welfare of the city, but undertaking new ones was not always advantageous, and at times commanders needed to be held back in their quest for glory.[7] The profits from conquests enriched the treasury, yet too ruthless a pursuit of booty could sometimes be inexpedient and have to be suppressed.[8] The splendor of religious festivals pleased the deities and secured their continuing

---

7. E.g. Cn. Servilius Caepio's attempts in 203 (Livy 30.24.1–4); C. Cassius Longinus' attempts in 171 (Livy 43.1.4–12, cf. 5.1–10); M. Aemilius Lepidus' attempts in 137 (App. *Iber.* 80, cf. 83).

8. E.g. M. Popillius Laenas in 173 (Livy 42.7.3–9.6), C. Lucretius Gallus and others in 171–170 (Livy 43.4.8–13, 7.5–8.10), and M. Aurelius Cotta in 71 (Memnon *FGrH* 3B no. 434 frg. 39).

support. However, aediles zealous to fete the populace could overburden subjects and allies alike with demands for contributions to their games. These tendencies had to be kept in check.⁹ The beauty and utility of public buildings enhanced the quality of life at Rome, but censors seeking the renown of constructing the city's first stone theater, in the eyes of some, threatened the moral fiber of the citizens by making it possible for them thereafter to watch the games sitting down. Such a thing could not be allowed.¹⁰ More troubling still was the prospect of too much success: in a system of government built on the race for status and power, there was always the danger that one person would attain a position of such dominance that he could bring genuine competition in the political arena to an end.¹¹ Conversely, some solution had to be found to the problem posed by the losers the contests inevitably produced.¹² The costs of failure could be high given the value of success and at times might drive men too far in their struggles to win. Polybius foresaw problems of this sort looming in the future, and events during the hundred years following 133 B.C. might appear to underscore his prescience.¹³ Catiline for one justified his attempted putsch largely in terms of his failure to win sufficient honor and the defeats he had suffered in his quest for a consulship.¹⁴

Like modern capitalism, therefore, the Republican system needed to be regulated to protect it from the dangers arising out of its own inherent contradictions. There had to be limits on aristocratic competition. And certainly they existed: throughout centuries of intense, often bitter struggles for office and honor, the system endured and the state prospered. In the end, of course, they failed to hold, and political rivalry degenerated into the chaos

---

9. On aediles, for Ti. Sempronius Gracchus in 182, see Livy 40.44.12; for M. Caelius Rufus in 50, see Cic. *Fam.* 78 (8.2).2; 81 (8.4).5; 82 (8.9).3; 84 (8.8).10; 88 (8.6).5.

10. On censors of 154, see Livy *Per.* 48; Val. Max 2.4.2; Vell. Pat. 1.15.3; App. *BCiv.* 1.28; Oros. 4.21.4. The structure was ordered torn down. Fears about the conduct of public assemblies in the theater may also have been involved: cf. Taylor, *Roman Voting Assemblies*, 29–32.

11. Cf. the remarks of Brunt, *Fall of the Roman Republic*, 327–30.

12. The high incidence of political failure under the Republic has recently been reemphasized: Brunt, *JRS* 72 (1982): 15–16; Hopkins and Burton, *Death and Renewal*, 107–16; cf. Earl, *Moral and Political Tradition of Rome*, 14.

13. Poly. 6.57.5–6.

14. Sall. *Cat.* 35.3–4; Syme, *Sallust*, 71–72.

and bloodshed of civil war. But to focus principally on their collapse in 88 and again in 49 B.C. is to miss their obvious and striking effectiveness over the long haul. For years they kept the competitive engine from overheating, breaking down, or going completely out of control and shaking the Republic to pieces. Their operation not only brought stability but also thereby helped propel the Roman juggernaut down the road to empire.

But what were these limits? How did they arise, and how did they keep the system functioning smoothly? More important, how could they be enforced? No authority existed outside of the political elite to insist that people restrain their ambitions, yet its own closely-knit character ensured that many, if not most, of its members were highly partisan observers of the contests. By what means, therefore, could such men agree to repress personal ambition when doing so might confer an advantage on one side or another in political struggles? How were the interests that needed protecting defined? And is it possible to describe how all the various specific restraints combined to form a coherent system of limits that allowed the Republic and its rulers to gain the benefits of vigorous aristocratic competition while at the same time avoiding its costs?

These are large and important problems, lying at the heart of Roman public life and central to any understanding of its dynamics. Yet they have seldom been addressed and never been answered.[15] Instead, scholars have tended to view the political history of the Republic, where competition among the elite is most readily apparent, largely in terms of clashes among the participants involved. There some have seen conflict focusing on ideals and principles; others have found only a thinly disguised struggle for power and factional advantage.[16] Yet without denying the inherent importance of this approach, it is also possible to view such events in a broader perspective, to see in them the workings of an intricate and finely balanced system for keeping such battles within ac-

---

15. A notable exception is Hopkins and Burton, *Death and Renewal*, 80–81, on individuation.
16. This point is well illustrated in the controversy over the motives behind the reforms of Tiberius Gracchus: See Earl, *Tiberius Gracchus*; Brunt, *Gnomon* 37 (1965): 189, reviewing Earl. The debate is well summarized by Badian, *ANRW* 1.1 (1972): 673–76.

ceptable limits without diminishing the vigor of the competition itself.

The present study is an attempt to understand the workings of this system by studying the fate of *imperatores victi*, defeated generals. This neglected problem has far-reaching implications for our understanding of how aristocratic rivalry was controlled at Rome. Military success at all times represented an abundant source of prestige and political strength. Those who led the Republic's armies to victory usually enhanced their chances of securing higher office and increased their influence among their peers and the public at large. It has commonly been assumed that the converse held true, that lost battles spelled trouble in court or at the very least constituted a serious liability at the polls.[17] But as I will demonstrate in chapter 1, defeated generals suffered no discernible ill effects in the political arena as a consequence of their failures on the battlefield. Very few generals were brought to trial on charges arising out of their defeats. More significant still, the *imperatores victi* as a group went on to win the Republic's most highly coveted and hotly contested offices, the consulate and the censorship, in proportions virtually identical to those of their undefeated peers. Of those who did not, many continued to be prominent in public affairs and enjoy the trust of the senate. The sons of *victi* gained consulates and praetorships in their turn about as often as the sons of men who had lost no battles. Thus by every conceivable test military failure had no impact at all on the long-term rate of political success of the commanders involved. Public anger was muted; ambitious rivals were unable to tap it for partisan ends. Yet in a deeply competitive aristocratic culture, and in a society that went to war almost every year, military defeat should have profoundly affected the course of political rivalry. It ought to have set a *victus* back significantly, if not knocked him out of the race altogether. Yet it did not. Something intervened to constrain his rivals' predatory instincts and keep his lost battle from turning into a serious handicap in subsequent contests. Clearly, whatever produced this anomalous state of affairs represents an important limit at work within aristocratic competition.

---

17. E.g. Astin, *Scipio Aemilianus*, 159; Gruen, *Roman Politics*, 136; Sumner, *Orators in Cicero's Brutus*, 110; Suolahti, *Arctos* 11 (1977): 149–50; Hackl, *Senat und Magistratur*, 84; and, implicitly, Morgan, *Historia* 23 (1974): 209.

Having uncovered this limit, the problem becomes understanding how it operated. For reasons to be discussed at the end of chapter 1, the obvious answers do not suffice: the structure of the *comitia centuriata*, an informal understanding among the senatorial class, the imperatives of factional politics, as well as other explanations in and of themselves all prove incapable of accounting for its effectiveness. Instead, solutions need to be sought at a deeper level, within the religious, military, and moral values of Roman political culture. It is necessary in the first place to apprehend what contemporaries believed caused a battle to be lost. Patently, generals were not being blamed for their defeats. For that to have consistently been the case, most of their peers in the senate and the public at large had to conceive of the causes of defeat as something over which a general exercised only limited control. Thus, even if errors in command had been made, these could be viewed as insufficiently critical in the overall genesis of events to warrant opponents raising the issue afterward. The Romans of the middle and late Republic recognized two paramount sources of military success: the state of their accord with the gods and the quality of their fighting men. Hence in the two chapters that follow I will examine the potential of each to limit rivalry over the question of who was to blame for a defeat.

Yet that analysis does not tell the whole story. Contention for offices and other marks of honor commonly turned on the voters' estimation of the contenders' moral worth: *virtus*, *gloria*, and *fama*, together with a host of similar qualities, had much to do with determining whom the public chose to support. The continued political success of *victi* demonstrates clearly that failure in war brought with it no particular stigma. But why should that have been so, particularly since victory demonstrated *virtus*, bestowed *gloria*, and enhanced *fama*? Something had to have prevented the mere fact of having led Roman arms to defeat from becoming a source of opprobrium and hence damaging a man's status in the eyes of his countrymen. In chapter 4 I therefore explore how the aristocratic ethos of Rome could shield the reputation of a *victus* from censure by offering strategies for winning glory and respect even in defeat.

Chapter 5 concludes the study by exploring this limit in relation to the broader workings of the Republican system. First it is necessary to gain a clearer understanding of the ways in which the complex of beliefs and expectations described in chapters 2 through 4 were transformed into the votes that produced the results uncovered in chapter 1. An awareness of the cultural foundations of the limit allows the role of well-known structures within Roman politics to emerge clearly. Second is the question of origins and development: when and how did this limit first arise, and did the elements that sustained it evolve to produce a change in the treatment of defeated generals? The cluster of *victi* brought to trial in the latter half of the second century or the rise in the first century of new ways of understanding the religious causes of victory might suggest that the traditional beliefs and mores underpinning the limit were beginning to erode. Last, an assessment of its place within the larger system of limits governing aristocratic competition is essential. Ultimately, only the contribution of this limit to the central task of bringing stability to the competition and protecting the interests of the Republic and the class that ruled it could enable a practice that ran directly counter to the natural tendency of political rivalry to withstand for centuries the pressures it had to contain.

1

Military Failure, Political Success

The link between war and politics is now axiomatic in studies of Republican Rome.[1] The glory and wealth that the city's conquerors gained by their victories paved the way to office, authority, and enhanced prestige when they returned to civilian life. But did that connection obtain in the other direction as well? Was military failure likely to bring serious political damage in its train? Athens in the fifth and fourth centuries seems to offer an obvious analogy. Then, too, successful war leaders enjoyed great influence in the political arena, but those whose operations failed regularly paid a heavy price. Thucydides is the best known but by no means the only politician to have had a career cut short by the domestic fallout from a military defeat. Prosecutions on charges brought by *eisangelia* were a constant danger to *strategoi* after battles were lost or when foreign-policy initiatives went awry. At Carthage the consequences could be even more frightening. The citizens there evinced a singular brutality when their armies met defeat: Punic commanders were crucified.[2]

Common sense might suggest that punitive measures would have been equally prevalent at Rome. Military failure affected the citizens directly. The soldiers who filled the legions and suffered

---

1. Harris, *War and Imperialism*, 17–38.
2. On *eisangelia* trials, see Hansen, *Eisangelia*, 66–120; on the prosecution of Athenian commanders generally, see Pritchett, *Greek State at War*, 2:4–33; Roberts, *Accountability in Athenian Government*. The phenomenon is not restricted to Athens, however: see Pritchett, *Greek State at War*, 31. On crucifixion at Carthage, see Poly. 1.11.5, cf. Zonar. 8.9; App. *Pun.* 24; Dio frg. 43.18, cf. Zonar. 8.11, 8.17; Livy 22.61.15, 38.48.13; Val. Max. 2.7 ext. 1; by Carthaginian soldiers, see Livy *Per.* 17, cf. Oros. 4.8.4. To what extent crucifixion was normal in the event of failure is not entirely clear: the impression that it was may arise from hostile Roman propaganda that developed into a literary topos. Note, however, that the sins of defeated fathers could be visited on their sons at Carthage: the general Hamilcar died in his defeat at Himera, but his son Gescon was still banished as punishment for the loss (Diod. 13.43.5, 59.5).

most when battles were lost voted in the assemblies, if they returned alive.³ And whether they did or not, their suffering touched relatives and friends, among whom the men also had votes. Even Romans with no personal ties to those in the ranks could be moved by anger and fear when defeat damaged the prestige of their city or imperiled its safety, and a hostile populace at Rome had effective ways of lashing out. The bulk of aristocratic competition took place under its arbitration, in elections for office or through the deliberations of judicial assemblies.⁴ Hatred and a desire for vengeance against the commander responsible therefore ought to have made themselves felt at the polls, ending his chances for further honors and perhaps even being visited on his descendants. Even greater danger could come from the courts. A military defeat might furnish grounds for a capital charge, and all such cases, until late in the history of the Republic, came before the voters in the *comitia centuriata* for trial. To be effective, of course, public animosity needed leaders to marshal and focus it, but candidates would not have been lacking. Working up popular rage and exploiting it for political advantage or to humiliate a rival was commonplace among ambitious aristocrats. Men eager for office ought not to have let the electorate forget an opponent's earlier failures. Enemies should have been quick to bring a rival to trial when he had led Roman soldiers to defeat.

Certainly, anecdotal testimony confirms what intuition would surmise, that defeat could stir great animosity against the men in command. Harsh criticisms fill the sources, often couched as judgments by an ancient author but possibly deriving ultimately from

---

3. Cf. Caes. *BCiv.* 2.31.3: *felicitas rerum gestarum exercitus benevolentiam imperatoribus et res adversae odia colligant.* Although the votes that mattered most in Roman assemblies were generally those of the wealthy and so not always reflective of the sentiments of the rank and file as a whole, it must also be kept in mind that the wealthy bore a disproportionately greater burden of military service throughout most of the middle Republic and did not cease to serve thereafter: Nicolet, *World of the Citizen,* 111. One would therefore expect them to have been more alive to the consequences of military defeat and quicker to vent their anger against the men perceived to be responsible. Even in the first century Cicero could present the influence of the soldiery as not negligible in elections for the consulate and assert that their opinions carried considerable weight with their friends and the public at large (*Mur.* 38, cf. Nicolet, *World of the Citizen,* 143; more cautiously, Brunt, *Fall of the Roman Republic,* 429).

4. Miller, *JRS* 74 (1984): 1–19; cf. Finley, *Politics in the Ancient World,* 70, 84–96.

contemporary opinions that found their way into later accounts.[5] Others, however, refer specifically to what was said at the time in the army or at Rome. We know that public opinion bitterly censured P. Claudius Pulcher following his defeat at Drepana in 249.[6] After a loss to Hannibal at the Ticinus in 218, many in Rome laid the blame on the rashness of the consul Ti. Sempronius Longus, whereas the men serving under the dictator M. Minucius Rufus two years later attributed their near destruction in an ambush by the same foe to their commander's "overboldness."[7] Little had changed by the late Republic. The proconsul L. Licinius Lucullus had to hide his legate C. Valerius Triarius from an enraged mob of soldiers to save his life following the latter's disastrous loss to Mithridates in 67, and when a series of failures in Macedon led to the arraignment of C. Antonius Hibrida in 59, one of his prosecutors dwelt on the fact that the general had been sleeping off the effects of a drunken debauch when the enemy attacked.[8] Even a win might not be sufficient to stifle criticism: in letters to the senate a legate faulted L. Cornelius Merula, the consul of 193, for mismanaging a victory over the Boii in Gaul.[9]

More telling evidence still comes from the *victi* themselves. Fears of stirring up anger and hostility at Rome certainly motivated Longus' efforts to gloss over the reverse he had sustained when he

---

5. For example, Polybius' criticisms of C. Terentius Varro at 3.116.13 perhaps derive from Fabius Pictor (Walbank, *Historical Commentary* [henceforth *Comm.*], 1.448); sources for Livy's judgments on M. Centenius Paenula (25.19.12), Cn. Fulvius Centumalus (27.1.4–5), and L. Coelius (43.10.3–5) are far less certain but may derive from the testimony of sources contemporary with the events through one or more intermediaries.

6. Poly. 1.52.2–3.

7. On Sempronius, see Poly. 3.68.9; on Minucius, see Poly. 3.105.8. Note also a similar charge leveled against Flaminius (Livy 22.3.4, 14; cf. 22.9.7 but also the analysis at 22.1.6–7). For discussion of the historiographic tradition, see Will, "Imperatores Victi," *Historia* 32 (1983): 173–82.

8. On Valerius, see Plut. *Luc.* 35.1–2; on Antonius, see M. Caelius Rufus *ORF*[4] 17 (= Quint. *Inst.* 4.2.123–24). Note too L. Furius Medullinus in 381 (Livy 6.25.4–5); Sp. Postumius Albinus and T. Veturius Calvinus in 321 (Livy 9.5.6–8, 7.7–10); Q. Fabius Maximus Gurges in 292 (Livy *Per.* 11; Dio frg. 36.30–31; Oros. 3.22.6–9); P. Valerius Laevinus in 280 (Plut. *Pyrrh.* 18.1); P. Cornelius Rufinus and C. Iunius Brutus in 277 (Zonar. 8.6); M. Livius Macatus (Poly. 8.30.5–6; Livy 27.25.3–5); Ap. Claudius Centho in 169 (Livy 43.11.10); Q. Titurius Sabinus in 54 (Caes. *BGall.* 5.52).

9. Livy 35.6.8–10. Cf. Cicero's criticisms of L. Calpurnius Piso's campaigns in Thrace (below, pp. 52–53) although Piso himself apparently considered them victorious.

wrote to the senate late in 218 as well as similar attempts at concealment on the part of Q. Marcius Philippus after his failures in 186.[10] Q. Pompeius' strenuous denials that his failures in Spain had led him to seek a treaty with the Numantines must also have stemmed from concern over a possible public backlash.[11] Undoubtedly, each hoped to avoid antagonism of the sort M. Claudius Marcellus encountered in 209 after a defeat by Hannibal or A. Manlius Vulso met in 178 when the Istrians drove him from his camp; for in a system like Rome's, where the *populus* bore the brunt of the mistakes made in command and yet was also the final arbiter in aristocratic competition, such outrage could lead to grave political consequences.[12] The bitter animosity that greeted the return of C. Hostilius Mancinus following his debacle at Numantia in 137 helped pass the bill to hand him over to the enemy; the anger aroused against A. Postumius Albinus in 110 fueled the popular agitation leading to the Mamilian *quaestio*; the tumultuous prosecution and exile of Q. Servilius Caepio in 104 grew out of the *luctus et odium* engendered by his defeat at Arausio.[13] These men felt the effects of the passions defeat could set loose, and they were not alone. All told, between twelve and fourteen men suffered criminal prosecution following military defeats between 390 and 49 B.C., and others feared the same treatment.[14]

A broader analysis tells a different story, however. In the same 340-year period between the disaster at the river Allia, which cul-

---

10. On Sempronius: Poly. 3.75.1; on Philippus: Livy 39.20.9–10, 23.1, and see further below, pp. 15–16.
11. App. *Iber.* 79, 83; cf. appendix 1.1, no. 69.
12. On Marcellus, see appendix 1.1, no. 18; on Manlius: Livy 41.6.1–3, 7.4–10; on the attack on his camp, see Livy 41.1.1–4.8, 5.1–2. Manlius and his colleague subsequently defeated the Istrians in pitched battle (Livy 41.10.1–13).
13. On Mancinus, see Cic. *De Or.* 1.181, *Har. Resp.* 43, *Brut.* 103; Plut. *Ti. Gracch.* 7.1; App. *Iber.* 80; on Postumius, see Sall. *Iug.* 39.2; on Caepio, see Cic. *De Or.* 2.124, cf. 199–203; *Part. Or.* 105; *Brut.* 135. Note also the outcry after the defeat at Lake Trasimene (Poly. 3.85.7–9; Livy 22.7.6–9).
14. Appendix 1.1, nos. 3, 4, 20, 35, 44, 46, 51(?), 65(?), 67, 69, 71, 74, 80, 81. On no. 65, see below, pp. 141–42. Not counted here are no. 43, who was tried and convicted before his father, who presided over a family tribunal; no. 75, who may not have been defeated and in any event escaped trial; and L. Cornelius Lentulus Lupus, who likewise probably never sustained a defeat in battle (below p. 186). On fears of prosecution, for L. Aemilius Paullus at Cannae, see Livy 22.49.11; for Q. Pompeius in Spain, see App. *Iber.* 79; cf. the remark of Cn. Pompeius Magnus in 67 (Dio 36.26.2). The authenticity of these reports is doubtful, but their presence in the literary tradition is significant. Note also the attempt to prosecute A. Manlius Vulso (Livy 41.6.1–3, 7.4–10).

minated in the sack of Rome by the Gauls, and the outbreak of the civil war between Pompey and Caesar as many as ninety-two commanders of varying ranks sustained defeat in battle against the foreign enemies of Rome, survived, and returned to the city having achieved no subsequent victory to offset the earlier loss. Fifty-eight of these men may, with some degree of certainty, be said to have been seriously defeated by the enemy.[15] Taking all these men as a group and those badly defeated as a subgroup, one might expect to find clear indications that members of one or both labored thereafter under a severe handicap in competition with other aristocrats. But surprisingly, none can be discovered. The most obvious test to determine the harm a military defeat could do to a general's political career is to ask how well such men did in later contests for election to high public office. Here no correlation between a lost battle and defeat at the polls can be established. Out of all these *imperatores victi*, roughly a quarter to a third (between twenty-six and thirty-three) went on to hold another elective magistracy, whereas of the fifty-eight who suffered major defeats, about the same proportion (between seventeen and twenty) won subsequent elections.[16]

The censorship represented the pinnacle of any aristocrat's political ambitions; as a result, contention was more strenuous here than for any other office. Military failure ought to have made a significant difference in a candidate's chances, but the evidence indicates otherwise. One of the censors for 136, Q. Fulvius Nobilior, had suffered a series of reverses with heavy loss of life at the hands

---

15. For a list of all commanders defeated in this period, see appendix 1.1. All those who exercised de facto independent commands, whatever their specific rank, are included in this study, and terms like *imperator*, general, etc., are to be understood as referring to *legati* as well as magistrates and promagistrates.

16. For all *victi* who held subsequent office, see appendix 1.1, nos. 2, 7, 8, 11, 13, 18, 19, 24, 26, 27, 32, 36, 38, 39, 41, 45, 52, 59, 60, 61, 69, 72, 75, 77, 82, 87; in addition, the following may have held higher office: nos. 23, 28, 43, 55, 76, 88, 91. The proportion is between 28 percent and 35.8 percent. Those who were seriously defeated and held subsequent office: nos. 2, 7, 8, 11, 18, 19, 24, 26, 36, 39, 41, 52, 61, 69, 72, 82; uncertain: 43, 55, 76, 91. The proportion is between 29 percent and 34 percent. In neither case are no. 4, censor in 42, or L. Cornelius Lentulus Lupus, the censor of 147, included in the reckoning. Note that many *victi* may have entertained no ambitions for election to further office. That would make the number of those who did and were successful an even larger percentage of the total group of *victi* who entered subsequent competition.

of the Celtiberians in Spain during his consulate in 153. Back at Rome, in the following year, he had even made a point of spreading stories about the damage his army had sustained in those battles and the prowess of the enemy. He became censor, notwithstanding his defeats.[17] One of the very next pair of censors, Q. Pompeius, had also fared badly in Spain as consul in 141, so much so that he feared he would be put on trial when he returned to Rome. He opened negotiations with the Numantines, which issued in what he asserted was a *deditio in fidem* by the enemy but they and even his own officers insisted was a *foedus*. The latter was anathema in the eyes of the senate, which rejected the agreement. In 136 Pompeius had to fight off an attempt to hand him over to the enemy as the senate sought to invalidate his treaty. But a mere five years later, in 131, he too won the Republic's highest office, the first occasion on which two plebeians were elected to serve together in that post. Here his poor record in Spain is of particular significance since he was initially running against another plebeian, Q. Metellus Macedonicus, for the single censorship traditionally filled by a member of that order. Macedonicus, moreover, had won a splendid victory in his praetorship against Andriscus and capped it with a triumph afterward. As consul he had also gained important successes in Spain, in striking contrast with Pompeius' failures there. Yet enough voters supported his opponent, despite the latter's miserable performance in Spain, to produce the unprecedented elevation of both men.[18]

In 70 B.C. L. Gellius Poplicola and Cn. Cornelius Lentulus Clodianus each secured election to the censorship, the first time anyone had filled that office in fifteen years. Yet when they had shared the consulate two years before, each had performed so poorly against Spartacus that the senate felt compelled to take control of

---

17. Appendix 1.1, no. 36. To be sure, he had been eligible for the censorships of 147 and 142 and apparently failed of election; but see below, p. 20.

18. Appendix 1.1, no. 69. On Macedonicus' victories, see the sources collected in *Magistrates of the Roman Republic* (henceforth *MRR*) 1:461, 467, 475. On the politics involved, see Astin, *Scipio Aemilianus* 237. There was no shortage of eligible patricians who might have sought the censorship at this election: Cn. Servilius Caepio, cos. 141; his brother Q. Servilius Caepio, cos. 140; P. Cornelius Scipio Nasica Serapio, cos. 138; M. Aemilius Lepidus Porcina, cos. 137 (himself defeated in Spain); and L. Furius Philus, cos. 136. That the voters chose to overlook their claims and instead break with tradition to elevate two plebeians clearly demonstrates lack of importance for them of a military defeat.

the war against him out of their hands altogether. Neither man could claim to be a potent force in politics in his own right; strong support was necessary—probably from Pompey and possibly from Crassus as well, the consuls of 70—to resurrect the office of censor and then put them in it. Pompey and Crassus, however, were not in a position to dictate to the assembly at that point. The situation was delicate and their potential enemies many, including one another. Electable candidates, not liabilities, were required. It would be strange and surprising indeed if Pompey and perhaps Crassus had thrown their weight behind two men whose defeats had otherwise ruined any further chances at the polls and now furnished a lightning rod for hostility and opposition. Instead, the support they received suggests that military failure had not ended the political usefulness of Gellius and Lentulus.[19]

At the highest level of political competition, therefore, lost battles did not prove decisive for the fortunes of these *imperatores victi* or the four or five others who also reached the censorship.[20] The same phenomenon is evident among those who went on to consulates following defeats. Q. Marcius Philippus, consul in 186, affords the most telling example: four thousand soldiers are said to have lost their lives to the Ligurians when he entered a wooded area without adequate reconnaissance and stumbled into an ambush on a narrow pass. Three legionary and eleven allied standards fell into the hands of the enemy, together with an abundance

---

19. Appendix 1.1, nos. 24, 39. On the question of collaboration between Pompey, Crassus, and the censors of 70, see Ward, *Marcus Crassus*, 104–5, cf. 24–25; Marshall, *Crassus*, 30; on doubts, see Brunt, *Fall of the Roman Republic*, 475. Yet if Pompey and Crassus did not promote the candidacy of Gellius and Clodianus, then their election on the strength of their own merits and in spite of their failures against Spartacus is all the more remarkable. On the political position of Pompey and Crassus in 70, see Sherwin-White, *JRS* 46 (1956): 5–9, contra, however, cf. Stockton, *Historia* 22 (1973): 205–18.

20. The others are P. Aelius Paetus, appendix 1.1, no. 2; L. Cornelius Scipio Barbatus, no. 27; P. Licinius Crassus, no. 45; L. Marcius Censorinus, no. 59; and M. Claudius Marcellus, no. 19, if the defeat he suffered came after, rather than before, his victory. Note too L. Calpurnius Piso Frugi, no. 13; L. Furius Medullinus, no. 38; Q. Marcius Philippus, no. 61; and C. Antonius Hibrida, no. 4, although this last censorship came during the second triumvirate and can hardly be considered the result of normal political competition. Note also the censorship of L. Calpurnius Piso Caesoninus, procos. 57–55, whom Cicero castigates repeatedly for military failures (*Sest.* 71; *Prov. Cons.* 5; *Pis.* 91–92), although he seems to have claimed victories (below, p. 52). L. Cornelius Lentulus Lupus, appendix 1.1, 186, was censor in 147 but probably did not sustain a defeat.

of weapons. So serious were his losses that Philippus thought it wise to disband his army well away from Rome to conceal their extent and absent himself from the city until his term of office expired. He became consul for the second time fifteen years later, in 169, and his *cursus* in the meantime hardly suggests that he found himself in the political wilderness as a result of his disaster. He served as an ambassador three years later in 183, became a *decemvir s.f.* in 180, and was sent once again on an embassy to Greece in 172–171 to conduct sensitive negotiations during the diplomatic crisis that preceded the outbreak of the Third Macedonian War.[21]

Another consul, Cn. Cornelius Scipio, unwisely attempted to capture Lipara in 260 during the First Punic War and quickly found himself surrounded by the enemy. According to Carthaginian sources, his predicament compelled his surrender, whereas in the Roman version he was lured to a conference and there treacherously made a prisoner. Neither tradition, however, denies that he had gotten himself and his forces into dire straits at the time. He returned to Rome in an exchange of prisoners soon thereafter and, bearing his new nickname Asina, became consul for the second time for 254. Now perhaps wiser, he once again set out to command a Roman army against the Carthaginians.[22]

Nor are these cases unparalleled. Cn. Baebius Tamphilius, praetor in 199, lost more than two-thirds of his forces when a rash attack on the Insubrian Gauls backfired. He won a consulship for 182, albeit after more than one unsuccessful attempt.[23] However, L. Calpurnius Piso and M'. Manilius, praetors in 154, had much less time to wait before advancing the next rung up the *cursus honorum* following a severe defeat at the hands of the Lusitanians. Manilius was consul in 149, Piso in 148.[24] Ser. Sulpicius Galba, praetor in 151, saw an important victory against the same enemy evaporate when the fleeing Spaniards rounded on their pursuers and chased the Romans from the field, cutting them to pieces in their turn. His opponents endeavored to bring him to trial in 149, but the charges

21. Appendix 1.1, no. 61.
22. Appendix 1.1, no. 26; on the divergent traditions regarding his capture, see Walbank, *Comm.* 1:76–77.
23. Appendix 1.1, no. 8.
24. Appendix 1.1, nos. 11, 52.

were treacherously murdering and enslaving the Lusitanians who had surrendered to him in 150. There is no indication that his earlier defeat played any part in the animosity stirred up against him at that time; in any event, the case never came to trial. But Galba did become consul in 144.²⁵ Even A. Postumius Albinus, the ill-omened legate left in charge of his brother Spurius' army, went on to become consul in 99 despite the degradation to which his foolishness had led: the Numidian king Jugurtha lured him into a trap in 110 and then forced him to capitulate along with all of his soldiers.²⁶ Altogether as many as seventeen men held consulships following military defeats either serious or minor, and four other commanders of varying ranks subsequently secured praetorships.²⁷

Noteworthy as well are two men who entertained hopes of winning the consulship after serious defeats but failed in their attempts. L. Manlius Vulso ran in 216 after having been routed and then besieged by the Boii in 218. Q. Arrius shared in the consul Gellius' defeat against Spartacus in 72 and aspired in 59 to one of the consulships for the following year. Both men were unsuccessful, but the very fact that they were in the running—in Manlius' case less than two years after his loss—suggests that they did not anticipate that public reaction to the defeats would block their election. Nor does the evidence offer any support for that notion: they were disappointed in their hopes owing to the broader machinations of politics rather than any animus against them personally. Arrius missed his consulate when the backing he expected from Pompey, Crassus, and Caesar failed to materialize and he had to drop out of the race. Manlius was compelled to stand aside along with his rivals by a consensus within the aristocracy in favor of a compromise candidate to meet the military and political crisis of 216.²⁸

---

25. Appendix 1.1, no. 82.
26. Appendix 1.1, no. 72.
27. The other consuls are appendix 1.1, nos. 7, 13, 18, 23, 28, 32, 38, 43(?), 60; and no. 75, if the tradition which reports his defeat is genuine. Not included in this reckoning of consuls are two very doubtful cases, nos. 55 and 76. The praetors are nos. 41, 77, 88(?), 91(?), the first and last of whom were being elevated to that office for the second time.
28. Appendix 1.1, nos. 5, 58. On the political crisis of 216, see Gruen, *CSCA* 11 (1978): 61–74; Twyman, *CPh* 79 (1984): 285–94.

Thus the assumption that military failure simply precluded a man's chances for further office is completely without foundation. Moreover, no simple correlation can be established between the magnitude of a defeat and subsequent chances for advancement. Men like Scipio Asina, Marcius Philippus, A. Postumius Albinus, and Q. Fulvius Nobilior went on to higher magistracies despite serious losses, whereas P. Sulpicius Saverrio, L. Calpurnius Piso, M. Fabius Hadrianus, and C. Claudius Glaber suffered only minor defeats yet never rose higher than the magistracies they held at the time. Indeed, no evidence suggests that as a group the defeated generals' chances of future electoral victory were any worse than their undefeated peers'. Forty-two men of consular rank lost battles without winning subsequent victories between 300 and 49 B.C., when the bulk of Roman defeats occurred. Six were exiled, and three died before they could stand for election to a censorship, leaving thirty-three to compete the next time a contest for that office took place. Of these, nine were victorious—about 27 percent. If the six exiled consulars are included in the pool, the proportion is about 23 percent.[29] If we restrict consideration to consulars who can with certainty be said to have sustained a serious defeat, two of these thirty commanders died, six were exiled, and six of the twenty-two who remained won censorships—again about 27 percent. If the exiled consulars once more are brought into the reckoning, about 21 percent (six of twenty-eight) of all seriously defeated consulars advanced to the apex of the *cursus honorum*.[30] With

29. For all defeated consuls, 300–49 B.C., see appendix 1.1, nos. 1–4, 6, 10, 12, 14, 18–20, 24–28, 33, 36, 39–42, 44, 45, 47, 51, 53, 57, 59, 61, 62, 65, 69–71, 74, 75, 78, 81, 84, 85, 89; those exiled: nos. 4, 7, 51, 71, 74, 81; those who died: nos. 18, 25, 62; those elected: nos. 2, 19, 24, 27, 36, 39, 45, 59, 69. Note too no. 61, elected after a second consulate. Leaving aside three doubtful defeats, nos. 1, 19, and 75, the proportions are, out of thirty consulars, eight censors (26.6 percent); including men exiled, out of thirty-six consulars, eight censors (22.2 percent). The percentages offered represent only very approximate orders of magnitude owing to the small numbers involved.

30. For consuls seriously defeated, 300–49 B.C., see appendix 1.1, nos. 2–4, 6, 14, 18–20, 24–26, 33, 36, 39, 41, 42, 44, 47, 51, 57, 61, 65, 69, 71, 74, 75, 78, 81, 85, 89; those exiled were the same as in note 29 above; those who died: nos. 18, 25; those elected: nos. 2, 19, 27, 36, 39, 61, 69. If two doubtful defeats, nos. 19 and 75, are left aside, the proportions are, out of twenty consulars, five censors (25 percent); if the men exiled are included, out of twenty-six consulars, five censors (19.2 percent). L. Cornelius Lentulus Lupus, censor in 147, is not included in any of these reckonings.

these figures may be compared an overall rate of about one in five of all consulars going on to become censors.[31]

A similar reckoning can be made one grade lower. Of the thirty-one men of praetorian rank who sustained defeats in that office or subsequently, eight or nine later became consuls.[32] This figure can be made more meaningful by restricting consideration to the years 197 to 81 B.C., when six praetors were elected annually. Hence about one in every three went on to hold a consulate during this period.[33] How did the twenty-one praetors who lost battles within these years fare as a group? Three were exiled; of the eighteen remaining, six or seven went on to become consuls, slightly better than a third. Of the thirteen who sustained serious defeats, three or four held subsequent consulates—23 or 30 percent, a little below average but still not much less than what a random distribution would produce.[34] In view of the smallness of the numbers involved, the difference is not significant. Thus the performance of defeated praetors mirrors that of defeated consuls. In neither case can it be said that overall the members of these groups were any less likely than undefeated men at the same rank to reach the next-higher office.

---

31. In this period 106 men won censorships; roughly five hundred consuls were elected, allowing for suffect consuls elected to replace those who died in office, whose elections were flawed, who served more than once, or who never entered office because of bribery convictions. It should also be noted that in the third century cases of nonconsular censors are known, as in 209, which means that the ratio of censors to consuls was actually slightly higher.

32. For the defeated praetors, see appendix 1.1, nos. 5, 7, 8, 11, 13, 16, 17, 21, 23, 29, 34, 35, 43, 46, 48, 49, 52, 54–56, 58, 60, 64, 66, 67, 72, 76, 79, 80, 82, 91; those elected consul: nos. 7, 8, 11, 13, 23, 43 (?), 52, 60, 82.

33. However, the ratio is only approximate owing to the fact that four praetors were elected in 179 and possibly 177: Livy 40.44.2; *MRR* 1:392, 398 and 399 and n.1. Note too that the chances of praetors elected in the late 80s going on to the consulship were diminished by the increase in the number of praetors elected annually after 80 B.C.

34. For all defeated praetors, 197–81 B.C., see appendix 1.1, nos. 11, 13, 16, 21, 23, 29, 43, 46, 48, 49, 52, 56, 60, 64, 66, 67, 72, 76, 79, 80, 82; those exiled: nos. 46, 67, 80; those elected: nos. 11, 13, 23, 43 (?), 52, 60, 82. The variation is due to uncertainty over the identity of no. 43. Those seriously defeated: nos. 11, 16, 21, 29, 43, 48, 49, 52, 64, 66, 67, 76, 82; those elected: nos. 11, 43 (?), 52, 82. If the exiled are counted, out of twenty-one *victi*, six or seven consuls (28.5–33 percent). None of those exiled sustained a serious defeat.

Yet apart from aggregates and averages, can a convincing argument be made that a defeat hindered any particular person from reaching the next rung on the *cursus honorum*? Caution is required: with information on any single electoral contest scarce for most of the history of the Republic, such questions more readily invite speculation than permit certainty. Still, common sense would seem to make the validity of the proposition self-evident, and therefore the issue is worth exploring in some detail.

The censorship offers little to support such a case. Contests here involved men whose political strength was already exceptional. Since so many contenders with impressive lineage, outstanding achievements, wealth, or popularity who had not lost battles went down to defeat or refused to run at all, it is well-nigh impossible to assert that the failure of any *victus* to win a censorship was due primarily to his lost battle rather than to the strength of the opponents he faced. Certainly, M'. Manilius' or L. Calpurnius Piso Caesoninus' lack of success in the war against Carthage during 149 and 148 was not primarily responsible for keeping either of them from becoming censor in 142. The triumph three years before of the victorious plebeian candidate L. Mummius over the Achaeans and the Corinthians would have tipped the balance decisively in his favor against virtually any rival.[35] This victory, rather than Q. Fulvius Nobilior's poor showing in Spain, also accounts for the fact that the latter had to wait until 136 for his censorship.[36] It cannot be plausibly maintained that Q. Fabius Maximus Servilianus failed to obtain the patrician place for the censorship of 136 (assuming that he ran) against Ap. Claudius Pulcher simply because he had been defeated by Viriathus. Claudius, it is true, had been victorious against the Salassi and celebrated a triumph, but the same enemy had badly defeated him previously, and either the senate refused to authorize the triumph or Claudius himself thought it prudent not to ask. He triumphed at his own expense and only by virtue of the protection afforded by his daughter, a vestal virgin,

---

35. Appendix 1.1, nos. 53, 13; sources on Mummius' triumph are collected in *MRR* 1:470; for its importance in securing his election, see Astin, *Scipio Aemilianus*, 113–14.

36. Appendix 1.1, no. 36. Fulvius also could have run in 147. Yet military failure cannot have been much of a handicap in that race since the successful plebeian was L. Marcius Censorinus, whose performance against the Carthaginians as consul in 149 had been dismal (appendix 1.1, no. 59).

against the threat of a tribunician veto. Yet the populace elected him censor and gave him as a plebeian colleague Q. Fulvius Nobilior, who himself had suffered serious defeats in Spain. Nobilior's success in reaching the censorship also makes it difficult to see M. Popillius Laenas' failure against the Numantines in 138 as the factor that kept him from being a viable contender for the plebeian seat in the same election.[37]

Similarly, in the elections for 131, discussed above, two plebeians were returned for the first time: one had celebrated a praetorian triumph and fought successfully in Nearer Spain, and the other had suffered a series of defeats in that same province. Is it, therefore, reasonable to suppose that M. Popillius Laenas, M. Aemilius Lepidus, Q. Calpurnius Piso, or any of the other commanders who had proved equally unsuccessful against the Spaniards failed to obtain election for this censorship owing to their defeats?[38] Losses at the hands of Spartacus cannot have meant much to the voters in 70 if C. Cassius Longinus was campaigning for the censorship in that year, seeing that they made censors out of two men who had received similar drubbings from the slaves.[39] Such examples make it nearly impossible to attribute the failures of P. Sulpicius Saverrio, Ti. Sempronius Longus, Cn. Papirius Carbo, M. Iunius Silanus, and others to reach the censorship to losses sustained against the enemies of Rome. The political strength of their opponents, about which the sources preserve too little information, is far more likely to have been decisive for these men in view of the fact that other *victi* not only won censorships over men who had not lost battles but also won them as often as their undefeated peers. Hence efforts to prove that a defeat kept any specific person from a censorship who would otherwise have won it seem doomed to failure without explicit evidence to the contrary, and none appears forthcoming.

---

37. Appendix 1.1, nos. 33, 36, 70; Servilianus' treaty with Viriathus may have been held against him, although it is important to remember it had initially been ratified by the *populus*. But if so, then it, not the defeat, was the key factor. For sources on Ap. Claudius' triumph, see Oros. 5.4.7; Dio frg. 74.2; cf. Cic. *Cael.* 34; Val. Max. 5.4.6; Suet. *Tib.* 2. On his defeat and subsequent victory, see Livy *Per.* 53; Dio frg. 74.1; Obseq. 21; Oros 5.4.7. A full discussion is in Astin, *Scipio Aemilianus*, 107–8.
38. Appendix 1.1, nos. 70, 2, 10.
39. Appendix 1.1, no. 14.

Rivalry for the consulship tells a similar story. Of the praetors who lost a battle in office or subsequently and did not go on to become consul, one must ask at the outset how many of them would have been strong contenders for that magistracy had they not suffered a military defeat?[40] Four should be put out of the reckoning at once: D. Iunius Silanus committed suicide; Cn. Fulvius Flaccus was condemned for cowardice in battle; L. Licinius Lucullus and C. Servilius, governors of Sicily in 103 and 102, both succumbed to prosecutions arising out of maladministration in that province.[41] Five others were without forebears who had achieved high office at Rome. These men had done well to reach the praetorship; *novi homines* could rarely hope for more.[42] Two others, L. Licinius Murena and P. Licinius Nerva, were from families that, although prominent recently and destined for greater things, had not advanced beyond praetorian rank at the time they held that office. Their chances of gaining a consulate would appear to have been slim under any circumstances.[43] The ancestors of C. and L. Plautius Hypsaeus, praetors in 146 and 135 respectively, had been eminent in the fourth century but not since.[44] Descent is difficult to trace for the various Manlii who held praetorships in 136, 79,

---

40. Some of the assumptions about the workings of Republican politics in what follows have come in for heavy criticism in recent years: see below, p. 51. The argument at this stage, however, does not require their validity. It is only necessary to show that even if one were to accept these hypotheses, one could still not make a convincing case that a defeat kept any particular *victus* from subsequently achieving public office. If one rejects the underlying assumptions, of course, then one is left without any specific cases with which to contest the general pattern described above.

41. Appendix 1.1, nos. 43, 35, 46, 80; on Lucullus and Servilius, see further below, chap. 4, pp. 142–44.

42. Q. Arrius, appendix 1.1, no. 5; Sex. Digitius, no. 29; L. Fufidius, no. 34; C. Nigidius, no. 64; P. Varinius, no. 91. The point is not vitiated by Hopkins and Burton's finding in *Death and Renewal*, 31–69, at table 2.4 that 26 percent of all consuls between 249 and 50 B.C. show no consular father, grandfather, great-grandfather, uncle, or previous consular brother or praetorian father. This figure takes into consideration only direct male ascendants on the paternal side of the family. Were it possible to include in it *any* family connection to a noble *gens* on either the paternal or maternal side, the percentage would in all probability have to be significantly reduced. On the strength of the bond between a mother's family and her children, see Hallett, *Fathers and Daughters*, 76–149.

43. Appendix 1.1, no. 48, 49. Note that according to Hopkins and Burton, *Death and Renewal*, table 2.4, only 5 percent of consuls between 139 and 50 B.C. are known to have had fathers who rose no higher than the praetorship.

44. Appendix 1.1, nos. 67, 68. Presumably the father of one or both men was L. Plautius Hypsaeus, who reached the praetorship in 189 but advanced no farther.

and 72, but even allowing for a direct connection to the great *gens* of earlier ages, that family went into decline following the first third of the second century. No Manlius appears in the consulate again until 65.⁴⁵ The plebeians Claudius Unimanus and C. Claudius Glaber probably had at best only distant links with the more illustrious bearers of that name and were not likely to have drawn strength from that connection.⁴⁶ It was certainly not impossible for any of these men to have reached the consulship; others similarly situated did. But many more did not. Unless bolstered by some splendid accomplishment or unusual political acumen or possessed of some other source of powerful support, the odds that men of such backgrounds would become consuls must be accounted long at the outset. Since none of them can be shown to have been likely to reach the consulate but for the fact of his having lost a battle, their cases offer no support to the notion that the battles they lost were the pivotal events in their political careers.

Four other men may have stood a somewhat better chance. L. Manlius Vulso reached the praetorship in 218 at a time when his family boasted many consuls. As noted, he ran for that office himself in 216 but was compelled to stand aside in favor of a compromise candidate. He ought to have tried again, but fate intervened: he fell into enemy hands after Cannae and probably spent much of the remainder of the war as a prisoner.⁴⁷ A praetor named Quinctius was defeated in 143 in Spain. Possibly he had some connection with the Quinctii Flaminini who held consulates in 150 and 126, but the matter hardly admits of certainty and hence cannot contribute to the argument one way or the other.⁴⁸ The consul Rutilius deprived C. Perperna, a legate in 90, of his command after a major defeat. The latter was the son of M. Perperna, consul in 130, and the brother of M. Perperna, who held that same office in 92 and would go on to become censor in 86. However, a consulate for Gaius would have been out of the question following Sulla's victory in 81 because of the family's Marian sympathies, whereas during the *Cinnae dominatio* in the 80s the political calculations of the re-

---

45. Appendix 1.1, nos. 56, 55, 54.
46. Appendix 1.1, nos. 21, 17.
47. Appendix 1.1, no. 58.
48. Appendix 1.1, no. 76. If, however, this man is to be identified as Q. Pompeius, then he became consul in 141, his defeat notwithstanding.

gime determined to whom such offices went. Gaius' failure to advance in these years owes more to the exigencies of those in power than to any disadvantage his defeat represented at the polls.[49]

Only Ap. Claudius Centho, cousin to the Pulchri and Nerones and, like them, able to trace his descent back through Ap. Claudius Caecus to the earliest years of the Republic, may have enjoyed strong chances of reaching the consulate at the start of his career.[50] Although his father had failed to win election as either praetor or consul, his paternal grandfather had been consul in 240, censor in 225, and dictator in 213.[51] Although the degree to which his defeat in Illyria impeded his further rise cannot be known with any certainty, Centho is nonetheless the only one out of all the defeated praetors for whom such claims can plausibly be made. Such an assertion hardly seems enough to support the hypothesis that defeat had a decisive impact on anyone else's political future, particularly in view of the normal rate of advance overall of defeated praetors to the consulate.[52] At the lower levels of the *cursus honorum*, among the various persons below praetorian rank who never reached even that stage, the story is much the same: they never climbed to the highest offices of the Republic because they were *novi homines* or from families obscure or eclipsed, or because their chances would for other reasons have been poor to begin with even if they had suffered no military defeat.[53]

But perhaps defeat affected the speed with which one could expect to move on to further offices, as the example of Cn. Baebius Tamphilius might suggest. He lost most of his army to the Gauls in northern Italy in 199 and only reached the consulate seventeen years later, in 182, after being defeated at least twice in contests for

---

49. Appendix 1.1, no. 66. On the political position of this man and his brother during the Cinnan period, see Badian, *Studies*, 55 and Gruen, *Roman Politics*, 239–42.

50. Appendix 1.1, no. 16.

51. Note, however, that Hopkins and Burton, *Death and Renewal*, table 2.4, calculate that only 16 percent of consuls between 194 and 170 B.C. and 11 percent between 169 and 140 B.C. had a consular grandfather but not a consular father.

52. It is of course fallacious to attempt to prove what happened in the case of any particular person by extrapolation from a general prosopographical pattern like the one traced earlier: cf. Linderski, *CPh* 72 (1977): 55–56. All one can do is present probabilities. The point to be stressed here, however, is simply that none of the cases discussed above affords any grounds for doubting the validity of the statistical norm.

53. Appendix 1.1, nos. 9, 15, 22, 31, 50, 63, 86, 87, 90.

that office.⁵⁴ However, other cases seem to indicate that Baebius' crawl up the *cursus* was exceptional.⁵⁵ By contrast, the voters elected M. Claudius Marcellus consul for 208 only a short time after the popular animosity stirred up following a defeat had forced him to return to Rome and rebut charges leveled against him on that score. His defense before the assembly was so successful that the vote to award him the consulate on the next day was unanimous. L. Manlius Vulso's run for the consulship of 216 less than two years after his defeat in Gaul is also significant here, particularly since the defeat did not account for his failure to win that office. The slaughter that P. Aelius Paetus' legate had suffered in 201, L. Marcius Censorinus' setbacks at Carthage in 149, and the thrashings inflicted on L. Gellius Poplicola and Cn. Cornelius Lentulus Clodianus by Spartacus in 72 did not prevent the elevation of each of these consuls to a censorship two years later.⁵⁶ The other consuls who lost battles and then went on to become censors likewise do not appear to have taken significantly longer at it than their contemporaries.⁵⁷

The group of six or seven defeated praetors who went on to become consuls between 197 and 81 B.C. might seem relevant to this question. After 180 the consulship could be held at the earliest only in the third year following a praetorship, hence this date affords a benchmark against which to measure the progress of these men, all of whom were praetors after 180, up the *cursus honorum*.⁵⁸ One or two reached the consulate in the third year after their praetorships, one in the fifth year, one in the sixth year, and three in the seventh.⁵⁹ Ideally their performances should be compared to the progress of undefeated praetors to decide whether these six

---

54. Appendix 1.1, no. 8.
55. Baebius may have been under instructions from the senate to maintain a defensive posture in Gaul during his command there as praetor. However, he ignored this advice and went on the offensive, which culminated in his defeat: cf. Eckstein, *Senate and General*, 5–6, 58–60. Hence disregard of the senate's instructions may have been the principal reason for the voters' antipathy, rather than simply his failure against the Gauls.
56. Appendix 1.1, nos. 18, 58, 2, 59, 39, 24.
57. Appendix 1.1, nos. 19, 27, 36, 45, 69.
58. Livy 40.44.1; see also Astin, *Lex Annalis before Sulla*, 7–19; contra, however, see Develin, *Patterns in Office-Holding*, 81–96.
59. Third year: appendix 1.1, nos. 13, 43(?); fifth: no. 52; sixth: no. 11; seventh: nos. 23, 60, 82. Note also, however, that no. 76, if he is to be identified with Q. Pompeius, won his consulate in the second year after his praetorship.

fared better or worse than others. Unfortunately, the average speed at which consuls reached that office following their praetorships in the mid-second century, when the consulships of these six occurred, cannot be established owing to the incompleteness of the praetorian *fasti* following 167. What we know of the rate of progress from praetorship to consulate before that date indicates that lengthy intervals were not uncommon.[60] But even if such a figure could be obtained, it would not allow us to answer the question of whether defeats caused these praetors to become consuls any more slowly than their undefeated or even victorious peers. Too many variables are involved to permit attaching decisive importance to any single factor. One simply cannot say whether Ser. Sulpicius Galba's failure to reach the consulship until 144 was due more to the battle lost in 151 or to public outrage at his butchery of the Lusitanians who surrendered to him in the following year.[61] M'. Manilius' minor defeat in 154 may have carried less weight with the electorate than his lack of distinguished forebears.[62] The same was perhaps true of C. Marcius Figulus: his father and grandfather do not appear to have held consulates.[63] L. Calpurnius Piso Frugi and perhaps P. Cornelius Nasica Serapio, on the contrary, each reached the same office *suo anno* notwithstanding a defeat.[64] The careers of L. Anicius Gallus and L. Mummius provide a contrast. They required eight and seven years respectively to reach their consulates, although each had triumphed as praetor. But undistinguished families seem to have handicapped these men too.[65] Ancestral eminence by no means tells the whole story, however. It took Q. Caecilius Metellus Macedonicus five years and two *repulsae* to win his consulship despite a praetorian triumph and consular progenitors. Harsh discipline had apparently made him unpopular with the voters.[66] Without similar basic information concerning the men who won consulships in these years—their personalities and

60. See Develin, *Patterns in Office-Holding*, 25–27.
61. Appendix 1.1, no. 82.
62. Appendix 1.1, no. 52.
63. Appendix 1.1, no. 60.
64. Appendix 1.1. nos. 13, 43.
65. Gallus was praetor in 168 and consul in 160; the dates for Mummius are 153 and 146; on their triumphs: Livy 45.43.1–8; App. *Iber.* 57.
66. *De Vir. Ill.* 61.3, cf. Livy, *Oxy. Per.* 52; Val. Max. 7.5.4; Astin, *Scipio Aemilianus*, 100.

political skills, their friends, and the opposing candidates—it is simply impossible to argue that a defeat slowed a particular career.

But even if one were inclined to attempt such an argument, it is difficult to conceive of a hypothesis that could adequately explain how defeated generals found it easier to get elected with the passage of time. If the voters refused to return a praetor to the consulate, say, two years after he had lost a battle but were willing to do so four, five, or six years afterward, what had changed in the meantime? Perhaps the voters' memories had grown dim, but surely the other candidates would have taken it upon themselves to refresh them before they went to the polls. In view of the speed with which several defeated consuls went on to become censors or consuls once again, it is hard to believe that different conditions obtained when the electorate considered raising praetorians to the consulate.

One more indication of how little importance both commoners and aristocrats attached to lost battles emerges from an examination of the circumstances in which some *imperatores victi* were elected or reelected to the consulship and others prorogued or otherwise allowed to remain in their commands. It is a commonplace that the Romans did not elect their magistrates on the basis of their military ability. Sufficient competence seems to have been assumed in all candidates for the consulate.[67] But what about men whose prior failures, it might have been argued, clearly indicated incompetence? In a number of cases their successes at the polls came as Rome found itself embroiled in major conflicts abroad, often when the military situation had reached a critical stage. If a poor military record was in fact ever a serious political liability, its effects ought to be most evident at such moments.

---

67. Sallust has Marius charge in 108 that his competitors for the office did not know the first thing about warfare from practical experience. For the charge to have been shocking and persuasive, Sallust must have been able to assume that Marius' imaginary audience of voters would normally have thought otherwise: *Iug.* 85.10–12. Cf. Astin, *Scipio Aemilianus*, 56. By contrast, a praetorian triumph was a great advantage in securing the consulate: see Harris, *War and Imperialism*, 31–33, 262–63, who suggests that a strong military reputation did play an important role in securing higher office.

Once again Q. Marcius Philippus, the unlucky consul of 186, furnishes a striking example. The Ligurian Apuani lured him into a narrow defile and ambushed his forces. Roman losses in the ensuing clash were severe. Accounts of the disaster are not detailed enough to allow one to say with certainty that Philippus' blunders were the cause of the fiasco, but responsibility for ensuring that the terrain was well scouted ought to have rested principally with the commander.[68] His efforts to conceal the extent of his losses as well as to keep away from Rome for the rest of the year strongly suggest that Philippus felt himself open to censure for his handling of the campaign. Therefore, what was known of his military talents can hardly have inspired confidence. Yet sixteen years later, when Philippus sought the consulate for the second time, Rome was at war with Perseus and, what is more, experiencing major difficulties in the conflict. In 170 news of defeats at Elimea and in Illyria and Epirus raised serious concerns in the senate about the conduct of the war there. A commission was dispatched to investigate. But when the fathers then ordered elections to be held, Philippus, a man with a clear record of failure as a general, garnered a majority of the votes; furthermore, no one challenged his right to cast lots for the province of Macedonia, which he obtained. Happily, Philippus proved himself a better general in his second consulate than in his first.[69]

The same cannot be said for M'. Manilius, praetor in 154. During his operations in Farther Spain, the Lusitanian commander Punicus beat him and another praetor soundly and killed some six thousand soldiers in the process, according to Appian. Five years later Manilius entered the consulship and together with his colleague received the province of Africa and conduct of the newly declared war against Carthage. Although Manilius sustained no serious defeat in the conflict, his operations against the city were anything but exemplary, even allowing for possible bias in the sources. Perhaps when Manilius was elected to the consulate of 149, the Carthaginians' abject and supine attitude may have led the voters and the *patres* to expect that they would capitulate without

---

68. Cp. Caes. BGall. 1.40; Livy 26.3.4.
69. On Philippus' earlier defeat, see above, pp. 15–16; on the military situation and senatorial concern at the time of the election, see Livy 43.11.1–12.2.

a struggle once war had been declared. Thus recollections of Manilius' earlier military ineptness may have generated little concern. However, the voters must have had few illusions about the ease with which the war against Carthage would be won and the need for a competent general in command by the time elections came round for the following year's consuls. Yet one of the men selected to fill that office was none other than L. Calpurnius Piso Caesoninus, praetor in 154 and partner in Manilius' Spanish debacle. To him fell the command of the troublesome African war for 148 after Manilius' disappointing performance. Caesoninus did scarcely better.[70]

A few other cases may be briefly noted: a force of rebellious slaves in Sicily defeated L. Calpurnius Piso Frugi during his praetorship there, apparently in 136. Three years later he was elevated to the consulate and allotted the task of crushing the same force of rebels. Cn. Baebius Tamphilius' rash attack on the Insubrian Gauls during his praetorship in 199 and his repulse with heavy casualties have already been mentioned. Yet during his consulship he went north once again, this time to fight the Ligurians. Also familiar is the consul of 260, Cn. Cornelius Scipio Asina, who sailed to Lipara with a few ships in hopes of having the city betrayed to him, only to find himself trapped in the harbor by superior Carthaginian naval forces. He then seems to have compounded his error by a naive reliance on *Punica fides*, which lured him to a conference with the enemy, where he was made a prisoner. Polybius, however, asserts that he simply surrendered. Astoundingly, despite this clear evidence of poor judgment, after once against securing election to the consulship in 254, he received the task of leading yet another army against the Carthaginians in Sicily.[71]

Overall the number of such instances is not high, owing in large part to the infrequency of repetition of the consulship and the fact that most praetors in the middle and late Republic did not see any

---

70. On Manilius and Piso in Spain, see appendix 1.1, nos. 52, 11; on their conduct of operations in Africa, see nos. 53, 12. Astin, *Scipio Aemilianus*, 55–56, rightly warns against accepting too much of the sources' characterization of Manilius' performance in 149 at face value owing to the possibility of bias in favor of Scipio Aemilianus' role in the Third Punic War.

71. Appendix 1.1, nos. 8, 13, 26. Note also M. Claudius Marcellus, no. 18 for 208; C. Marcius Figulus, no. 60 for 156; and M. Aurelius Cotta, no. 7 for 74, if he is the praetor defeated in 80.

serious fighting in their *provinciae*. Yet the examples adduced here indicate how little concerned the voters could be to insist on a history of success in the men they selected to command the armies of which they themselves often made up the rank and file—even when major wars were afoot, even when these wars were not going well. To be sure, the opposite was sometimes true. At times of crisis the need to put affairs into the hands of the city's most talented generals led to the elevation of P. Cornelius Scipio Aemilianus to the consulate in 134 as well as the selection of his father L. Aemilius Paullus to command against Perseus in 168 and of his grandfathers L. Aemilius Paullus to lead the Romans against Hannibal at Cannae and P. Scipio Africanus to undertake the invasion of Africa in 205. Others cases too spring readily to mind.[72] But against them must be set the contrary examples of failures like Philippus, Caesoninus, and Asina, elected at times when one might expect the military situation abroad to have made the voters particularly attuned to the candidates' records in command. Their readiness at moments of real crisis to turn to men of demonstrable ability only underscores the contradiction. Only the lack of significance of a military defeat in their eyes can explain this peculiar state of affairs. Although the voters certainly were often cognizant of a candidate's victories, no stigma attaching to military failure seems to have influenced their choices at the polls.[73]

Blindness to past defeats was not restricted to the voting assemblies, however. Much of the blame for allowing *victi* once again to take command of major wars can be laid to the operation of the lot when the two new consuls determined at the outset of their year in office which of the two consular provinces each would obtain.

---

72. Sources for the elections of these men are collected in *MRR* under the appropriate years. Note also C. Marius' second consulate in 104 and the election of M. Claudius Marcellus in 215 and of P. Cornelius Rufinus in 277. See, generally, Develin, *Patterns in Office-Holding*, 14–16, 94–95; idem, *Practice of Politics at Rome*, 107–118.

73. An apparent exception makes the same point. According to Livy, Q. Fabius Maximus urged in a speech at the electoral assembly of 215 that one of the candidates for the following year's consulate, T. Otacilius Crassus, should not be elected because of his poor performance in command of the fleet off Sicily; he would not be up to the challenge of leading an army against Hannibal (Livy 24.8.14–20). However, the *centuria praerogativa* had already cast its vote for Otacilius when Fabius spoke, and his efforts to browbeat them into reconsidering certainly sprang from a fear that the rest of the centuries would follow their lead.

On the surface, at least, the outcome was the result of chance or the will of the gods. The senate almost never saw fit to intervene, even on those occasions when a prior defeat might have raised doubts about the wisdom of allowing an important command to go to one of the new consuls. Whatever the fathers' misgivings, they deferred to the will of the *populus* and the luck of the draw. To be sure, scholars have in the past frequently believed that the senate regularly manipulated provincial assignments for partisan or pragmatic ends.[74] This view is no longer widely held; yet even allowing that the lot may have been fixed on occasion, the evidence presented above concerning the *victi* who subsequently obtained important commands shows that the senate did not trouble itself to do so in order to prevent someone of questionable competence from receiving charge of a major war. Therefore, even assuming the hypothesis of senatorial intervention in the allocation of provinces, these findings refute the belief that defeat had any impact on the choices the fathers made in such cases.

On only one occasion did the senate trouble itself over whether a previously defeated commander ought to be allowed to lead an army once again. Ser. Sulpicius Galba had so badly handled the pursuit of Viriathus following an initial victory that he lost seven thousand men, according to Appian, and was forced to flee the field. He became consul in 144 together with L. Aurelius Cotta, and the two men each contended vigorously for the command in Farther Spain against Viriathus. Their dispute led to a serious division among the senators—something difficult to understand if the *patres* were ordinarily unwilling to assign wars to unsuccessful generals. In that case there ought to have been no controversy at all; a consensus among the senators would have forced Galba to stay home. When the question was finally decided, the issue of who would prove the better commander against the Spaniards is striking by its absence. Ultimately the fathers kept Galba from taking charge of the war, but they refused to give the job to Cotta either, and not because they thought one of them any less capable of conducting the campaign than the other: they made their deci-

---

74. E.g. Badian, *Flamininus*, 31–32; the thesis is rejected by Eckstein, *Phoenix* 30 (1976): 122–124, but reappears implicitly in Dyson, *Creation of the Roman Frontier*, and Develin, *Practice of Politics at Rome*, 107.

sion on moral grounds. The senators were convinced that each would use his tenure in the province to enrich himself. In the case of Galba the reference is plainly to charges of treachery and profiteering during his previous tour of duty.[75] The senate may well have been sensitive here to the extent to which a governor's treatment of the natives could expedite or impede the speedy and successful conclusion of a war, but even so, such thinking nevertheless reflects the lack of importance the fathers attached to Galba's earlier *military* failure.[76]

Yet the *patres* exerted far more control over the determination of who would lead the Romans to war than this apparently passive acceptance of the will of the voters and the choice of the gods might suggest. For most of the history of the Republic they had a preponderant influence in the creation of promagistrates, whether by appointment or prorogation. Here too they exhibited a willingness to nominate men with far less than immaculate military records. Thus P. Cornelius Scipio's defeat at the Ticinus in 218 did not stand in the way of his repeated prorogation as one of the two Roman commanders in Spain from 217 until his death in 211.[77] Likewise the senate kept C. Terentius Varro, who presided over the disaster at Cannae, in command of Picenum from 215 until 213. Perhaps the desperate need for commanders after the appalling losses at Cannae accounts for these instances, but surely the shortage was

---

75. On the controversy, see Val. Max. 6.4.2; on Galba's earlier command in Spain, see Appendix 1.1, no. 82.

76. One other well-known case might be mentioned in this context, although it does not concern a *victus*. L. Cornelius Scipio was elected consul in 190 during the war with Antiochus. There was controversy over whether he or his colleague should take command. Cicero contends it was because he was neither vigorous nor strong enough (*Phil.* 11.17), whereas Livy reports that political favoritism was the cause (37.1.7–9). Livy's account is likely to be correct here: see Dorey, *Klio* 39 (1961): 196–97; Balsdon, *Historia* 21 (1972): 224–34.

77. Appendix 1.1, no. 25. The command of Ti. Sempronius Longus, vanquished at the Trebia by Hannibal, Appendix 1.1, no. 78, was not prorogued, which De Sanctis, *Storia* 3.2²: 33, ascribes to poor generalship. But the explanation is simpler: Scipio's army had gone on to Spain after its commander had returned to Italy to meet Hannibal there, whereas Sempronius' army had returned from Sicily with him to northern Italy. In 217 the senate elected to continue prosecuting the war in Spain with the army already in that province and placed Scipio in command, in keeping with standard practice in selecting promagistrates. But Africa, Sempronius' province in 218, was not assigned to anyone for the following year, eliminating the possibility of appointing Sempronius proconsul to command there, and the remnants of his army in Gaul went to one of the new consuls for 217 (Livy 21.63.1; discussion in Walbank, *Comm.* 1:410–11).

a good deal less pressing by 208, when the *patres* again appointed Varro to a promagistracy in Etruria (he remained in that post into 207).⁷⁸ Ap. Claudius Centho seems to have been retained in command of Illyria into 169 notwithstanding a serious loss in the previous year.⁷⁹ During the late Republic the fathers extended Q. Lutatius Catulus' command an additional year despite what appears to have been a defeat by the Germans in 102.⁸⁰ In 79 and apparently 78 as well Q. Caecilius Metellus Pius lost badly to Sertorius; his colleague after 77, Cn. Pompeius Magnus, fared no better in 76 and 75. Yet the senate made no attempt to remove either man from his command, instead proroguing each until they managed to bring the war in Spain to a successful conclusion in 71.⁸¹

The men who decided which generals to place or continue in a promagistracy were well aware of the prestige attached to wielding *imperium* and the opportunities for glory that conduct of the *res publica* bestowed. Inevitably, therefore, such determinations were to a large extent political in nature, and these cases again reveal the failure of military defeat to have any significant impact on this process. But during the fourth and third centuries the senators had other ways of controlling who was in charge of the Republic's wars. Had they so wished, the appointment of a dictator offered an easy way of removing a commander whose defeat had demonstrated he

---

78. Appendix 1.1, no. 85.
79. Appendix 1.1, no. 16.
80. Discussion of the defeat and its reflection in the sources is in Carney, *Biography of C. Marius*, 37 and n. 183.
81. Sources on Metellus and Pompeius in Spain are collected in MRR 2:83, 86, 94, 99, 104. The same Galba defeated by Viriathus in 151 and passed over for command of that war in 144 was prorogued in Spain for 150 (appendix 1.1, no. 82); D. Iunius Brutus Callaicus was continued in Spain following his defeat at Pallantia with Lepidus (appendix 1.1, no. 42); C. Sentius lost to the Thracians in 91 but was prorogued in Macedonia until 87 (appendix 1.1, no. 79). He finally won a victory over King Sothimus and the Thracians in 88 but saw his province overrun by Mithridates in the following year, when he was replaced. He had already served five years, however, and was by then long overdue to return home. The forces of Mithridates badly defeated M. Aurelius Cotta, consul in 74, and forced him to take refuge in Chalcedon until he could be rescued by his colleague. The senate prorogued him until 70, however. On his defeat, see Cic. *Mil.* 33; Sall. *Hist.* 3.23–24M; Livy *Per.* 93; *Corpus Inscriptionum Latinarum* (henceforth *CIL*) 1². 196; Plut. *Luc.* 8.2; App. *Mith.* 71; Memnon, *FGrH* 3B no. 434 frg. 39; Eutrop. 6.6.2; *De Vir. Ill.* 74.4; Oros. 6.2.13. On his continued command: Memnon, *FGrH* 3B no. 434 frgs. 42–43, 47–52. It is not clear whether the prorogation of A. Manlius Vulso occurred before or after the senate learned of his defeat (Livy 41.6.1–3). Note also the prorogations of nos. 40 and 70 (appendix 1.1) until successors arrived.

could no longer safely be left at the head of his troops. But in practice the office was rarely so used. In 390, following the disaster at the Allia, the senate appointed Camillus dictator to rescue the city from the Gauls. But their intent was not to depose from command Q. Sulpicius Longus, the military tribune with consular power who had just led the Roman forces to defeat. He was among those besieged on the Capitoline in Rome, where he continued to exercise command in defense of the citadel even after the nomination of the dictator.[82] Similarly, the appointment of C. Sulpicius Peticus as dictator in 358 had nothing to do with the defeat the consul C. Fabius Ambustus sustained against Tarquinii in the same year. The senate made its decision because it feared a Gallic attack around Praeneste and Pedum in the south earlier in the year, before Fabius' loss had even taken place.[83] When the Volsci cut a Roman army to pieces in 379 owing to the incompetence of its commanders, the senate resolved to appoint a dictator, but as the enemy remained quiet thereafter, nothing further was done to replace those in charge.[84] Unsubstantiated reports of a defeat following a battle against the Samnites in 310 led to L. Papirius Cursor's elevation to the dictatorship. Yet the *patres* in this case were almost certainly reacting to rumors that the consul, C. Marcius Rutilus, had been seriously wounded in the fighting. At the time the decision was made, the senators were uncertain whether Marcius was still alive. Appointing a dictator to replace an injured or deceased consul was common in the fourth century, and nothing suggests that this case ought to be viewed any differently.[85] Q. Fabius Maximus was made dictator after the Roman debacle at Lake Trasimene in 217, but there was no question here of taking control out of the hands of the unsuccessful commanders. Hannibal had already seen to that: C. Flaminius died at Trasimene, and C. Centenius, the propraetor in charge of a cavalry force ambushed by the Carthaginians shortly thereafter, perished in that attack. The surviving consul, Cn. Servilius Geminus, had yet to demonstrate his abilities one way or the other.[86]

---

82. Appendix 1.1, no. 83.
83. Livy 7.12.7–9.
84. Livy 6.30.6–7.
85. Livy 9.38.4–14; cf. the cases in 362, 340, 325, and 312 B.C. (sources in *MRR* under the appropriate years).
86. Sources are in *MRR* 1:242, 245.

Only in three instances might it seem that the senate had recourse to a dictator to remove those responsible for a defeat from command. In 321, following the *foedus Caudinum*, it ordered the consuls who had presided over the surrender, T. Veturius Calvinus and Sp. Postumius Albinus, to appoint one to hold elections for two new consuls; during the first Punic war P. Claudius Pulcher was instructed to nominate another following a disastrous loss at sea in 249 made infamous by his defiance of the auspices; and after the crushing defeat at Cannae the appointment of a dictator relieved C. Terentius Varro of any further responsibility for conducting operations against Hannibal.[87]

But these examples are not to be taken simply at face value. The defeat at Cannae had ushered in the most serious crisis the Republic had ever faced, and the senate's demand for the appointment of a dictator in 216 was completely in keeping with its practice of utilizing the office in an emergency to place in command men capable of meeting it. Yet what distinguishes this case is the senate's continued confidence in Varro's abilities. They left him in charge of Apulia for the rest of the year and prorogued his *imperium* for 215. He was later sent to take charge of Picenum, where he stayed until 213.[88] To be sure, the *provinciae* to which the *patres* assigned Varro proved to be military backwaters during the remainder of the struggle, but the senate can hardly have known that at the time. Varro's treatment was really no different from that accorded Cn. Servilius Geminus, the consul of the previous year displaced by Fabius Maximus' appointment as dictator: he spent much of 217 in command of the fleet.[89] In giving Varro charge of a subsidiary, but not necessarily unimportant, part of the war effort, the senate used him in much the same way. Despite the heavy censure he endures in the sources, Varro's promagistracy was in effect a vote of confidence in the man himself, quite in keeping with the famous vote of thanks he received following Cannae.[90] True, he would no longer face Hannibal, but in such a crisis this task could only be safely left to Rome's best generals. Indeed, the

---

87. Appendix 1.1, nos. 92, 73, 20, 85. Note that in 321 the two dictators nominated were each appointed *vitio* and compelled to resign. Elections were held by an interrex. However, this fact does not invalidate the hypothesis regarding the intent of the appointment.
88. Appendix 1.1, no. 85.
89. Sources are in *MRR* 1:242.
90. Livy 22.61.13–14; other sources are in *MRR* 1:247.

readoption of the strategy of *cunctatio* itself may testify to the senate's belief that *no* commander it could appoint could win a set battle against the Carthaginian, at least for the present.[91]

By contrast, there are clear indications that Calvinus, Albinus, and Pulcher no longer enjoyed senatorial confidence in their abilities as war leaders. After the first two returned to Rome, the fathers insisted that a dictator be appointed to hold elections at once and that the newly elected consuls enter office immediately and resume prosecution of the war.[92] Likewise a formal recall and Livy's notice that the dictator who replaced Claudius Pulcher, A. Atilius Caiatinus, was the first to lead an army outside Italy suggest that the senate's aim was to remove Claudius from command altogether. But the events attending these defeats set them apart. After their army had been trapped, Calvinus and Albinus agreed to lay down their arms, swear to a treaty of peace, and lead their army under the yoke. The consuls had brought upon Rome the greatest possible humiliation and therefore could no longer be trusted to conduct the *res publica* as was fitting.[93] Claudius Pulcher's defiance of religious convention revealed not only his contempt for the gods but also culpability in bringing about the defeat since failure to secure divine support deprived Roman arms of that vital precondition for their success. This reckless behavior demonstrated his incompetence as far as the *patres* were concerned and fueled their resolve to strip him of his *imperium*.[94] These outrages made issues out of the battles these three men lost and roused the normally quiescent senate to take steps to replace them.

There can be no doubt that the senators were regularly concerned during the fourth and third centuries to ensure effective leadership in times of crisis by elevating men of proven ability to the dictatorship. Yet ordinarily they were just as reluctant to use

---

91. The Republic's best general in 216, M. Claudius Marcellus, happened to be holding a second praetorship. Appointment of M. Iunius Pera, a man apparently without significant military laurels, as dictator seems to have been intended to enable Marcellus to take charge of the main Roman effort after Cannae notwithstanding his rank (Livy 22.57.1, 7–8; Plut. *Marc.* 9.1–2; App. *Hann.* 27; other sources in *MRR* 1:248).

92. This account may be legendary: Rome may have abided by the treaty for some time; see Crawford, *PBSR* 41 (1973): 1–7.

93. Appendix 1.1, nos. 92, 73.

94. Appendix 1.1, no. 20. On the religious causes of victory and defeat, see chapter 2.

the same office as a means of replacing generals whose defeats might have raised doubts about the wisdom of leaving them in command. The defeat sustained by P. Claudius Pulcher's predecessors, the consuls of 250, had produced no call for the appointment of a dictator; neither had serious losses in 292 and 280 or a number of others during the first half of the third century.[95] This apparent contradiction in effect mirrors the ambiguity in the voters' choices for the consulate. In neither the *curia* or the *comitia* did past failure have any discernible impact on the choices made there, yet both the senators and the voters could make strenuous efforts to put the Republic's best generals at the head of its armies when grave dangers threatened. Such measures clearly indicate that both the senators and the centuriate assembly could view a person's past successes as holding out the promise of victories in the future. Previous performance in these cases guided political decisions—but only in emergencies. The reverse, that a prior failure augured ill for the future, never obtained in the normal course of aristocratic rivalry. Or if such doubts arose, they nonetheless never affected the outcome of struggles over who was to lead the Romans to war.

Yet poor conduct of current military operations did on some occasions intrude into the political arena. More than once there were calls to abrogate a magistrate's *imperium* following a defeat. However, the outcomes of the ensuing conflicts offer a fair appraisal of just how reluctant the Romans were to see such steps actually taken. Only rarely could the senate or the people be prevailed upon to follow through on these proposals. Q. Fabius Maximus Gurges' defeat at the hands of the Samnites in 292 was serious enough for the question of his recall to be broached in the senate, yet on the plea of his father to spare his son this humiliation, along with his promise to serve as a legate, the senators were persuaded to forgo abrogation.[96] Twelve years later, in 280, when P. Valerius Laevinus lost badly to Pyrrhus, an opponent directed criticism specifically at the consul's handling of the battle: the Epirotes had not beaten the Romans, but Pyrrhus had conquered Laevinus. Yet no motion to rescind his command followed in the senate. The fathers

---

95. Appendix 1.1 nos. 6, 50. On 292, see the following note; on 280, see appendix 1.1, no. 89. Other failures were in 295, 279, 277, 260, 255.

96. Livy *Per.* 11; Dio frg. 36.30–31, cf. Zonar. 8.1; Eutrop. 2.9.3; Oros. 3.22.6–9. See also Val. Max. 4.1.5, 5.7.1; Polyaenus 8.15.

sent his colleague south to lend assistance, and in due course the following year's consuls succeeded to the command and resumed warfare.[97] The tribune M. Metilius in 217 called for the abrogation of Q. Fabius Maximus' dictatorship for failing to bring Hannibal to battle, but it was never carried into law. Instead, the assembly elevated Fabius' master of horse to the position of codictator—a vote of no confidence and a slap in the face for Fabius, certainly, but that was as far as the matter was allowed to go.[98] One night in 178 the Istrians surprised the army of the consul A. Manlius Vulso and drove it in a panic from its camp. Once news of this rout reached Rome, two tribunes set up a vigorous outcry for cancellation of the prorogation of his command, which was tantamount to formal abrogation. Their efforts met with a veto from one of their colleagues, which prevailed after a good deal of controversy.[99]

Only in a handful of late cases did attempts at abrogation succeed. In 136, following his failure to capture Pallantia and serious losses on the retreat, M. Aemilius Lepidus Porcina was deprived of his command in Spain and forced to return to Rome as a civilian, according to Appian.[100] Thirty-one years later a vote of the people abrogated Q. Servilius Caepio's proconsulship after the disaster at Arausio.[101] In 72 the senate told the consuls of that year, L. Gellius Poplicola and Cn. Cornelius Lentulus Clodianus, to "keep quiet" after their failures against Spartacus and handed the war over to the praetor M. Licinius Crassus. This action may represent a formal abrogation of their commands, although the matter is disputed.[102] Mention should also be made in this context of the recall of C. Hostilius Mancinus following his surrender to the Numantines. The senate sent his colleague Lepidus Porcina to replace him in Spain. However, there is no indication of any formal effort to

---

97. Appendix 1.1, no. 89, although Degrassi, *Inscr. Ital.*, 13.1 40–41, 113, suggests that Laevinus may have died in office or abdicated.
98. Sources are in *MRR* 1:243.
99. Livy 41.1.1–4.8, 5.1–2, 6.1–3, 7.4–10, 10.1–13. Note also that after M. Claudius Marcellus' army fled following a defeat by Hannibal, and Marcellus thereupon went into winter quarters, a tribune in Rome began proceedings to abrogate his command. However, Marcellus was able to refute the charges so effectively that he was elected consul unanimously on the following day (appendix 1.1, no. 18).
100. Appendix 1.1, no. 3. However, Bauman, *RhM*, n.s., 111 (1968): 37–50 at 45–50, argues that no formal abrogation in fact took place.
101. Appendix 1.1, no. 81.
102. For sources and bibliography, see appendix 1.1, nos. 39, 24.

abrogate his *imperium*. Instead, the fathers seem to have been content to allow his year of office to run its course before they took action against him.[103]

But as with the replacement of Calvinus, Albinus, and Pulcher via dictators, some specific transgression beyond simply losing battles was needed to trigger the removal of these generals. Lepidus had flouted a senatorial directive to abstain from attacking Pallantia, a clear breach of the deference to the *auctoritas patrum* expected of a consul. This defiance is likely to have been the primary factor motivating the ignominious termination of his *imperium*. However, the other commander in Spain, M. Iunius Brutus Callaicus, who had cooperated with Lepidus and shared in the defeat, not only was not deprived of his command but also was prorogued and eventually awarded a triumph.[104] Mancinus' decision to surrender and furthermore agree to the humiliation of a treaty dictated by the enemy had far more to do with rousing senatorial ire against him than his failure against Numantia, even if it did not lead to abrogation.[105] Caepio's obstinate refusal to cooperate with his colleague against the enemy, sacrificing two Roman armies and the safety of the Republic to *inimicitia*, along with charges of disgraceful cowardice in battle were primarily responsible for bringing about his deposition. Cn. Mallius, his partner in the disaster of 105, was apparently left to complete his term of office unmolested.[106] Only in Gellius and Clodianus' case does abrogation, if that is in fact what took place, seem to have resulted from no other cause than simple incompetence. Yet here the proximity of the threat posed by Spartacus was responsible for goading the fathers to a step they were otherwise reluctant to take.[107]

In these four instances, therefore, the grounds for actually removing an unsuccessful general by either abrogation or recall were essentially those that had obtained during the fourth and third

---

103. Appendix 1.1, no. 41. Hackl, *Senat und Magistratur*, 83–84, asserts that Claudius Unimanus' command was abrogated after his defeat by Viriathus. There is no evidence for this in the sources, however; see also appendix 1.1, no. 21.

104. Appendix 1.1, no. 42. Astin, *Scipio Aemilianus*, 147, 259, suggests that a move was afoot to recall Brutus at this time, regarding which Scipio delivered a speech. If so, however, nothing came of it.

105. Appendix 1.1, no. 41.

106. Appendix 1.1, nos. 81, 51.

107. Appendix 1.1, nos. 39, 24.

centuries, when the senate accomplished the same thing through the appointment of a dictator. Porcina, Mancinus, and Caepio had committed egregious transgressions in connection with their defeats, much like those of Calvinus, Albinus, and Pulcher, and these justified the measures taken against all of them. The only case that does not conform, that of Gellius and Clodianus, parallels Varro's in 216. The threats that in each instance they failed to stem were, if not of equal magnitude, equally immediate and posed a direct danger to the *res publica* close to home. Swift, competent action was required, and this necessity justified setting aside the normal structure of command.

Otherwise, removing someone from a position of great honor, such as the command of a Roman army and conduct of the *res publica*, was to inflict signal disgrace. It was never easy for an aristocracy that valued *dignitas* above virtually all else to support such an action against one of its members save when he had already dishonored himself by flight, surrender, or some other grave personal misconduct.[108] Nor was it any easier for voters to do so, in so far as they operated within the same moral universe and were obligated to listen to the *patres'* collective *auctoritas* or the advice of individual patrons. No stigma attached to defeat in and of itself; hence it could never furnish a reason to deprive a *victus* of the honor he currently enjoyed. Neither did it constitute grounds for withholding further *honores* to unsuccessful generals, even if these were consulships that brought with them the charge of important wars. The Romans simply did not order their priorities so as to decide questions of prestige and status on the basis of probable competence, at least most of the time. To have made it an issue would have meant withholding or withdrawing positions carrying with them great honor from men who might otherwise claim to deserve them. The same point is relevant to the remarkably normal rate of success that *victi* achieved in advancing to higher magistracies that did not entail military responsibilities, particularly the censorship. If a lost battle involved no disgrace, then its failure to

---

108. Cf. the plea of Q. Fabius Maximus Gurges' father as the senate debated his recall: *pater deprecatus hanc fili ignominiam eo maxime senatum movit* (Livy *Per.* 11; Oros. 3.22.6).

make an impact in contests where moral worth and dignity bulked large in the voters' minds can hardly surprise.

———|———

Where we can glean evidence for the activities of those *victi* who did not go on to higher office, it gives further support to the thesis that military defeat had little or no impact on personal status at Rome. Such men played precisely the roles in public affairs one would expect of those who had achieved similar rank and whose honor was without stain. C. Fabius Ambustus held the post of *interrex* in 355.[109] Ti. Sempronius Longus apparently was a legate in command of troops in 215 despite his loss to Hannibal at the Trebia.[110] M. Minucius Rufus' near-fatal rashness in attacking Hannibal in 217 did not prevent his serving in the next year with the army of the consuls at Cannae. As a senior consular, he undoubtedly sat on the generals' *consilium*, where the most critical decisions of the campaign were hammered out.[111] Sex. Digitius' disaster in 194 was apparently of no concern to L. Cornelius Scipio four years later: he appointed Digitius to be his legate for the campaign against Antiochus in Asia Minor. Digitius later served on an embassy to Macedon in 174 and on a commission to purchase grain in 172.[112] M. Terentius Varro, M. Baebius Tamphilus, and Q. Marcius Philippus all acted in similar capacities following their defeats.[113] So too did L. Gellius Poplicola and Cn. Cornelius Lentulus Clodianus in 67.[114]

Stature and influence of a more general sort, as distinct from public service in specific posts, are attested for a number of others: M'. Manilius perhaps intervened in the political drama of 133 to urge Tiberius Gracchus to bring his proposed *lex agraria* before the curia. Evidently he was a man of considerable esteem and author-

---

109. Appendix 1.1, no. 30.
110. Appendix 1.1, no. 78.
111. Appendix 1.1, no. 62.
112. Appendix 1.1, no. 29.
113. Appendix 1.1, nos. 85, 8, 61. Note also A. Postumius Albinus, in command of a fleet in 89 (appendix 1.1, no. 72).
114. They were legates under Pompey in the campaign against the pirates (appendix 1.1, nos. 39, 24). Note that Gellius apparently was placed in active command of the Etruscan Sea.

ity at the time, an impression confirmed by his appearance in Cicero's *De Republica*.[115] As noted above, M. Aemilius Lepidus Porcina's defeat before Pallantia led to recall by the senate, and subsequently he was fined. Yet his financial ostentation, which drew the ire of the censors of 125, suggests he made efforts to keep himself in the public eye after his return.[116] In 114 C. Porcius Cato lost heavily to the Scordisci in Thrace and succumbed to charges of *repetundae* soon thereafter. But a prosecution and condemnation before the Mamilian *quaestio* in 110 indicates that he had remained influential in the meantime and perhaps had secured a place on one of the embassies to Numidia during those years.[117] L. Licinius Lucullus' legate, C. Valerius Triarius, disappears from the record following his defeat by Mithridates in 67. However, Lucullus' own supersession by Glabrio later in that same year had nothing to do with the defeat, and Lucullus emerged from retirement in 62 to lead the fight in the senate against his old nemesis Pompey.[118] Two or possibly three men even went on to secure triumphs from the senate despite involvement in serious defeats: D. Iunius Brutus Callaicus, who shared in the repulse at Pallantia in 136, and L. Licinius Murena, who triumphed in 81 notwithstanding a thrashing administered by Mithridates two years before.[119] In addition, M. Claudius Marcellus' triumph in 196 may have come on the heels of a loss to the Boii in Gaul.[120]

To be sure, most *victi* are not known to have held office subsequently or otherwise involved themselves in political affairs. But given the nature of the sources, this is no more than one would expect. Generals who lost no battles—even generals who won them—are usually difficult to trace after they leave office. Most consuls, after all, would not become censors, most praetors would not become consuls, and the record of personnel who served on embassies and legations and in other such capacities is patchy at

---

115. Appendix 1.1, no. 53.
116. Appendix 1.1, no. 3.
117. Appendix 1.1, no. 71.
118. Appendix 1.1, no. 47.
119. Appendix 1.1, nos. 42, 48.
120. Appendix 1.1, no. 19. Note also the naval triumphs of the consuls of 255, Ser. Fulvius Nobilior and M. Aemilius Paullus, and of C. Sempronius Blaesus, cos. 253, despite the fact that all of them had lost most of their fleets owing to disastrous shipwrecks (sources in *MRR* 1:209–11).

best. Yet it is usually only through the holding of public office that we can follow the progress of individuals for all but the very last decades of the Republic. The fact that where we can track the careers of *victi* they appear in the main no different from what one would expect had no defeat occurred demands the presumption of a similarly normal *cursus* in the case of those *victi* who subsequently vanish from our sources. Such men certainly spent their remaining years on the front benches of the senate actively participating in the conduct of the *res publica* along with others of similar rank and dignity.

One additional finding sheds further light on the lack of any long-term effect arising from lost battles, and that is their failure to mar the political fortunes of the descendants of *victi*. The reverse, however, has sometimes been maintained—that in some cases of particularly egregious failure the stigma of defeat was passed on to successive generations of the commander's family, denying them access to office and authority.[121] Perhaps it is so, for no direct evidence exists to refute the notion that, for example, the absence of C. Hostilius Mancinus' progeny from the *fasti* after 137 or of T. Veturius Calvinus' relatives for a century following his disaster at the Caudine Forks in 321 was owing to the unwillingness of the voters to return descendants of these men to office. Yet the overall pattern of office holding among the sons of defeated generals argues against this view. Lost battles did not make a noticeable difference in a family's ability to maintain high status at Rome by securing the election of its scions to the city's top magistracies.

As mentioned above, during his consulship in 249 P. Claudius Pulcher sustained a severe defeat at sea made memorable by an act of singular impiety preceding it. On his return he was tried, convicted, and heavily fined. Yet neither the battle he lost nor the verdict that followed prevented a succession of descendants from winning consulships in every generation down to the end of the Republic and beyond. His son Appius, praetor in 215 and consul in 212, was the first.[122] One of the praetors serving in the year of

---

121. Specifically in reference to the descendants of Mancinus, appendix 1.1, no. 41, see Wikander, *Opuscula Romana* 11, no. 7 (1976): 103 n. 165; in reference to the descendants of Veturius, no. 92, see Münzer, *Real-Encyclopädie der classischen Altertumswissenschaft* (henceforth *RE*) 8A col. 1888.

122. Appendix 1.1, no. 20.

the latter's consulate, Cn. Fulvius Flaccus, failed ignominiously against Hannibal and capped his defeat by leading the flight of his men from the battlefield. Even his brother Quintus' immense prestige could not save him from condemnation in the following year. Nevertheless, Gnaeus left behind a son who held the consulship in 180 and a grandson who later won the same office for 134.[123] Also condemned on account of his cowardice following a defeat was C. Plautius Hypsaeus, praetor in 146. No children of his are known to have attained high office, but a L. Plautius Hypsaeus was praetor in 135, and a M. Plautius Hypsaeus reached the consulate ten years later. The exact relationship of these men is uncertain, but their names are rare enough to place them plausibly within the same family, either as brothers or cousins. If so, Gaius' disgrace did not prove an obstacle to Lucius' election, nor did the fact that Lucius too met with defeat in the field keep Marcus from becoming consul in 125.[124]

Likewise the offspring of other *victi*, who more typically had suffered no ill effects after their defeats, also managed to follow their fathers into high office. A good measure of this phenomenon can be obtained by comparing what has been termed the rate of family status maintenance for all consuls—that is, the percentage of them with at least one son who won election to the consulate or praetorship—with similar figures for defeated consuls. Hopkins and Burton have calculated that 38 percent of all consuls for the period 249–50 B.C. had sons who gained this same office in their turn, whereas the sons of another 19 percent rose only as high as the praetorship and no further, producing a combined rate of 57 percent.[125] In the same two-hundred-year period forty-five consuls lost battles that were not followed by other victories. This figure includes not only those who survived, returned to Rome, and resumed participation in political life but those who died in their defeats as well.[126] Of them, between eighteen and twenty-one produced consular sons, 40–46.6 percent, the variation being due to uncertainties in identifying the fathers of some later consuls. In addition, another group of between four and six persons had prae-

---

123. Appendix 1.1, no. 35.
124. Appendix 1.1, nos. 67, 68.
125. Hopkins and Burton, *Death and Renewal*, 61, table 2.6.
126. See the list in appendix 1.2.

torian sons who never became consuls, 8.8–13.3 percent, which yields a combined succession rate of 48.8–59.9 percent. If only serious defeats are taken into account, thirty-seven consuls had between fifteen and seventeen consular sons, 40.5–45.9 percent, and between four and six praetorian sons besides, for a total rate of 51.3–62.1 percent.[127] These figures can be further refined. The total number of consuls for the period in question is 364, and they had 138 consular sons.[128] By subtracting the forty-five defeated consuls and their eighteen to twenty-one consular sons from these totals, it is possible to derive succession rates for those consuls who never suffered a defeat and compare them with the rates established for defeated consuls. The percentage obtained for undefeated consuls, 36.6–37.6 percent, is not significantly different from the 40–44 percent succession rate for the defeated consuls.[129] If only those who sustained serious losses are left aside, the succession rate for undefeated consuls and those who sustained only minor reverses remains about the same, 37.6–38.8 percent.[130]

The rate at which sons of defeated consuls won consulships, then, is not much different from that at which the sons of all consuls, and especially the sons of undefeated consuls, equalled their fathers' rank. There is roughly a 4–9 percent difference between

---

127. For all defeated consuls or men of consular rank, 249–50 B.C., see appendix 1.1, nos. 2–4, 10, 12, 14, 18, 19(?), 20, 24, 25, 33, 36, 39, 40–42, 44, 45, 47, 51, 53, 59, 61, 62, 65, 69–71, 74, 78, 81, 85, and those listed in appendix 1.2. M'. Acilius Glabrio, appendix 1.1, no. 1, is not included since it is not certain that he commanded the forces allegedly defeated by the Gauls in 154, nor is L. Cornelius Lentulus Lupus, appendix 1.1, p. 186. Consular sons: appendix 1.1, nos. 2, 12, 18–20, 25, 33, 39, 40, 42, 44(?), 45, 53(?), 65, 69, 78; appendix 1.2, nos. 1, 4(?), 5, 6, 11; praetorian sons: appendix 1.1, nos. 14, 24, 81(?), 85; appendix 1.2, nos. 7, 12(?). Consuls or consulars seriously defeated: appendix 1.1, nos. 2–4, 7, 14, 18, 19(?), 20, 24, 25, 33, 36, 39, 41, 42, 44, 47, 51, 61, 65, 69, 71, 74, 78, 81, 85; appendix 1.2, all except no. 10; consular sons: 2, 18, 19, 20, 25, 33, 39, 42, 44(?), 65, 69, 78; appendix 1.2, nos. 1, 4(?), 5, 6, 11; praetorian sons are the same as above. If M. Claudius Marcellus, appendix 1.1, no. 19, is left out of the reckoning, the figures are as follows: out of 44 consulars defeated, 17–20 consular sons (38.6–45.4 percent), 4–6 praetorian sons (9–13.6 percent), combined succession rate, 47.6–59 percent; out of 36 consulars seriously defeated, 14–16 consular sons (38.8–44.4 percent), 4–6 praetorian sons (11.1–16.6 percent), combined succession rate, 49.9–61 percent.

128. The number 138 is arrived at by multiplying 364 by 0.38; Hopkins and Burton give no figure for the total number of sons.

129. There were 117–120 sons of 319 undefeated consuls.

130. There were 123–127 sons of 327 consuls undefeated or with minor reverses. This grouping includes M. Claudius Marcellus, appendix 1.1, no. 19, as a seriously defeated consul. Leaving him and his consular son out of the count does not significantly alter these results.

the proportion of all consuls' sons who only reached the praetorship and that for defeated consuls' sons alone—19 percent versus 8.8–13.3 percent. The difference is not statistically significant given the very small number of praetorian sons of defeated generals involved—between four and six. In view of the close correlation between rates for defeated and undefeated consuls' consular sons, it would be unwise to make much of the divergence in the case of praetorian offspring.[131]

No general pattern can be detected indicating that a military defeat passed any stigma on to succeeding generations. Considering the many losing generals who subsequently went on to win high public office, this result is not surprising. Of course, it cannot be ruled out that a specific defeat suffered by a father made it impossible for a son to win election, but in support of this argument the record is silent. No evidence indicates that this is why Mancinus, for example, was the last of his family to make his mark on the *fasti*, whereas counterexamples of the sons of P. Claudius Pulcher, Cn. Fulvius Flaccus, and many others demonstrate that exclusion from office was by no means inevitable. Even in the case of Mancinus' family one would be forced to argue that although the Romans were unwilling to elect a descendant to office, they were ready to raise Mancinus himself to a second praetorship following his defeat—an absurdity on the face of it. The burden of proof, therefore, is on those who would contend that military defeat had any impact whatsoever on the future of a defeated general's son.

Thus a paradox emerges: despite all the censure, criticism, and outrage that a defeat could provoke, these had no overall effect on aristocratic competition. Numerous defeated generals went on to hold the highest elective offices in the Republic, the consulate and censorship; proportionally, about as many of them did so as their

---

131. The calculations offered here need to be treated with some caution. Hopkins and Burton give no indication of how they determined who was a son of whom, nor do they list the persons involved. It is impossible to be certain that they are counting the same father-son pairs identified here, and therefore some overcounting or undercounting ought to be assumed. For the criteria used to determine the sons of *victi*, see below, appendix 1.1.

undefeated peers, and, as nearly as can be determined, their advancement to these offices came with roughly the same rapidity. Notwithstanding their poor military performances in the past, they secured consulships that would entail important military responsibilities, gaining election even at times when wars abroad were not going well. They were also continued in, or reappointed to, similar posts by the senate. Almost never did they suffer the indignity of having the conduct of a war taken out of their hands simply because they had lost a battle. Those who did not hold another elective office or promagistracy nevertheless continued to be selected by the senate to conduct the city's business or otherwise remained active in public life. Defeated consulars saw their sons achieve the praetorship and consulate about as often as the sons of other men who had held the consulship. By every conceivable measure, therefore, military defeat did not usually damage a political career. The contradiction is glaring, and isolated examples of apparent judicial retribution only sharpen the paradox. Yet even these exceptions make the same point: of the twelve to fourteen men brought to trial, two or three escaped punishment altogether.[132]

One acquittal deserves special emphasis in this context. M. Iunius Silanus, consul in 109, faced prosecution in connection with the defeat he suffered at the hands of the Cimbri. His trial is of the utmost importance, for it is the one instance in which the sources clearly connect defeat in battle with the criminal prosecution that followed: *M. Silanus . . . adversus Cimbros rem male gesserat: quam ob causam Domitius eum apud populum accusavit.*[133] Yet it is highly significant that the trial took place in 104, four years after the defeat.[134] Nothing happened in its immediate aftermath, when one might expect the issue to have stirred the greatest passions. Only after the spectacular disaster at Arausio in 105 had enraged public opinion did a tribune, Cn. Domitius, bring charges against Silanus. Patently the prosecutor sought to play upon that anger. He alleged

---

132. Those convicted: appendix 1.1, nos. 3, 4, 20, 35, 46, 51(?), 67, 71, 74, 80, 81. Those acquitted: nos. 44, 65(?), 69. On nos. 51 and 65, see below, chap. 4, p. 126 n. 47 and pp. 141–42.
133. Asc. 80 C.
134. On the date, see Badian, *Mélange Piganiol*, 913 n. 3; Marshall, *Historical Commentary*, 277–78.

that Silanus had been responsible not just for his own defeat but also for instigating the whole series of calamities that were then threatening to engulf the Republic.[135] No other charge supervened to cloud the case. If ever there was a trial in which responsibility for a military disaster was clearly the issue laid before the public, this was it. And if ever disaster had brought the Romans to the point of visiting their wrath upon those responsible, the time was now: in the very next year these same enraged citizens would condemn to death one of the two generals who presided over the debacle at Arausio and compel the other to flee into exile. Yet for Silanus the verdict was not even close: every tribe except two voted in favor of the defendant.[136]

Nothing points up the ambiguity of military failure more forcefully than this case. Leading Roman arms to disaster ought to have had a profound impact on a general's subsequent political fortunes, and yet mostly it did not. Silanus' escape despite crisis and outrage epitomizes the general unwillingness at Rome to bring the backlash from a defeat to its logical conclusion in the public arena. Other men, indeed the vast majority, never faced remotely similar consequences despite defeats equally or even more severe, and a sizable number even went on to enjoy signal success in contention for the highest offices of the Republic. How, therefore, could a deeply competitive political culture in a society regularly at war so mitigate the impact of a military defeat as to rob it of all significance for a *victus'* subsequent career? What blocked the efforts of rivals to bring the weight of public anger to bear against a vulnerable opponent? What, in other words, imposed limits on aristocratic competition in such cases?

Pragmatism might seem to offer one plausible solution. Moments of acute crisis and the simple need to survive impel people to suspend their differences and pull together. But although in the wake of some defeats this cooperation may have helped limit partisan rivalry, it cannot have been a factor consistently since by no means every defeat the Romans suffered was catastrophic, and elections for the most part took place long after any emergencies

---

135. *Criminabat (sc. Domitius) rem cum Cimbris iniussu populi gessisse, idque principium fuisse calamitatum quas eo bello populus accepisset* (Asc. 80 C).
136. Asc. 80 C; further sources are in appendix 1.1, no. 44.

had passed. Nor does the model fit the facts of the two most relevant cases: without doubt the Romans buried their differences in the wake of Cannae, the most dangerous military situation the Republic ever had to face; but the Arausio disaster in 105 was nearly as threatening, and it ushered in a particularly intense period of political conflict.[137]

However, under ordinary circumstances other considerations may have helped a consensus emerge. All senators hoped for the honor of leading a Roman army; hence no one of them may have wished to create precedents from which he might suffer if in his turn he met with defeat. A sense of shared advantage might well have brought about a conscious decision to avoid obloquy in all such cases, perhaps couched in terms of a noblesse oblige demanding that honorable men refrain from lowering themselves to conquer political enemies temporarily embarrassed by military failures of this sort. This scenario is plausible enough but too simplistic. Aristocrats had other, equally pressing interests to consider as well. Self-promotion regularly required beating rivals in contests for office, launching an attack in court, or helping relatives and friends do the same. Roman political culture encouraged and rewarded the pursuit of *inimicitiae*, and aspiring figures might hope to make their mark by prosecuting judiciously chosen feuds with powerful men.[138] If an issue so easily raised against an opponent lay ready to hand, why should an immediate, personal advantage have taken a back seat to the more general one? True, the latter involved self-interest as well, but at a greater remove: the situation in which one man exploiting another's defeat found himself subsequently attacked on the same grounds might never arise. Most generals going off to war anticipated victory, not defeat; and many aristocrats, having already conducted their campaigns, were safe from whatever dangers such a failure might bring. No gentlemen's agreement could have withstood several hundred years of fierce partisan rivalry without firmer underpinnings than notions of decorum or remote class advantage. These factors may well have con-

---

137. In addition to the prosecution of Silanus, discussed above, note also those of Q. Servilius Caepio, appendix 1.1, no. 81, and possibly Cn. Mallius Maximus, appendix 1.1, no. 51, both in 105; and L. Licinius Lucullus, appendix 1.1, no. 46, and C. Servilius, appendix 1.1, no. 80, in 102 and 101 respectively.

138. Epstein, *Personal Enmity*, 19–21.

tributed to the political immunity *victi* enjoyed, but they were not themselves the cause. Stronger foundations were needed.

The constitutional machinery at Rome perhaps could have supplied such foundations. The wealthier citizens in the equestrian and first-class centuries exercised a disproportionately large, if not decisive, influence on the outcome of contests in the *comitia centuriata*. Yet during the second and especially the first centuries the lower classes increasingly came to comprise the bulk of the legions and so largely took the brunt of the physical suffering any defeat entailed.[139] If, therefore, the poor citizens who made up most of the rank and file exerted little influence on the choice of consuls or censors, perhaps that is why public unhappiness with someone who had led the legions to defeat failed to prove a liability at the polls. But throughout the middle Republic men drawn from the first and equestrian classes continued to serve as soldiers, and if as time went on they came to represent a smaller and smaller percentage of the men in the ranks, as a group they still bore a greater military burden as the price of their electoral predominance.[140] Even after Marius' reforms at the close of the second century and the growing proletarianization of the army, they did not cease to serve. Grief and anger at a military defeat were not restricted to voters in the second class and below. The richer citizens should have been no less cognizant than the poorer of a candidate's prior failures. Nor is any dramatic rise detectable in the political fortunes of *victi* during the second and first centuries as military service, and thus the suffering entailed by defeat, shifted increasingly to men without real power in the *comitia centuriata*. Therefore, although the structure of the Roman electoral assembly cannot be ignored, since it ensured that the judgment of only a small segment of the population would actually elevate *victi* to further magistracies, it in fact explains nothing.

But perhaps the informal structures of politics can supply an answer. It might be argued that the men who rose to high office and military command in the Republic drew their strength from

---

139. Gabba, *Republican Rome*, 1–69; Brunt, *Fall of the Roman Republic*, 240–80; Smith, *Service in the Post-Marian Army*, 1–10, 27, 44–45.

140. See above, n. 3.

the support of other prominent members of the senatorial class. Firm, long-standing bonds of *amicitia* or marriage links among such men, together with the tight control they exercised over the votes of their clients, could have provided the means necessary to block the public's ability to reject those who had lost battles when they next stood for higher office. Members of a *factio* depended on one another for personal advancement and protection from their enemies, so that the simple need to win and retain political power would have led them to close ranks when one of them came home from the wars in defeat. Because their clients did what they were told at the polls, patrons could use their control over great blocks of them to secure the election of a *victus* or protect him in court, thereby preserving the cohesion of the alliance on which their own chances for office and authority depended. In this way a faction might ward off the efforts of its rivals to turn public animosity into political capital. The convictions of those few *victi* unlucky enough to find themselves brought to trial resulted, on this hypothesis, from political weakness and demonstrate by counterexample how important the backing of powerful friends was.

This model of how politics worked during the Republic has come under increasing fire from critics, but for the sake of argument the existence of the sort of factional groupings it posits and their collective dominance of the political landscape may be momentarily accepted.[141] Yet it still leaves critical problems unresolved. It is not self-evident why a client's loyalty to a patron outweighed his sorrow and outrage at the loss of a son or brother or his own suffering in a defeat when he was later instructed to cast his ballot for the person who had been in command. Nor is it clear how political allies could have remained loyal to their friends if they themselves came to share in the unpopularity and ignominy when they urged voters to support the man responsible. And it is far from obvious how a faction could win enough new adherents within the aristocracy to get its members into office if the men it put up for the consulate or censorship were objects of indignation

---

141. Brunt, *Fall of the Roman Republic*, esp. chaps. 1, 7–9; Wiseman, ed., *Roman Political Life*, 13–16, cf. 27–38; Millar, *JRS* 74 (1984): 1–19, cf. idem, *JRS* 76 (1986): 1–11. Develin, *Practice of Politics at Rome*, esp. chap. 3; Carney, *Phoenix* 27 (1973): 156–79; Seager, *JRS* 62 (1972): 53–58.

and contempt. To ascribe the continued success of the *victi* to the imperatives of factional politics begs the question of what ordered priorities and colored perceptions where defeat was concerned.

Perhaps, therefore, the military situation holds the key. One might assert that the Republic's long record of victories made any single defeat seem a matter of small concern, particularly when the empire reached an extent great enough to put events on the frontiers well beyond the immediate concerns of most people.[142] Hence because the actual danger it presented to the state was minimal, the significance of a military defeat could be greatly depreciated. In the abstract and broadly speaking, such an analysis may have some merit: the Romans won many more battles than they lost and so could afford to be generous toward their failures. But it still does not solve the problem of why such generosity was forthcoming in the first place. In a deeply competitive political culture one would not normally expect much compassion toward weaker rivals. Ambitious men ought to have been quick to exploit any vulnerabilities they perceived in their opponents. Why, then, did defeat not constitute a political liability? Moreover, not all the defeats sustained during the city's acme presented little immediate danger to its vital interests. Certainly the revolt of Spartacus posed an urgent threat to much of Italy, yet the unsuccessful generals in that conflict suffered no punishment, and some went on to garner higher offices.[143] Conversely, political difficulties followed military failures for more than one general in the remote province of Spain, yet these scarcely shook the foundations of the Republic.[144] There is simply no correlation between where a defeat took place or the extent of Rome's overseas possessions at the time and the fate of the *victus* in command. Nor is it correct to assume that events on distant frontiers always failed to stir passions at Rome. In the late Republic, when there was little need to worry about the city's security against threats from beyond the confines of the empire, Cicero could make extravagant claims about the defeats his enemy L. Calpurnius Piso had allegedly suffered in Thrace in a clear bid to rouse *invidia*

---

142. Cf. Sall. *Cat.* 31.3.
143. Those defeated: appendix 1.1, nos. 5, 14, 17, 24, 37, 39, 54, 63, 77, 87, 88, 91; offices: 24, 39, 77, 87(?), 88, 91(?).
144. Appendix 1.1, nos. 3, 41, 67, 69, 82. See further below, chap. 4.

against him. His resort to such charges indicates that he believed his audience was hardly inclined to indifference in such matters.[145]

Thus the obvious features of political life are unable to explain the continued success of the *imperatores victi*. Instead, it is necessary to turn to more fundamental elements of Roman culture to find solutions.

---

145. Cic. *Pis.* 91–92; *Sest.* 71; *Prov. Cons.* 4–5. Cicero's claims appear to have been false: Piso erected trophies and was acclaimed *imperator* by his troops, making it difficult to see his campaigns as a total loss (Nisbet, ed., *In L. Calpurnium Pisonem Oratio*, 178–80; Brunt, *Italian Manpower*, 469–70).

2

Defeat and the *Pax Deorum*

War and religion were inseparable at Rome. The connection was already firm early in the city's history when the annual cycle of festivals came to be laid down. The celebrations in the spring and fall that marked the opening and close of the campaigning season remained fixed points in the religious calendar long after that document had ceased to reflect the solar year and the rhythms of ancient warfare with any precision.[1] At an equally distant date the fetial priests took charge of the diplomatic preliminaries to any conflict to ensure that Roman actions remained within the bounds of *religio*.[2] Sacrifices, vows, and prayers at the commencement of each war sought to elicit the active cooperation of the gods, and taking the auspices before any important action in the field, especially offering battle, furnished assurance that their support remained firm. Further vows came on the eve of combat or in its midst. Victory brought forth offerings of thanks and the fulfillment of promises. For an especially splendid success, celebration of a triumph paid tribute to Jupiter Optimus Maximus for his help in battle.[3] Temples built from the spoils gave permanent, physical expression to the central role of divine support in the ideology of Roman conquests.[4]

---

1. On the Equiria, the dance of the Salian priests, the Armilustrium, the "October Horse," and the various other festivals in March and October and their connection with warfare, see Wissowa, *Religion und Kultus der Römer*, 144–53; Degrassi, *Inscr. Ital.* 13.2: 366; Dumézil, *Archaic Roman Religion*, 1:205–45; Latte, *Römische Religionsgeschichte*, 114–16.

2. On the fetial procedure, see Rich, *Declaring War*, 56–58; Harris, *War and Imperialism*, 166–71; Wiedemann, CQ 36 (1986): 474–90. It matters little that by the second century such concerns may have come to be honored more in the breach than in practice. The initial impulse as well as vestigial survivals clearly sprang from a sense of the importance of the gods in war.

3. See, most conveniently, Le Bonniec, "Aspects religieux," 101–15; on the triumph generally, see Versnel, *Triumphus*.

4. On temple construction as a result of victory, see Strong, BICS 15 (1968): 99–100; Stambaugh, ANRW 2.16.1 (1978): 583–84.

Conversely, the shock of defeat gave rise to the belief that the support of the gods had vanished, and obviously this conviction played a considerable part in limiting competition in its wake. Conceiving of defeat as fundamentally the outgrowth of a religious problem severely curtailed its potential to become an issue in future political rivalry. To be sure, the Romans never believed that human action was irrelevant to war, that they could simply stand aside and let the gods do their fighting for them. They were realists: in practical terms the men on the ground won or lost their battles. Therefore, strictly speaking, no religious explanation of a defeat could ever serve as a direct alternative to a human one. But in effect the admission of a divine component into the mechanics of its causation allowed something very much like that to happen. Although the support of the gods alone was never sufficient to achieve victory, it was nonetheless essential. If absent, failure was inescapable and indeed came to be seen as tantamount to proof of that absence. Thus, whereas the human and divine factors involved operated simultaneously and, as it were, on parallel levels of reality, the latter had the potential to diminish radically the significance of the former. The gods were superior and infinitely more powerful than men. As a result, whatever a general's mistakes had contributed to the outcome of a battle, these had been vastly overshadowed by the consequences of failing to secure divine support for the enterprise. Coupled with the widespread perception that the principal human cause of defeats was the inadequacy of the soldiers rather than that of their leaders (to be explored in chapter 3), tracing the causes of a defeat to some religious problem could absolve a commander of almost all responsibility for what had happened. If the gods' disposition toward the Republic had really been the decisive factor, then questions about competence or calls for vengeance against a *victus* became meaningless as rallying cries in future contests.

But there were problems in making this scheme work. The corporate power of the aristocracy within the state as well as the ascendency of the noble families that comprised its core rested heavily on control of the means by which the state maintained its *pax deorum*. If the origins of battlefield disasters were to be found in the mechanics of cult back in Rome, then there was a real possibility that finger pointing and recrimination by persons both outside the religious establishment and within its ranks would fuel conflict, not moderate it. The resulting strife could affect defeated generals directly since almost all of them had held magistracies that entailed discharging a variety of religious duties connected with their wars. By contrast, a sufficiently dramatic loss could bring the entire system into doubt, for much of its validity in the last analysis rested on the success it was believed to have engendered for the Republic. The common danger such a crisis of confidence posed might have spawned efforts within the ruling class to sever military defeat from its religious roots at precisely those moments when *victi* were most in need of the protection the connection afforded. Thus for the *pax deorum* to have limited aristocratic competition effectively in the wake of defeat and shielded generals from its political backlash, a way of understanding its religious causes was needed that traced these back to some failure within the operation of cult but at the same time avoided the issue of accountability altogether and strengthened rather than diminished belief in the system as a whole.

———|———

The Romans never assumed that a fundamental benevolence guided the gods' dealings with men.[5] Their deities were austere, powerful forces—inscrutable, capricious, and frequently destructive but also capable of being controlled and utilized if one knew their secrets. The relationship was in a sense contractual: in return for worship the gods furnished their cooperation and support to the Roman people. *Do ut des* epitomizes the principle, and the *pax deorum* describes the condition resulting when benefits were mutually and reciprocally conferred between the Romans and their heavenly protectors. The lines of communication that this crucial nexus implied constituted the bedrock of the city's prosperity and success, and maintaining the gods' participation in the agreement was the raison d'être of the city's public cult. One of the most distinctive characteristics of that cult was the enormous stress laid on the meticulous execution of all ritual acts. In Republican theology the mental or emotional state of the worshipers counted for noth-

---

5. On what follows, see Jocelyn, *JRH* 4 (1966–67): 89–104, esp. 100–103.

ing; all that mattered was that the Romans fulfilled their obligations to the letter. They undertook no vow, offered no prayer, made no sacrifice without the greatest efforts to get the language and procedures exactly right. The smallest error or irregularity vitiated the whole event, necessitating its repetition until a flawless execution could be accomplished. Only precision on the part of the Romans could induce the gods to fulfill their part of the agreement, and so enormous care was taken to ensure that no mistakes occurred.[6]

This feature of Roman worship suggests an obvious model for religious dysfunction and its effect in war:

> Failures could be explained on the ground that the techniques had not been properly carried out, or they were simply forgotten. As a rule the mechanical performance of ritual would receive little attention. Neglect of some detail would scarcely be noticed, except retrospectively, in the case of a disaster following. Then any defect would be remembered and the importance of meticulous observation would be confirmed.[7]

Defeat, in other words, would lead to a review of the cult activities preceding it until someone recollected an error in the recitation of a formula, a disruption in the ritual silence, a slight hesitation as a victim had approached the altar, or some other little *vitium* that no one had caught at the time. Although apparently trivial, its effect had been to invalidate the entire ceremony of which it had been a part. This rupture in the flow of benefits from one side brought about their corresponding cessation on the other. The state of *pax* ceased to exist. Thus Roman arms were on their own as they entered battle and perhaps even had to contend with the active opposition of the gods as well. Military failure in this conception becomes easily comprehensible as the result of a breakdown in relations with the heavenly powers.

Yet the lack of explanations along these lines in the sources is

---

6. E.g. Cicero, *Haru. Resp.* 23; Plin. *HN* 13.10; Dio 12.51; cf. Tromp, *De Romanorum Piaculis*, 59–62, 71–77; Jocelyn, *JRH* 4 (1966–67): 92; North, *PBSR* 44 (n.s. 30) (1976): 1–12 at 1–3; Scheid "Le délit religieux," 117–71; Wardman, *Religion and Statecraft*, 1–21.

7. Liebeschuetz, *Continuity and Change*, 28, cf. 56. Liebeschuetz is here speaking specifically of auspication, but his hypothesis is in fact more appropriate for vows and sacrifices since whatever was reported to the auspicant by his assistant was held to constitute binding auspices: see below, pp. 64–65.

striking. Only once does an unnoticed, trivial error in ritual form appear as the cause of a major defeat. In 217, following the destruction of Flaminius' army at Lake Trasimene, the very first item the senate heard from the decemvirs after they had consulted the Sibylline books was their discovery that a vow to Mars undertaken on account of the war had not been correctly made.[8] Even this case, though, does not conform to expectations as closely as it might at first appear. The need to appease Mars was only one of a number of propitiatory steps recommended by the decemvirs; Jupiter, Venus Erycina, Mens, and other gods all received attention.[9] The flaw in the vow to Mars did not seem at the time sufficiently egregious to have brought on the catastrophe at Trasimene by itself.[10] Tradition concurred, and a host of religious transgressions by the consul Flaminius in time came to be viewed as its real cause.[11] There are no other cases on record in which the Romans responded to a defeat with a search for undetected errors in the mechanical performance of ritual. Precisely where one would expect intense hunts for unnoticed slips and their frequent discovery, this failed to occur.

The reason lies in the fact that although the model could explain why defeats happened, it was incapable of fulfilling the other tasks a central role in limiting competition demanded of it. This insufficiency existed because fundamentally the explanation hinged on somebody's blunder. As noted, the Romans went to great lengths to guarantee the meticulously correct execution of cult. Therefore,

---

8. Livy 22.9.9.
9. Livy 22.9.9–10.
10. The origins of this error are problematic. Livy's language at 22.9.9 suggests that the vow to Mars had been made in 218 in connection with the Roman declaration of war against Carthage: *quod eius belli causa votum Marti foret, id non rite factum* . . . ; but he makes no mention of it either in that context, at 21.17.4, or at 21.62.1–6, where, according to Klotz, *RhM* 85 (1936): 84, Livy placed the religious events properly belonging to the opening of 218 (cf. Zonar. 8.22). Generals departing for the front did not regularly undertake offerings to Mars, and this one was probably exceptional; note the sacrifice to whatever gods the consuls thought appropriate at the outset of the war with Philip in 200 (Livy 31.5.3–4). If so, then possibly the ritual formulas employed were incorrect or the sacrifices promised inadequate; cf. the uncertainties over the precise form a vow of games and a gift for Jupiter should take at the inception of the Second Macedonian War (Livy 31.9.6–8).
11. Coelius Antipater, frg. 20 P (= Cic. *Div.* 1.77), cf. Coelius frg. 19 P (= Cic. *Nat. D.* 2.8); Livy 21.63.5–14, 22.1.5–7, 3.7–14; Val. Max. 1.1.6; Plut. *Fab.* 3.1. See below, pp. 77–78, for further discussion.

if defeat were seen as the product of unnoticed mistakes in performance, it might follow that failure on the battlefield could have been avoided if only more care had been taken in carrying out the ceremonies properly. Instead, someone had allowed a small but crucial step to be either incorrectly performed or omitted altogether. This negligence, then, became the real reason failure had ensued, and it immediately raised the question of who was to blame and possibly suffer punishment for the tragic consequences of his inattention. Therein lay the germ of a political contest, for there were as many places where blame could be laid as cult procedures in which unnoticed errors could occur, and the aristocracy was not averse to discovering or devising little technical mistakes in the rituals at other times when some personal advantage might be gained from doing so.[12]

A struggle over who was responsible for such *vitia* could jeopardize the *victus* directly. A considerable number of religious duties fell to army commanders, particularly those holding the office of consul at the time, as the bulk of defeated commanders in the period under study did.[13] On the morning of his first day in office a new consul took the auspices, then led a procession to the Capitoline temple, where he offered sacrifice to Jupiter and announced his vows to the same deity.[14] Consuls also celebrated the Latin Festival and sacrificed to Vesta and the *penates* at Lavinium.[15] Each took

---

12. *Instaurationes* (repetitions) of the *ludi* are among the best-attested examples: see the lists in De Sanctis, *Storia*, 4.2.1^2: 335 n. 951; Taylor, *TAPhA* 68 (1937): 284–304, at 291; discussion in Tromp, *De Romanorum Piaculis*, 70–71; Eisenhut, *RE* 14: 198–206. Note too the *instauratio* of the Great Games in 194 in connection with errors in the celebration of the *ver sacrum* in the preceding year (Livy 34.44.1–3). Not all *instaurationes* were necessarily the result of errors in procedure, although this seems to have been the most common reason (Taylor, 294–96; Tromp, *De Romanorum Piaculis*, 66–69). On *instaurationes* in Cicero's day, see, e.g., *Haru. Resp.* 21. They were still a feature of the games during the reign of the Emperor Claudius: Dio 60.6.4–5. The discovery of *vitia* in auspication for legislation, elections, and the entry of magistrates into office was also frequent, e.g. Val. Max. 1.1.5; Plut. *Marc.* 5.4, 12.1; Livy 23.31.13–14; Cic. *Nat. D.* 2.10–11; *Div.* 1.33, 2.75; *QFr.* 6 (2.2).1; Val. Max. 1.1.3; Gran. Licin. 28.24–26 C.
13. See in general Le Bonniec, "Aspects religieux," 106–10; R. Combès, *Imperator*, 387; Keaveney, *AJAH* 7 (1982): 162–64.
14. Ov. *Fast.* 1.79–84; *Pont.* 4.4.23–35; Livy 21.63.7–8.
15. On the Latin Festival, see Wissowa, *Religion und Kultus der Römer*, 124–26; on Lavinium, see Varro *Ling.* 5.144; Asc. 21 C.; Val. Max. 1.6.7; Serv. *Aen.* 2.296; Macrob. *Sat.* 3.4.11; discussion in Weinstock, *JRS* 50 (1960): 112–14; Alföldi, *Early Rome*, 246–71.

the auspices and sacrificed before the meetings of the senate, over which he presided.[16] Auspication was again necessary when proclaiming a date for an army to assemble and when leaving the city for a province, along with more offerings and additional vows to Jupiter Capitolinus.[17] On arrival in camp the army had to be purified.[18] Sacrifice and auspication continued to be required during operations in the field, especially prior to joining battle.[19] Vows in the midst of combat might also prove necessary.[20] The religious duties of promagistrates and praetors assigned a military *provincia* were similar, although not as extensive. They had charge of no festivals but did have to take the auspices, offer sacrifice, and announce vows when they left the city.[21] The requirements for lustration, sacrifices, and auspication while in the field were also probably similar.[22] Perhaps, therefore, carelessness here had broken the *pax deorum* and led to defeat.

But many more people were involved in securing the cooperation of the gods, and responsiblity tended especially to cluster around the apex of Rome's political hierarchy, shared out among the powerful and the well connected. The urban praetors had charge of the *ludi Apollinares,* and the Roman games and the *ludi Megalenses* fell to the curule aediles. The plebeian aediles supervised the *ludi Ceriales* and the Plebeian games. Praetors also undertook other sacrifices, especially in the absence of the consuls when the senate typically placed a praetor in charge of whatever extraordinary religious measures it deemed necessary in the course of the year.[23] Annual tenure of these offices ensured that over time a substantial number of men took a turn supervising such events. Certain other rites, the need for which had been discovered on consultation of the Sibylline books, were discharged by the decem-

---

16. Varro ap. Gell. *NA* 14.7.9; cf. Cic. *Fam.* 377 (10.12).3.
17. On the proclamation, see Livy 45.12.10; on departure, see Cic. *Phil.* 3.11, 5.24; Livy 21.63.9, 41.10.5–13, 41.27.3, 42.49.1.
18. See Latte, *Römische Religionsgeschichte*, 119.
19. On sacrifice, see Livy 8.9.1, 9.14.4, 27.16.15, 27.26.13–14, 38.26.1. On auspication, see Livy 9.14.4, 10.40.5–11, 23.36.9–10, 27.16.15, 38.26.1, 41.18.14.
20. E.g. Livy 40.52.4.
21. Cic. 2 *Verr.* 5.34; Dio 39.39.6.
22. On the auspices of promagistrates, see appendix 2.
23. E.g. Livy 21.61.10, 25.12.12–14, 45.16.7–8; App. *BCiv.* 1.54; Val. Max. 9.7.4.

virs.²⁴ In addition, the annual worship of the dozens of other gods and goddesses who occupied places within the Republican pantheon was parceled out to various groups: the duties of the pontifical college seem to have been extensive in this area.²⁵ Older bodies, such as the Salii, the vestal virgins, and the *flamines* undertook more limited obligations. Some foreign deities, captured along with other booty from the enemy, were apparently given over to noble families to tend.²⁶

The participation of so many eminent Romans in the cult made a search for ritual error something of a loose cannon on the quarterdeck of the Republic and might furnish a *victus* under attack with an opportunity to lay the blame elsewhere. C. Hostilius Mancinus alleged that his campaign against Numantia had been vitiated from the start because the war had been renewed in violation of Rome's *fides* and hence without the support of the gods. The pontifical and augural colleges as well as the whole senate ought to have seen that a terrible religious error was being committed, particularly since warnings had been raised at the time Pompeius' agreement was rejected.²⁷ Yet the temptation to raise similar charges would not have been limited to *victi*. In the highly volatile atmosphere following a serious defeat, accusations of mistakes or malfeasance in conducting the city's dealings with the gods could be powerful weapons in the hands of intensely competitive aristocrats well accustomed to the practice of destroying rivals through prosecution. In the anxious months following the Roman debacle at Arausio, M. Aemilius Scaurus, a priest as well as the *princeps senatus*, was accused of being responsible for the improper celebration of the rites to Vesta at Lavinium.²⁸ He came within an ace

---

24. E.g. *CIL* 1² p. 29; Livy 37.3.6; Dio frg. 74.
25. Szemler, *RE* Suppl. 15:356–58.
26. Arn. *Adv. Pag.* 3.38. See van Doren, *Historia* 3 (1954): 487–97.
27. App. *Iber.* 83; Cic. *Off.* 3.109; *Rep.* 3.28. Full discussion and sources are in Rosenstein, *CA* 5 (1986): 239–50.
28. In 104: Asc. 21 C. Scaurus' priesthood is much disputed. On the basis of Suet. *Ner.* 2.1, Geer, *CP* 24 (1929): 292–94, argued that Scaurus was a *pontifex* and that Asconius is wrong in calling him an augur. Badian, *Arethusa* 1 (1968): 26–46 at 29–31, defends Asconius as the better source. See Marshall, *Historical Commentary*, 129–132, for a summation of the problem and other scholarship, as well as Keaveney, *AJAH* 7 (1982): 150–54, and Scheid, "Le délit religieux," 168–71. On Scaurus' career generally, see Bates, *PAPhS* 130 (1986): 251–88.

of condemnation. The goddess' role was central to the very existence of the Roman state.[29] Only improprieties in observances so vital could account for a disaster of such magnitude—or so the prosecution might allege.[30] A paradigm in which battlefield failures could be traced to undetected slips thus had the potential to bring about more conflict among the elite, not less.

But this kind of model implied a broader threat to the aristocracy as well. Its monopoly over religious authority was one of the critical props sustaining senatorial dominance in the Republic.[31] Raising questions about whether correct ritual procedure had been followed automatically brought up the problem of who was to judge. Customarily all religious matters touching the *res publica* were the prerogative of the senate, which generally acted on the advice of the appropriate *collegium*. Presumably such matters would be resolved within the *curia*.[32] However, this solution was not inevitable, only preferable from the *patres'* point of view. Others might see things differently. Scaurus' accuser brought him to trial before the assembly, thereby asserting the right of the *populus Romanus* to pass judgment on whether sacrifices undertaken on its behalf had been rightly performed.[33] Treating an issue like this one outside the confines of the senate was utterly without precedent at Rome; yet had contests over whose errors had been responsible for a defeat become a regular feature of political rivalry, it is difficult to see how this step could have been long avoided. Once the populace led by

---

29. On the Lavinian cult, see Macrob. *Sat.* 3.4.11; Serv. *Aen.* 2.296. On Vesta and the Di Penates generally, see Wissowa, *Religion und Kultus der Römer*, 156–66.

30. Scheid, "Le délit religieux," 125. No source explicitly connects Scaurus' prosecution with the defeat at Arausio, but the sequence of the two events cannot be mere coincidence. Note that the prosecutor, Cn. Domitius Ahenobarbus, was playing up the question of who was to blame for the crisis in the north in another of his prosecutions in the same year: Asc. 80 C; see further above, chap. 1, pp. 47–48. His tribunate is dated to 104 by Asconius, 80–81 C, and 103 by Velleius Paterculus, 2.12.3. G. Niccolini *I fasti*, 191 argues for Asconius' date; Sumner, *Orators*, 97–100 defends Velleius' at length but is answered by Marshall, *Historical Commentary*, 277–78; see also Badian, *Mélange Piganiol*, 913 n. 3. The anniversary of the Arausio defeat, October 6, later was considered a *dies ater*: see Plut. *Luc.* 27.7, cf. Gran. Licin. 33.15–17 C.

31. For a careful analysis of one aspect of the interplay of aristocratic power and control over religious affairs, see Linderski, *PP* 37 (1983): 12–38. On religion and politics generally, see most recently Wardman, *Religion and Statecraft*, 1–62.

32. E.g. Livy 22.9.9–10; Cic. *Nat. D.* 2.10–11; *Div.* 1.33; Val. Max. 1.1.3; Plut. *Marc.* 5.1–3.

33. Asc. 21 C: *diem ei [Scauro] dixit apud populum et multam irrogavit*.

ambitious men had seized control of this traditional bulwark of the political status quo, the consequences were bound to diminish the collective power of the aristocracy.[34]

Hence simply ascribing defeats to trouble in the *pax deorum* would not necessarily have protected *victi* or limited political rivalry. To accomplish these tasks, two additional refinements were necessary. First, there had to be methods of interacting with the gods that eliminated as far as possible the kinds of undetected slips in ritual out of which political controversy could grow. Second, a means was needed of discovering types of religious errors that would allow the Romans to trace disaster to a lapse in the city's accord with the deities but at the same time avoided the dangers that could arise from trading charges over who to blame for it.

———|———

Precisely because the effects of minor ritual errors could be so deleterious, the religious establishment went to great lengths to prevent them in practice. Their cost, in both political and military terms, was simply too high; hence mechanisms intended to keep them from occurring pervaded the whole apparatus of Roman cult. Any ritual formula required for a ceremony was first recited by an assistant to the celebrant, who then repeated what had been spoken to him. A second assistant stood by listening to catch mistakes, while a third man was in charge of making certain that strict silence was preserved throughout. Finally, a flautist performed to obviate the possibility of extraneous sounds being heard by the celebrant and thereby vitiating the ceremony.[35] They made their offerings to the gods in the same spirit of punctiliousness.[36] For blood sacrifices, for example, technicians known as *victimarii* undertook the

---

34. As it was, Scaurus' trial certainly gave rise to the *lex Domitia* requiring popular election of priests to the four great *collegia*. This law asserted an unprecedented public role in religion since it established that an election by part of the voters, rather than co-option, ought to determine who was most worthy to serve in this capacity and hence wield the considerable power that it entailed. See Rawson, *Phoenix* 28 (1974): 193–212 at 209, and Scheid, "Le délit religieux," 125 n. 26.

35. Plin. *HN* 13.10; cf. also Livy 31.9.9, 36.2.3.

36. Note, e.g., the text of the vow of a *ver sacrum* in Livy 22.10.2–6 with its numerous provisos; discussion in Eisenhut, *RE* 8A cols. 913–15. Cf. the uncertainties over the exact terms under which to vow a gift to Jupiter in 200: Livy 31.9.6–8.

crucial roles. They conducted the *probatio* to determine an animal's suitability, led the victim to the altar, and there struck it dead, for an acceptable animal not only had to be physically "right" but had to approach the place of sacrifice willingly and die properly once struck. An animal that bolted at any point, particularly after being hit, was regarded as a terrifying portent.[37] The actions of the celebrant himself at this stage were restricted primarily to sprinkling the animal with *mola salsa* and touching it with a knife, which symbolically accomplished the offering. Keeping the actual slaughtering of large sacrificial animals out of unskilled hands not only avoided a bloody mess but ensured that the offering would be effective in pleasing the gods and thus sustaining the state of *pax* that resulted. Since everything depended on flawless execution of the rites, no chances could be taken: after the victim had been dispatched, the *victimarii* or *haruspices* recovered the *exta* and carefully inspected their condition. The viscera indicated whether or not the offering had been a *litatio*, that is, one acceptable to the gods.[38] The discovery of irregularities meant repetition of the sacrifice until the gods indicated through the *exta* that they were satisfied.

In case all these precautions failed, two additional safeguards were in place. One was prophylactic: on the day before any sacrifice a special anticipatory offering, the *hostia praecidanea*, was made to offset any errors that might have escaped the assistants' vigilance.[39] Second, not all errors were necessarily fatal. A central tenet in pontifical law was the proposition that only mistakes committed knowingly and intentionally, *scienter et dolo malo*, were inexpiable.[40] Others could be atoned for.

However, a magistrate never presumed the support of the gods would attend whatever public business he was intent on. He sought a demonstration that the lines of communication were still open by means of the *auspicia impetrativa*.[41] Favorable signs did not,

---

37. E.g. Livy 21.63.13–14; note also Obseq. 47. On the behavior required of the victim at the sacrifice, see Tromp, *De Romanorum Piaculis*, 60.

38. In other cases *haruspices* examined the entrails as a means of divining the future. On the different meanings of the *exta*, see Schilling, "A propos des 'exta,'" 1371–78. That the *haruspices* were involved in both types of extispicine seems indicated by Livy 31.5.7.

39. See Tromp, *De Romanorum Piaculis*, 72–77.

40. See below, n. 86.

41. On the regulations governing augurs and the auspices, see the excellent study of Linderski, *ANRW* 2.16.3 (1986): 2146–2312.

of course, guarantee success, only that the gods had given their permission for what was about to take place.[42] Yet such approval was an essential element in the preservation of the *pax deorum*. Here too the crucial job of observing the signs went to an assistant. The magistrate himself never based his understanding of the gods' will on what he had seen with his own eyes.[43] Furthermore, the auspices were whatever he was told they were, not the signs actually observed. It made no difference if a celebrant later discovered that the man on whose report he depended had made a mistake or even lied about what he had seen.[44] It was possible, in other words, to ensure favorable auspices even if none occurred.

The primary aim of such arrangements was to guarantee that the ceremonies passed off flawlessly. They may also have represented an attempt to protect an aristocratic celebrant from any harm mistakes could bring.[45] But in effect they rendered the magistrate a passive participant in the rites, and actual responsibility devolved onto his assistants. Most seem to have been men of humble station and could, at least in theory, have served as scapegoats in the event calamity raised doubts about the integrity of the ceremonies.[46] But not all were so modestly situated. The *pontifex*

---

42. However, favorable auspices might be taken to imply that divine support, and hence success, would attend whatever the person had in mind, whereas unfavorable signs could be held to constitute a qualified glimpse into the future, in that if the gods withheld their permission, whatever was about to take place would likely turn out badly: see Linderski, *PP* 37 (1983): 30–31; idem, *ANRW* 2.16.3 (1986): 2200–2202.

43. Clear in Cicero's description of the *auspicatio tripudii* at *Div.* 2.71–72. This procedure was the one regularly employed prior to battle (Livy 10.40.4, 22.42.7–10; Cic. *Div.* 1.77) and, apparently, on departure from the city (Livy frg. 12). Note also the magistrate's reliance on assistants in watching for signs from the heavens: Cic. *Div.* 2.74; Dion. Hal. 2.6.2–3.

44. Demonstrated by the well-known case of L. Papirius Cursor's auspication in 293: see Livy 10.40.4–14; cf. Linderski, *PP* 37 (1983): 32.

45. Tradition recorded the story that the third king of Rome, Tullus Hostilius, died as a consequence of errors in carrying out certain rituals. Having found in the commentaries of his predecessor Numa what he believed were the rites necessary to free his people from a plague, he bungled them and brought down Jupiter's wrath in the form of a thunderbolt: see Calpurnius Piso, frg. 13 P (= Plin. *HN* 28.14); Livy 1.31.5–8.

46. However, no evidence indicates such scapegoating in fact occurred. Possibly the lowly status of assistants placed them beneath the notice of those who preserved historical accounts at Rome, so that censure and punishment simply go unrecorded in the sources. But it seems more likely that they made conscientious efforts to carry out their responsibilities properly and that the number of people involved at the various ceremonies and their awareness of the need for precision combined to cut down the incidence of undetected slipups to virtually nil. Fur-

maximus not infrequently pronounced the required formulas for the consul to repeat when the latter undertook vows on behalf of the state.⁴⁷ A member of the decemvirs on occasion fulfilled a similar role, apparently in connection with rites commanded by the Sibylline books.⁴⁸ Individual augurs might be summoned to assist at auspication, particularly at legislative and electoral *comitia*, but a magistrate could go outside their ranks for someone to declare the auspices to him if he so choose.⁴⁹ In a more general sense, however, all celebrants acted under the guidance of one of the three great colleges of priests, which between them controlled all authoritative sources for correct ritual and whose members tended to be drawn from among the most prominent *gentes* of the city.⁵⁰ High status and serious political clout among his assistants could give a celebrant powerful allies to support an assertion that nothing had gone wrong in the ceremonies he had performed.

Thus the Republic's way of doing business with the gods was so constituted as to shield a *victus* from criticism when disaster raised suspicions of mismanagement. The same held true for other celebrants, and these procedures helped limit rivalry and deflect the issue of accountability. By itself, however, technique could not make these problems go away entirely. Notwithstanding the most elaborate precautions undertaken by the most eminent members of the state, lost battles still demanded a religious explanation. Given the enormous stress placed on the formal requirements of cult, this need meant that mistakes would have to be found some-

---

thermore, the effect of the *hostia praecidanea* may have been felt to have nullified the consequences of any inattention on their part: Tromp, *De Romanorum Piaculis*, 72–77. As will be discussed below, the kinds of religious mistakes the Romans tended to discover following defeats were such as to eliminate the need to find minor errors in the rites and someone to blame for them.

47. E.g. Livy 4.27.1, 31.9.9, 36.2.3, 42.28.9; cf. Suet. *Claud*. 22. See Szemler, *RE* Suppl. 15 col. 358.

48. E.g. Livy 41.21.11; Pliny *HN* 28.12 with Livy 22.57.6; Plut. *Mor*. 284B–C.

49. Cic. *Div*. 2.71; Valeton, *Mnemosyne* 18 (1890): 209; contra, however, cf. Βάσης, ΑΘΗΝΑ 7 (1895): 142–44. Hard evidence is regrettably scarce: Linderski, *ANRW* 2.16.3 (1986): 2190–295.

50. On the membership of the colleges of *pontifices*, *augures*, and *decemviri s.f.*, see the lists in Szemler, *Priests of the Roman Republic*.

where. The real key to controlling political backlash, therefore, lay not in suppressing their discovery but in uncovering only the kinds of errors that were safe and sometimes even useful to the political establishment.

Time and again following defeats the Romans came to realize that some religious transgression was at the root of the problem, and these transgressions fall into two basic categories. The distinctive feature of the first is the fact that the violations were not recognized at the time and in most cases could not have been, thus making them and the defeats they caused all but inevitable. The earliest example appears in connection with the disaster at the River Allia in 390. Following the recovery of the city in the year after its sack by the Gauls, Livy reports that the senate became aware of a coincidence of dates between the defeat in the previous year and the disaster that overtook the Fabii at the Cremera almost a century earlier. It became clear that failure in both cases had resulted from entering battle on an unpropitious day, and for that reason the fathers set aside the day in question, July 18, as a *dies religiosus*.[51] Although the story may be suspect in some of its details, the incident itself is probably genuine.[52] For our purposes the point to emphasize is that recognition that a violation of ritual law had occurred came only after the battle, in the light of its results. Proclaiming July 18 a *dies religiosus* clearly represented an effort to ensure that the same mistake would not happen again.[53] But patently no one had been aware of the dangerous quality of the day

---

51. Livy, 6.1.11; cf. Cicero, *Att.* 171 (9.5).2; Varro, *Ling.* 6.32; *Fasti Antiates Maiores* a.d. XV Kal. Sextilis (= *Inscr. Ital.* 13.2: 15); *CIL* 9.4192; 11.1421, 25; Tac. *Hist.* 2.91; Plut. *Cam.* 19.1, cf. 19.8; *De Vir. Ill.* 23.7.

52. The fact that July 18 was a *dies religiosus* is beyond question, and the decision to make it one certainly required official sanction from the senate and *pontifices*. Such a step would have been taken only for some good reason, and the most plausible is that soon after the battle the defeat at the Allia was believed to be connected with the dangerous character of the day itself. There is no other obvious explanation for this step; the character of other *dies religiosi* is outwardly quite different: see Degrassi, *Inscr. Ital.* 13.2: 361–62; Michels, *Calendar of the Roman Republic*, 63–65. It was not the only version of the story, however: the question of why exactly the *pax deorum* had disappeared before the Allia was a live issue in the mid-second century: see below, pp. 73–74.

53. For the actions prohibited on the *dies religiosi*, see Varro, quoted in Macrob. *Sat.* 1.16.18: *Propterea non modo proelium committi, verum etiam dilectum rei militaris causa habere ac militem proficisci, navem solvere . . . religiosum est*, and Degrassi, loc. cit., and Michels, loc. cit.

on July 18, 390, and that therefore entering battle on that date violated a fundamental religious principle. Nor could anyone have been: the other *dies religiosi* are of quite a different kind.[54] Thus comprehension could only come after the fact and, accordingly, too late.

Likewise in the case of C. Hostilius Mancinus' fiasco at Numantia in 137: his explanation for the events that brought about his capitulation to the enemy turned on the assertion that his predecessor Q. Pompeius' agreement with the same foes had possessed the religious status of a treaty and thus engaged the *fides* of the Republic. Therefore, the rejection of that pact by the senate and its renewal of the war violated the obligation of the city in the eyes of the gods to respect pledges of its good faith. That requirement was of course well understood by everyone at Rome; what had not been realized until then was its applicability to an arrangement never formally ratified by the voters, such as the one made and later denied by Pompeius. But Mancinus' failure provided strong support for his point, and the bills the senate promulgated to hand him and Pompeius over to the Numantines demonstrate that he had convinced a majority of the *patres* of the soundness of his analysis. The sole justification for the legislation was the need to remove the religious impediments to a successful resumption of the war that the treaties each man had made represented.[55]

The pivotal elements in these cases were not mechanical errors—crucial little mistakes that had somehow slipped by those who ought to have caught them had they only exercised greater vigilance; quite the reverse. The rituals involved in entering battle or marching off to war were all highly public. Everyone was aware of what was being done, but no one seems to have understood that the procedures involved in these particular instances were incorrect and so had provoked a break in the *pax deorum*. It might appear that we come close to having a minor technical flaw cause a defeat with the curious story of C. Terentius Varro, the commander at Cannae, who had angered Juno by placing a pretty young male

---

54. See n. 52.
55. App. *Iber.* 83; Cic. *Off.* 3.109; *Rep.* 3.28. Full discussion and sources are in Rosenstein, *CA* 5 (1986): 239–50.

actor into Jupiter's chariot when he was in charge of offering games to that deity, apparently during his aedileship.[56] But the boy was there for all to see, and no one had deemed his presence improper at the time. He fulfilled a legitimate role in the celebration of the rites by carrying the *exuviae*. His beauty honored and pleased the god. The only source for this puzzling episode recounts that the act was only remembered many years later when it was expiated. Although it is not stated explicitly, the presumption must be that if this event is genuine, recognition of the error occurred only after, and in the light of, Cannae, when it was determined that Varro's action had been improper.[57]

The pattern was similar when a failure to obey a sign caused the Romans to lose. Communications from the gods could take several distinct forms, but all required of their recipients either compliance with their dictates or at least some step to neutralize their effects. To act otherwise was courting disaster. But often such warnings went unheeded because they could not be understood as such until after a defeat in battle had revealed their significance. The best illustration occurred as the meaning of the vestals' unchastity unfolded after Cannae. At some point before the battle two of the vestal virgins were found to be in violation of their vows and pun-

---

56. Val. Max. 1.1.16, cf. August. *De Civ. D.* 2.12. Varro held both the plebeian and curule aedileships (Livy 22.26.3), therefore it is not certain whether his error was at the Plebeian or the Roman games. Both center on the cult of Jupiter Optimus Maximus. The *ludi Plebei* however may not have existed when Varro served as plebeian aedile: Mommsen *CIL* 1².335; Wissowa, *Religion und Kultus der Römer*, 454.

57. Expiation suggests a prodigy was involved; there were many associated with Cannae, according to Livy 22.57.2, cf. Poly. 3.112.8. Perhaps one of them led the decemvirs to uncover this particular error in the course of examining the Sibylline books. Note too the prominence of Juno in the *prodigia* in the early years of the war and the efforts to expiate them undertaken in response: Livy 21.62.4, 8; 22.1.17–18; see also Dumézil, *Archaic Roman Religion*, 2: 463–70, on the cult of Juno at this time. The tale itself is highly suspect: it holds Juno's wrath, not Jupiter's, responsible for Cannae although he, not she, was the deity whom the festival addressed. In terms of Roman doctrine any ritual error ought to have frustrated its intended effect on Jupiter and thus ruptured the *pax deorum*, not angered Juno. The absence of the incident in Livy's narrative also casts some doubt on its veracity, although he does not include all religious events in the wake of Cannae; note 22.67.2, 67.6. If there is some kernel of truth here, the story has been drastically reshaped to introduce the Ganymede parallel and anthropomorphize the deities involved far more than was common at Rome (although note that the *lectisternium* of 217 seems to indicate a significant degree of hellenization in the Romans' religious outlook by that date: Dumézil, *Archaic Roman Religion*, 2: 476–78).

ished. The crime itself does not seem to have been viewed as imperiling the community's relations with the gods, although it was considered a grave offense. But after the catastrophe, when proof of the gods' anger against the Romans was clear for all to see, the unchastity was understood to have been a *prodigium*—a sign indicating a serious crisis in the *pax deorum*.[58] In all such cases immediate expiation was necessary to restore the favor of the gods.[59] Yet the Romans had failed to carry out this vital step and, far worse, had gone on to commit the ultimate folly of risking everything on one great, decisive battle with Hannibal, which, not surprisingly, they had lost. In its aftermath the Romans began to understand that the disaster had come about as a result of their failure to placate the gods, but it is equally obvious that the pivotal error had been their failure to recognize the indications of divine anger until it was too late. That failure made the cataclysm that followed all but inescapable.

Tradition focused on similar blindness to the meaning of warning signs in accounting for a series of early Republican disasters. In 310 the dictator L. Papirius Cursor brought voting in the *comitia curiata* to a halt when the *curia Faucia* won the privilege of giving its vote first: it had done so, he asserted, prior to the Allia, the Caudine Forks disaster, and the Cremera. Papirius recognized that the *curia Faucia* voting first constituted a *triste omen*, and so, quite properly, he broke off the proceedings and began afresh on the

---

58. Contra, however, see Cornell, "Some Observations on the *Crimen Incesti*," 27–37. He argues that the vestal scandal of 114, in which three of the virgins were convicted of unchastity, did not constitute a prodigy but was itself a religious transgression that angered the gods and nullified the effect of the sacrifices they carried out. If so, then since the events of 114 clearly parallel those in 216, in both cases the unchastity itself would have appeared as the cause of the defeats that followed, rather than failure to expiate the *prodigium* it represented. However, Cornell's argument must dismiss not only the testimony of Livy concerning the meaning of the vestals' unchastity in 216—which obviously is relevant to 114—but also Plutarch's explicit statement that the terrible nature of the vestals' crime in 114 caused the senate to order consultation of the Sibylline books. This was the customary response to a *prodigium* and was done to discover some means of expiation: Varro, *Rust.* 1.1.3. Plutarch further reports that the books enjoined an extraordinary sacrifice to avert an impending disaster, which was the usual means of restoring relations with the gods following a *prodigium* demonstrating their anger: *Mor.* 284B-C; Eckstein, *AJAH* 7 (1982): 71–73.

59. Livy 22.57.2–4: *duae Vestales eo anno . . . stupri compertae . . . altera . . . necata fuerit, altera sibimet ipsa mortem consciverat. . . . Hoc nefas cum inter tot, ut fit, clades in prodigium versum esset*. On the meaning of *prodigia* and the necessary response, see Wissowa, *Religion und Kultus der Römer*, 390–91.

following day.⁶⁰ Omens were unlike *prodigia* in that they referred to action, not status; they revealed nothing about the condition of the *pax deorum*. They merely indicated that the proceedings about to take place did not enjoy the endorsement of the gods on that day, although on another day it might be forthcoming. Like the auspices, however, they could offer a qualified prediction of the future insofar as they foretold what would happen if their warning was disregarded.⁶¹ Manifestly, earlier failures to perceive the ominous quality of this same event were believed to have helped bring about the disasters Papirius enumerated; but without precedent to guide them, comprehending its meaning on these earlier occasions was virtually impossible. Two and a half centuries later some ascribed M. Licinius Crassus' disaster at Carrhae to his failure to perceive that he left Rome *contra auspicia* when he refused to heed the *dirae* announced by the tribune C. Ateius Capito in 55.⁶² At the time

---

60. Livy 9.38.15–39.1 (= Licinius Macer frg. 17 P). Macer was the only one of Livy's sources to add the Cremera. Papirius' dictatorship in this year is regarded as spurious: Hartfield, *Roman Dictatorship*, 455–57. Whether the dictatorship is genuine or not, however, does not deprive the story of its importance for this discussion.

61. On this critical distinction, as well as on the proper steps for dealing with unfavorable oblative signs, see Linderski *PP* 37 (1983): 30–31; idem, *ANRW* 2.16.3 (1986): 2195–98. It was a well-established principle of religious law at Rome that the force of an omen could be avoided if a magistrate or an augur refused to accept it or denied he had observed it: Pliny *HN* 28.17, cf. Cato *ORF*⁴ 73. This does not mean, however, that failure to recognize an omen invalidated its meaning. Clearly in this instance the magistrates at the *comitia curiata* that preceded the Allia and the Caudine Forks were thought to have observed the *curia Faucia* vote first and not to have either denied the fact or announced that it was not an omen having to do with them. Otherwise, the proceedings would have been halted and renewed on another day, when another *curia* would have voted first. Livy could hardly have termed the *curia Faucia* "abominanda" if tradition had not assigned it a crucial role in the disaster.

62. Cic. *Div.* 1.29–30; Plut. *Crass.* 16.3–6; Dio 39.39.5–7; other sources in *MRR* 2:216. This enormously complex incident has been penetratingly analyzed by Valeton, *Mnemosyne* 18 (1890): 440–43. Unfavorable omens such as *dirae* announced either by a private person or another magistrate were not binding on a magistrate if he took no notice of them, as Crassus pointedly did not. Hence ignoring them ought not to have contributed to his defeat in any way. Moreover, the signs announced had been invented, so that they did not even represent the gods' true wishes. Yet Valeton argues that since even the invention of fictitious signs represents an act of impetrative auspication, what were announced to Crassus were not *dirae* but unfavorable auspices, and these ought to have been binding on Crassus since the auspices were not what was actually seen but whatever was announced to a magistrate: see above, pp. 64–65. Thus the proconsul unwittingly committed the fatal error of departing the city *contra auspicia*. See also Bayet, "Les malédictions," 31–45 (= *Croyances et rites dans la Rome antique* 353–365); Linderski, *ANRW* 2.16.3 (1986): 2200–2202.

Crassus' actions may have seemed proper and the episode merely undignified, but in the aftermath of the battle the case for a religious error became much stronger.[63]

Locating the source of a break in the *pax deorum* in transgressions due to ignorance rather than simple negligence made an important contribution to the task of protecting *victi* and suppressing competition after a defeat. Like explanations based purely on flaws in the execution of the rites, this type of rationalization also translated what had gone wrong into religious terms, shifting the principal locus of causality away from the battlefield and into the heavenly sphere. That shift could go a long way toward insulating the human decisions involved from criticism and protecting the general in charge. If the absence of the gods' support had prevented success, then nothing within the power of any man could have altered the result. This frame of reference trivialized human actions and rendered the question of a general's relative skill or wisdom in discharging the responsibilities of his office nugatory. Even if he had made mistakes, their contribution to the outcome of the battle can only have appeared minor compared to the effects of the gods' opposition. Such an outlook easily became a *victus'* first line of defense against recrimination and the wrath of his fellow citizens. Moreover, it obviated the entire issue of punishment. When a breakdown in the *pax deorum* was held to have denied Rome success, prosecution or a repulse at the polls was pointless. The electorate's and the senate's readiness to place a *victus* once again in charge of important military affairs also becomes readily comprehensible, for there was no good reason not to if the state of the city's relations with its gods, rather than incompetence, served to explain failure. Since presiding over an earlier defeat implied nothing about a man's strategic capabilities or the probable outcome of the war to be entrusted to his care, the purely political factors that

---

63. On Crassus' undignified departure, see Cic. *Att.* 87 (4.13).1, mid-November, 55. Note the attempt by the censor Ap. Claudius Pulcher to stigmatize Ateius in 50 on the grounds that he had been responsible for the false auspices that caused Crassus' defeat; Cicero thought this attempt foolish but nevertheless believed a reasonable case might be made for laying the blame for Carrhae on Crassus' neglect of the omens (*Div.* 1.29). Cicero himself did not believe that signs from the gods had had anything to do with the defeat since for him they had no existence; here he merely presents Quintus' arguments. But these certainly represent the case Marcus would make were he to accept their validity.

normally influenced how such assignments were made operated with their usual results.

But the distinct advantage this schema enjoyed was its ability to protect the rituals and personnel of the cult from criticism when defeat appeared to reveal that something had gone badly wrong in its operation. It explained the problem in a way that stifled calls for accountability, for who could be held responsible in such cases? No one had apprehended that an error was being committed until it was too late because the errors were generally impossible to spot until after disaster had indicated the crisis they had caused in the *pax deorum*. Defeat thus became both their result and the essential catalyst for comprehending what had gone amiss. The hindsight on which these rationalizations were based finds clear parallels in the field of augural law.[64] *Observatio* enabled the augurs as well as *haruspices* to comprehend the meaning of signs on the basis of a long line of previous observations that taken together comprised the foundation of divinatory *scientia*. This resembles what the senate did to understand the cause of the Allia: it drew on a store of knowledge about the circumstances of former defeats, enabling it to recognize that the loss to the Gauls had happened on the same date as the destruction of the Fabii at the Cremera. The principle is even more pronounced in an alternative version of the story appearing in Cassius Hemina's history in the mid-second century. According to him, the *patres* summoned L. Aquinius, a *haruspex*, to analyze the problem. Aquinius announced that the defeat had been caused by undertaking sacrifice on the day following the Ides, having deduced this from the fact that the same thing had happened before the battle at the Cremera and at many other times and places as well.[65] Clearly, the story assumes a body of haruspical lore compiled by earlier practitioners on which Aquinius drew to

---

64. On *observatio* and *coniectura*, see the excellent discussion of Linderski, *ANRW* 2.16.3 (1986): 2230–41.

65. Cassius Hemina frg. 20 P; Cn. Gellius, frg. 25 P (both=Macrob. *Sat.* 1.16.21–24): *ex praecepto patrum Lucium Aquinium haruspicem in senatum venire iussum religionum requirendarum gratia dixisse Quintum Sulpicium tribunum militum ad Alliam adversus Gallos pugnaturum rem divinam dimicandi gratia fecisse postridie idus Quintiles; item apud Cremeram multisque aliis temporibus et locis post sacrificium die postero celebratum male cessisse conflictum.* Therefore the days after the Kalends, the Nones, and the Ides were each decreed to be a *dies ater*, on which no battle should be fought, sacrifice made, or election held. Cf. Verrius Flaccus *ap.* Gell. *NA* 5.17.2; Livy 6.1.12; Plut. *Cam.* 19.8; *Mor.* 269F. On the *dies atri*, see below, n. 91.

establish a pattern of occurrences into which the events leading up to the battle could be fit.[66] But in either version only a coincidence in the dates provided the essential clue, and obviously there could have been no coincidence prior to the second defeat.

Coniectura, by contrast, was used to establish the meaning of signs or portents that had never been seen before, or at least not in similar circumstances. Here, however, the parallel is not as close as with *observatio*, for the employment of *coniectura* required first of all the recognition that a sign had appeared, whereas in cases like the vestal scandal it was precisely the Romans' inability to perceive this vital fact that had led them into error and consequent disaster. Only from that result could the existence of a *prodigium* be deduced, placing the possibility of avoiding the error entirely out of reach. There had been earlier instances of vestals caught violating their vows, but none was associated with a military crisis.[67] Yet once the disaster at Cannae led the Romans to expect a warning from the gods, the significance of the vestals' unchastity and the Romans' lack of appropriate response became suddenly and terribly clear.

These types of errors, therefore, were intrinsic to the structure of the cult itself. One might expect the *pontifices* and the *augures* to have known such things as which days were proper for sacrifice and battle or what constituted a *prodigium*, but Roman religion was not a revealed one for which some authoritative text had set down the rules once and for all. Religious knowledge at any given moment was inherently limited by prior experience, by what the ancestors had discovered about what the gods demanded in exchange for their cooperation with Rome. There could be no certainty that such information would remain definitive for the future; the terms of the bargain could change at any time. Situations might

---

66. Although Aquilnius' role here may well be an invention of later writers (cf. MacBain, *Prodigy and Expiation*, 45), it nevertheless provides an important instance of how subsequent generations thought the process of analyzing the religious causes behind the catastrophe ought to have been carried out and furnishes exceptionally good testimony for the carryover of conceptual frameworks from one area of religious thinking to another.

67. The closest parallel might seem to be the military crisis of c. 228, when human sacrifice was undertaken in the shadow of an impending Gallic invasion. A vestal had previously been condemned for unchastity, but this condemnation does not seem to have been connected with events leading up to the invasion. For sources and discussion, see Eckstein, *AJAH* 7 (1982): 75–81.

arise that the *maiores* had never faced, or the deities could simply elect to alter the terms of the accord in keeping with their capricious and unfathomable natures. Augural *scientia* too was restricted by what had been seen before or could be conjectured on the basis of the current state of affairs.[68] Any other posture would ultimately have been self-defeating to the credibility of a system founded on the premise that the correct application of ritual could secure the active support of the gods for the *res publica*. Sooner or later defeat was going to prove this view false. Thus the system had an inherent need for the tacit expectation that eventually the simple lack of knowledge would lead the city into error through failure to fulfill some previously unsuspected requirement or the inability to recognize a warning of trouble in the *pax* when it came.

In a sense, then, the realization that mistakes of this sort were to some extent inevitable also had to be built into the Roman religious outlook. It is reflected in the elaborate mechanisms for expiation when portents indicated that the Romans were no longer in a state of accord with the gods. Such procedures clearly represent an effort to limit the deleterious consequences of this inherent weakness within the structure of the cult. But this expectation is even more obvious in the surprising fact that no religious body or functionary was specifically charged with the all-important task of detecting warning signs.[69] Individuals, particularly augurs, might announce them to magistrates conducting their duties or, in the case of *prodigia*, to the senate, and specific rules governed acceptance of these reports, but that is not the same thing as formal investment with responsibility. Those most concerned with such matters, the *decemviri* and *haruspices*, went into action only on instruction from the senate after a suspected *prodigium* had been reported to it. Where a celebrant did have a specific responsibility to ascertain the disposition of the gods, in auspication, favorable results indicated only the current status of relations with the gods and signified their approval to proceed. They did not guarantee a successful result. There was good reason for an absence of account-

---

68. See above, pp. 73–74.
69. Magistrates, of course, had to take the auspices, but these required impetrative, not oblative, signs. They indicated only whether or not the gods gave permission to proceed and, strictly speaking, implied nothing at all about the state of the *pax deorum* (Linderski PP 37 [1983]: 30–31).

ability in this whole area. Because the cult both asserted that by means of signs it could scan the state of the *pax deorum* and yet had to cope with the problem of finding an explanation when defeat or other disaster demonstrated that this early-warning system had failed, no one could assume responsibility for a task that would eventually lead to his being blamed for not spotting the anticipated premonitions of some public tragedy. Thus, this state of affairs also necessitated the assumption that occasionally crucial communications from the gods would slip by unnoticed, with predictably dire results.

This sense of the inescapability of failure was not necessarily a bad thing for the religious establishment or the suppression of rivalry. Far from manifesting the bankruptcy of the system, disaster imagined to have originated in this fashion could strengthen the cult at the very moment when Rome's heavenly protectors might seem to have abandoned the city. It confirmed the fundamental premises of the religious system by demonstrating what would happen when signs were ignored or obligations to the gods were incorrectly fulfilled. A heightened sense of dependence on the priests and their rituals followed, for even though their ability to preserve the *pax deorum* might not be perfect, nonetheless they represented the sole means the Republic had of understanding and furnishing what its restoration required. The senate possessed both the resources and will to foreclose any possible alternative means of access to the gods that might arise to challenge the legitimacy of the state cult in troubled times.[70] Enhancing the stature of the cult and those who controlled it, coupled with the senate monopoly on religious authority, strengthened the political status quo precisely at those moments of crisis when the wisdom of the traditional leadership was most open to doubt. The *patres* set in motion the mechanisms that would identify and supplicate the appropriate deities, demonstrating that they were in control of the situation and that something was being done about it.[71] Furthermore, the highly public nature of such steps as well as the regularity with which the senate took them must have accustomed the public to the notion that the cult represented only an imperfect

---

70. E.g. in 213: Livy 25.1.6–12.
71. E.g. Livy 21.62.6–11, 22.1.14–18, 10.1–10; cf. Poly. 3.88.7; Livy 22.57.2–7.

instrument for satisfying the gods. Lapses in the *pax deorum* were bound to happen, and the general awareness of that fact would have helped cushion the shock when failure on the field of battle drove it home once again, mollifying any public hostility against the religious establishment that ambitious men might exploit. Underpinning this expectation was the tendency to focus far more on the restoration of the *pax deorum* than the apportioning of blame. That tendency was valuable for the obvious reason that the religious tensions disaster could engender would find their release here rather than in the persecution of those alleged to have borne responsibility for the errors, whether religious or military, that had caused it.[72] Of course, had defeats occurred too frequently, their ability to enhance credence in the religious system would have been seriously eroded, and that in turn would have diminished the ability of the system to limit public outcry and suppress contention. But as long as the Romans won more battles than they lost, the cult could claim credit for restoring the *pax deorum* and so bringing about victory. That success too strengthened the position of the ruling class. Certainly winning was always better than losing, but even defeat could have its occasional uses if properly managed.[73]

Undetectable mistakes were not the only type of ritual error the Romans saw as the cause of their defeats, however. Improprieties of another sort are amply represented in the sources, and these too worked to suppress rivalry over blame while at the same time enhancing the authority of the cult and those who controlled it. Here also mistakes and unheeded signs constitute the mainspring of events, but instead of being the result of imperfect religious knowledge, they stem from the willful violation of well-understood requirements. The portrait of C. Flaminius on his way to catastrophe

---

72. Cf. Liebeschuetz, *Continuity and Change*, 9–10.
73. Compare this Roman attitude to the modern view of air travel, where occasional crashes do not shake our faith in the principles of flight. Disenchantment would only happen if an unacceptably high percentage of planes went down. Instead, accidents by their terrible consequences emphasize the need for safety and our dependence on the system that provides it through correct management of the airline industry. I owe both the point and the analogy to the acuity of Jerzy Linderski, in a private communication.

at Lake Trasimene in 217 exemplifies the paradigm perfectly. Expediency and cynicism allegedly led him to slip out of the city before the Ides of March and the official commencement of his magistracy, thereby shirking the religious duties incumbent on a new consul.[74] He made no offerings or vows to Jupiter on the Capitoline, none to Jupiter on the Alban Mount at the Latin Festival, and ignored the rites to Vesta and the Penates at Lavinium altogether. Furthermore, he had failed to take the auspices on the morning of his entry into office or before he marched off to war. His *imperium* was defective; he could even be said not to possess the auspices. Once in the field, he refused to take cognizance of repeated omens warning of the gods' wrath or be bound by the announcement of unfavorable auspices.[75] Disaster thus became the ineluctable consequence of his actions.[76]

The sources present Flaminius' errors as flagrant and public, not undetected little slips in the rituals. Everyone knew the reasons for his defeat and where to lay the blame. From a systemwide perspective, accounting for defeats in this way served the interests of the religious establishment quite nicely by implicitly validating the performance of everybody else involved with the cult and at the same time underlining the crucial importance of the rites they performed. Moreover, recrimination no longer posed a threat since it was perfectly clear who the guilty party was. But of course for the *victus*, casting what had gone wrong in these terms could only have sealed his doom since far from repressing the issue of accountability, it actually invited retribution, not for the impiety itself—that was the gods' business—but for its consequences.[77] Concern over this possibility figured prominently in the calculations of P. Lentulus Spinther, proconsul in Cilicia in 56 B.C. In a letter Cicero advised him in no uncertain terms of the likely results if he disregarded the Sibylline injunction not to restore Ptolemy to his

---

74. On expediency and cynicism, see Livy 21.63.5; 22.3.7–14; Coelius frg. 20 P. On the duties of a new consul, see above, pp. 59–60. On the veracity of the event, see below, n. 122.

75. Coelius Antipater frg. 20 P (= Cic. *Div.* 1.77), cf. Coelius frg. 19 P (= Cic. *Nat. D.* 2.8); Livy 21.63.5–14, 22.1.5–7, 3.7–14; Val. Max. 1.1.6; Plut. *Fab.* 3.1.

76. Note esp. the verdict of Q. Fabius Maximus in Livy 22.9.7: *Q. Fabius Maximus dictator . . . vocato senatu, ab dis orsus cum edocuisset patres plus neglegentia caerimoniarum auspiciorumque quam temeritate atque inscitia peccatum a C. Flaminio.*

77. Scheid, "Le délit religieux," 142–43.

throne with an army: although no one would criticize a success, the religious prohibition would prove dangerous in the event of a failure.[78] That was precisely what happened to P. Claudius Pulcher, consul in 249. After departing for his province in defiance of the auspices, he lost most of his fleet to the Carthaginians at Drepana.[79] The consul escaped this fiasco only to face a capital trial for treason back in Rome.[80]

Yet except for Pulcher, all *victi* accused in the sources of similar negligence were long past the point of caring, having perished in their defeats. Flaminius died at Trasimene. Crassus, who might have been blamed for neglecting the announcement of adverse omens when he departed from Rome, was treacherously slain in the aftermath of Carrhae.[81] A report circulated that the consul P. Rutilius Lupus perished in 90 along with much of his army because he ignored warnings conveyed through the livers of his victims.[82]

---

78. Cic. *Fam.* 18 (1.7).5: *si rem istam ex sententia gesseris, fore ut absens a multis, cum redieris ab omnibus collaudere; offensionem esse periculosam propter interpositam auctoritatem religionemque video.* Even that prognosis proved overly sanguine: A. Gabinius eventually effected the king's return and sustained no losses, but devastating floods followed at Rome, which many saw as punishment for violating the Sibyl's pronouncement and which helped fan the flames of public resentment (Dio 31.64.1–4). On his prosecutions, eventual condemnation, and the political stakes involved, see Gruen, *Last Generation*, 322–28; Seager, *Pompey*, 136–38.

79. Cic. *Div.* 1.29; 2.20, 71; *Nat. D.* 2.7; Livy frg. 12 (=Serv. *Aen.* 6.198), cf. *Per.* 19, 22.42.9; Val. Max. 1.4.3; Suet. *Tib.* 2.2; Flor. 1.18.29; Schol. Bob. 90 St. The truth of the incident is variously appraised: see below, n. 122.

80. Poly. 1.52.2–3; Cic. *Div.* 1.29; *Nat. D.* 2.7; Val. Max. 8.1. abs. 4; Schol. Bob. 90 St. For an analysis of the legal issues, see Bauman, *Crimen Maiestatis*, 27–29; Linderski, *ANRW* 2.16.3 (1986): 2176–77 nn. 110–111. Public antagonism was not appeased by a fine nor even by Claudius' death soon thereafter. His sister was prosecuted and fined for a flippant and insensitive remark, made while caught in the crush of people leaving a festival, to the effect that she wished her brother were still alive to lose another fleet and so ease congestion in the city (Livy *Per.* 19; Val. Max. 8.1. damn. 4; Suet. *Tib.* 2.3; Gell. *NA* 10.6.2). Discussion is in Suolahti, *Arctos* 11 (1977): 133–51.

81. Cic. *Div.* 1.29: *M. Crasso quid acciderit videmus dirarum obnuntiatione neglecta.* On the death of Crassus, see Marshall, *Crassus*, 160–61.

82. Obseq. 55. Cf. the reported fate of L. Genucius Aventinensis, the first plebeian consul to conduct a war under his own auspices: in 362 the Hernici ambushed and routed his army and killed the consul himself. According to Livy, the patricians complained that entrusting him with the command had violated religious law (Livy 7.6.7–12, esp. 10, cf. 6.41.4–12). Likewise with other generals: according to one tradition, the consuls of 208, M. Claudius Marcellus and T. Quinctius Crispinus, paid no attention to the concern of a *haruspex* over anomalies in the *exta* prior to embarking on a reconnaissance mission. The consequences were fatal, as the two rode into an ambush laid by Hannibal (Livy 27.26.13–27.11; Val. Max. 1.6.9; Plut., *Marc.* 29.4–9). Marcellus was killed in the attack, and Crispinus died of his wounds sometime later (Livy 27.33.6). On the various traditions regarding the death of Mar-

Obviously accounts such as these placed the blame for a defeat on someone who, conveniently, was no longer able to defend himself—a useful ploy in moderating the potential repercussions at Rome. But more was involved. The auspices and other signs did not technically reveal the future; they simply advised a magistrate of the status of the gods' disposition with regard to what was about to take place.[83] Paying no attention to them when they appeared was thus a species of religious transgression, like open contempt for sacrifices or other rituals, for it violated a firm tenet of the *pax deorum* that all public business could proceed only with the express approval of the gods. However, it was an equally firm tenet within Roman theology that the gods would deal with religious malefactors themselves.[84] The deaths of generals who acted in defiance of the auspices or other signs or who, like Flaminius, neglected ceremonies altogether therefore were both the result and a confirmation of this principle. Even the one apparent exception to the rule, Pulcher's sailing *contra auspicia*, conforms in that the gods intervened at his trial to prevent the Romans from condemning the accused to death: that was their prerogative.[85] The lives of generals

---

cellus, see Caltabiano, *CISA* 3 (1975): 65–81. A similar story was told of Ti. Sempronius Gracchus, proconsul in 212, who, when sacrificing in anticipation of breaking camp, watched the livers of his victims be eaten by a pair of giant snakes. The *haruspices* announced that this omen portended hidden dangers, but Gracchus was apparently undeterred. He was later betrayed by a Lucanian guest-friend and killed (Livy 25.16.1–24; Val. Max. 1.6.8). Livy, however, knew several different versions of how Gracchus met his end (25.16.24–17.7). Note a similar story concerning this man's homonymous nephew (Cic. *Div.* 1.36).

83. See above, n. 42.

84. Cic. *Leg.* 2.19; Tac. *Ann.* 1.73; Cornell, "Some Observations on the *Crimen Incesti*," 29–30. Note esp. the verdict of the consul L. Papirius Cursor, whose *pullarius* was caught falsifying the auspices: *qui auspicio adest si quid falsi nuntiat, in semet ipsum religionem recipit* (Livy 10.40.11). However, the Romans were not averse to making the deities' task a little easier: the consul placed the offending chicken-keeper in front of the legions as the battle began. He was killed by an enemy spear, and his death was taken by the consul as a sign that the gods were present (Livy 10.40.13). Vestal virgins were not specifically put to death, only entombed, so that it could be said that the gods decided their fate.

85. As the voting commenced, thunder was heard; a *vitium* supervened. Prosecution went forward at a new trial, but on different charges, and the defendant sustained a heavy fine instead (Val. Max. 8.1. abs. 4; *Schol. Bob.* 90 St.; for other sources, see above, n. 80).

who deliberately angered the gods were forfeit to the deities.[86] Within a system that allowed the causes of a defeat to be traced back to a willful violation of religious law, such a belief was vital to the protection surviving *victi* enjoyed because it implied that their dealings with the gods had been entirely sound—otherwise they would have died. Such an endorsement was absolutely essential precisely because of the Romans' willingness to play fast and loose with regulations governing the *pax deorum*.

Chicken-keepers in Cicero's day customarily starved the birds to make them eat greedily and so deliver favorable auspices.[87] Conversely, the *augur optimus* M. Claudius Marcellus regularly traveled in a closed litter when he wished not to be impeded by contrary signs, for auspices had no validity if the magistrate concerned announced that he would not see them.[88] When the Romans vowed a *ver sacrum* to Jupiter in 216, they could order Jupiter to overlook any irregularities when its terms were fulfilled ten years later.[89] Such practices involved no irreverence toward the gods because those versed in religious law saw nothing inconsistent in honoring their power while at the same time trying to control it to the advantage of the Republic in any way they could. They understood that both sides were bound by the rites governing the *pax deorum* and made every attempt to exploit that fact.[90] Thus it comes as no surprise that the men commanding Roman armies also made similar efforts to get around the rules when these came into conflict with what they believed the *res publica* required. In 69 B.C., as a Roman army was about to join battle with an Armenian force, it was pointed out to its general, L. Licinius Lucullus, that the day was *ater* and hence unfit for warfare since the defeat at Arausio had occurred on the same date. He responded by announcing that

---

86. Cicero, *Phil.* 2.83. Knowingly committing a religious transgression rendered a person *impius*, and the act itself was inexpiable: Q. Mucius Scaevola, quoted in Varro, *Ling.* 6.30, and Macrob. *Sat.* 1.16.10–11, in regard to a praetor who deliberately held court on an improper day, but there is no reason why the principle should not have extended to other types of willful violations.

87. Cic. *Div.* 2.73.

88. Cic. *Div.* 2.77; Plin. *HN* 28.17.

89. Livy 22.10.2–6; cf. above, n. 36.

90. Jocelyn, *JRH* 4 (1966–67): 102–3; North, *PBSR* 44 (n.s. 30) (1976): 5–8; Linderski, *PP* 37 (1982): 32.

he would make it henceforth a lucky day for the Romans, as indeed he did: the Romans went on to win the battle.[91] Lucullus' readiness to engage Tigranes on October 6 may indicate that the date had not been officially removed from among the *proeliares*, or perhaps it shows his own religious skepticism; but these are not the only possible explanations. Consider Scipio Africanus' advice to his brother Lucius, who commanded the Roman forces in 190, to attack Antiochus at Magnesia on a *dies religiosus* when it became clear that bad weather would hamper the enemy's resistance.[92] The ensuing victory proved him right—and Africanus was anything but a skeptic, much less unaware of the character of the day.[93] Failure was not inevitable if commanders ignored the dictates of cult; victory might prove that the gods had been tractable in the interests of the *res publica*.[94] Even Flaminius could vouch for that fact: during his first consulship he had refused to accept official word from Rome that his election had been religiously flawed when his army was on the verge of battle, and he had gone on to win.[95]

---

91. Plut. *Luc.* 27.7-8, although Plutarch may be confusing *dies atri* with *dies nefasti* here: cf. *Cam.* 19.7. For the date, cf. Gran. Licin. 33.15-17 C. On this and the following incident, see also Holladay and Goodman, *CQ* 36 (1986): 160-62. Like all other public business, Roman warmaking was subject to temporal constraints. Most days in the calendar were *proeliares*, that is, suitable for commencing a battle, but custom and experience had demonstrated that some were not: the *dies atri* following the Kalends, Nones, and Ides of each month, and the *dies religiosi*. On *dies proeliares*, see Macrob. *Sat.* 1.16.16; for *dies atri* and *religiosi*, see Michels, *Calendar*, 63-66. Generals who went into action on such days could find themselves bereft of the gods' support: cf. Livy 6.1.12 in reference to the cause of the defeat at the Allia—*quod postridie Idus Quintilis non litasset Sulpicius tribunus militum neque inventa pace deum*, although he rejects this particular version of events. For authors who accepted it, see above, n. 65.

92. Frontin. *Str.* 4.7.30. On the prohibition of warfare on such a day, see above, n. 53.

93. Africanus was certainly a man who observed the dictates of the city's cult. In that very year he spent the month of March on the western side of the Hellespont while the rest of the army crossed into Asia because as a Salian priest he was constrained if absent from the city to remain in one place while the sacred shields moved in Rome. As a result the legions remained in camp instead of marching against the enemy. Poly. 21.13.10-14; Livy 37.33.6-7; cf. Holladay and Goodman, *CQ* 36 (1986): 163-64.

94. Possibly Scipio chose to interpret the advantageous weather as an auspicious sign and hoped by announcing it to his brother the consul to constrain the gods to act in accordance with it, the religious character of the day notwithstanding. Lucullus' response may have been both apotropaic and at the same time intended to constitute a favorable omen. Undoubtedly the auspices for both had been favorable. On the conditional nature of such violations of the religious rules, see Scheid, "Le délit religieux," 148-49 n. 115.

95. Plut. *Marc.* 4.2-3; Zonar. 9.20, cf. Livy 21.63.7, 12.

Thus commanders at times faced a conflict between the need for scrupulous obedience to the demands of cult and an awareness that subordinating these to what they believed were the military imperatives facing them might be legitimate. Roman religious sensibilities encompassed both positions, and this fact can put Flaminius' behavior during his second consulship in a different light. He may have failed to make the proper sacrifices before he left the city, but that does not mean he refused to do so at all. Livy depicts him offering sacrifice on his entry into office.[96] He also purified his army and took the auspices before setting out in pursuit of Hannibal, although he ignored their results.[97] Clearly he is presented as a man prepared to uphold the city's end of the *pax deorum*, but only on his own terms and in keeping with the needs of the Republic as he saw them.[98] If he had won, the victory would have demonstrated that once again the gods had been willing to overlook irregularities, and all would have been forgiven.[99] But he lost, and perhaps fortunately for himself, died at Lake Trasimene, thereby obviating the possibility that he would face retribution for the consequences of his neglect and removing the issue from the political arena at Rome.

But suppose a *victus* who broke the rules survived: might that not leave him vulnerable to the charge of being responsible for a

---

96. Livy 21.63.13: *Paucos post dies magistratum iniit, immolantique ei vitulus.* Whether the offering was made to Jupiter or some other deity is unclear.

97. Coelius Antipater, frg. 20 P (= Cic. *Div.* 1.77).

98. Flaminius' position before the defeat may actually have been more defensible than is generally thought. After he left the city preceding the first day of his term of office, the senators asserted, according to Livy, that a consul took the auspices with him from Rome and did not possess them if he assumed his office elsewhere: 22.1.6-7. Flaminius' disaster subsequently became a demonstration of the truth of that proposition, but at the time the matter may have been far more cloudy. Who was to say that such an innovation was illicit before the events at Trasimene decided the issue? On the difficult problem of how exactly a magistrate received the auspices, see most recently Keaveney, *AJAH* 7 (1982): 161–62. Although Flaminius ignored the inauspicious feeding of the chickens, saying that it only indicated the condition of the birds' bellies, the augurs themselves were somewhat ambivalent about the meaning of such ceremonies. Some held that although they could constitute warnings, they implied no fixed prediction of what was to come: Linderski, *PP* 37 (1982): 31. As far as the dire omens were concerned, magistrates were entitled to ignore their announcement by anyone except augurs: Linderski, *ANRW* 2.16.3 (1986): 2195–96.

99. Note Cicero's remark to Lentulus Spinther in regard to the likely consequences of violating the Sibylline prohibition against restoring Ptolemy with an army, quoted above, n. 78.

disaster brought about by religious malfeasance? The issue was not merely hypothetical. Pulcher lived to face the consequences of his actions, and so did C. Terentius Varro, who commanded the Romans at Cannae. He had chosen to fight Hannibal on a *dies ater*.[100] But while Pulcher underwent trial and conviction, Varro escaped that fate, although the *dies atri* were common knowledge, and everyone was aware of when the battle had been fought.[101] The disaster in 216 ought to have been traceable at least in part to this error, for that was how the Romans in one version of events had explained the Allia.[102] Yet Varro's choice of a day for battle was apparently never an issue either at the time or thereafter. No source censures him for this oversight—not even Claudius Quadrigarius, who alone takes note of the date. Furthermore, it was well established that knowingly undertaking public action on a forbidden day was an inexpiable act that rendered a magistrate impious.[103] Yet not only is there no mention of this error in the sources, but after the battle the senate passed its famous public decree of thanks on Varro's behalf for "not having despaired of the state" and entrusted him with important responsibilities for the remainder of the war.[104]

Thus survival, though important, was not the key to protecting *victi* who had consciously violated the terms of the *pax deorum* in the course of fighting their wars. In this regard Varro was as guilty as Pulcher, who, even if he did manage to escape capital charges, was heavily mulcted.[105] The crucial difference between their transgressions lay not so much in the issue of volition as in the kind of violation committed. Both men had broken rules, but Pulcher

---

100. Varro ordered his troops into battle on August 2, the day following the Kalends, which was *ater* and hence unsuitable for combat. The date is preserved only in Claudius Quadrigarius, frg. 53 P (=Gell. *NA* 5.17.5 and Macrob. *Sat.* 1.16.26): *a.d. quartum ante nonas Sextiles*. On the *dies postriduanus*, see above, n. 91. On his responsibility for the decision to offer battle on that day, see Poly. 3.110.1-4; Livy 22.45.5-6.

101. Note Livy 22.10.6 in 217 B.C.

102. See the account of Cassius Hemina above, n. 65. Although Hemina's floruit is the mid-second century, the story is undoubtedly much older. On the prohibition against offering battle on a *dies ater*, see above, n. 65.

103. See above, n. 86.

104. See Appendix 1.1, no. 85. Significantly, tradition later made his rashness, not his impiety, the chief cause of the disaster. See Will, *Historia* 32 (1983): 173-82.

105. For sources, see above, n. 80.

had violated the auspices. All accounts agree on this point.[106] Varro had deliberately elected to ignore one of the restrictions attached to a *dies ater*, but he had probably sought confirmation of this decision through auspication. We are not told that he had in so many words, but the sources preserve no indication that Varro had acted *contra auspicia* at Cannae, a point unlikely to have dropped out of the tradition. Admittedly, this argument is merely *ex silentio*; however, a curious story in Livy lends credibility to the surmise. Livy relates that Varro nearly rushed into an ambush set by Hannibal shortly before Cannae, from which he was saved only by the refusal of the chickens to eat when his colleague took the auspices. Varro therefore stayed his attack.[107] Obviously Livy means to illustrate Varro's rashness, but on a more subtle level the story demonstrates that Varro was no Flaminius or Pulcher.[108] Unlike them, he heeded the auspices when the gods withheld permission to act. It is difficult to imagine how such a tale could have arisen if there was the slightest belief that Cannae had happened because he had entered battle without the express approval of the gods.[109] Hence we may be relatively certain that on the morning of battle Varro ordered the chickens fed and learned that they had eaten auspiciously. In and of itself the appetite of the birds promised nothing since favorable auspices did not guarantee success.[110] But they did absolve Varro of all responsibility for the religious consequences of his decision. As far as he knew at the time, the action he was about to undertake accorded with the wishes of the gods even though it would occur on a *dies ater*. Pulcher could make no such claim, and that fact exposed him to the public desire for vengeance.

Auspication thus represented a crucial advertisement of a general's respect for the *pax deorum*, shielding him from popular outcry in the event of defeat. But his immunity from criticism in itself would only have led to a search elsewhere for a place to lay the

---

106. See above, n. 79.
107. Livy 22.42.7–9, cf. 41.1–42.12; App. *Hann.* 18.
108. Note esp. Livy 22.42.9: *Quod quamquam Varro agere est passus, Flamini tamen recens casus Claudique consulis primo Punico bello memorata navalis clades religionem animo incussit.*
109. One can in fact imagine that the tale was originally invented by Varro's supporters precisely to remove all traces of doubt on the point.
110. See above, n. 42.

blame had previously undetectable signs and errors not been available to suppress the hunt. In 216 they came into action smoothly with the sudden discovery that the unchastity of the vestals represented not just a crime but a *prodigium* as well, which, having gone unexpiated, led the Romans into catastrophe on the battlefield. Conveniently these women were already dead, so involving their transgression in the genesis of the disaster injured no aristocratic interest any further than it had been already in their punishment itself. But even this transgression was not the cause of the disaster; instead, the Romans' failure to recognize it as a warning from the gods of serious trouble in the *pax deorum* had led the city to the brink of ruin. Possibly it was fated for the Romans to suffer the disaster at Cannae.[111] Or perhaps some previous unwitting mistake had led the gods to break off their *pax* with the Romans, so that they refused to furnish their support on that day.[112] The important point, however, is that whatever the cause, both it and the detection of the vestals' crime antedated the battle and hence Varro's decision to fight on a *dies ater*. The heavenly genesis of the catastrophe had already taken place. For failing to realize it no one was at fault—unless perhaps the senate as a whole, which had responsibility for acknowledging events reported to it as *prodigia* and ordering their expiation. No member of that body, therefore, was likely to make an issue out of a shortcoming for which they all bore some measure of the collective responsibility. Joint complicity dampened the potential for political conflict latent in tracing the origins of defeat to the gods.

Thus both ways of conceptualizing how religious errors had occurred could be effective in protecting *victi* from the political consequences of their defeats because each drove home the same points: the *pax deorum* could not be taken for granted; the results of its breakdown were always catastrophic; and the sole means of remedying this situation or avoiding it altogether rested in obeying the dictates of the state cult. It was highly advantageous to the religious establishment and the senatorial class generally to insist on drawing these lessons from a disaster, for they emphatically

---

111. This is clearly the meaning of the first Marcian prophecy discovered some years later: Livy 25.12.5–6.
112. This is perhaps the implication of the discovery of Varro's alleged error in conducting the *ludi* while he was aedile: see above, pp. 68–69.

underscored the need to respect the authority of those who controlled the traditional means of access to the gods. Yet such explanations left little room for the efforts of particular aristocrats to pin the blame on the general himself for what had gone wrong in the city's relations with the heavenly powers. As long as the *victus* had discharged his obligations to the gods or at least heard favorable auspices reported before the battle, he bore no blame if the results showed that the gods had turned against Rome. The religious causes would have to be sought elsewhere. Their discovery and the steps that senate ordered to correct them introduced an explanation into the public arena that became a real factor in subsequent political debate. Whatever transpired thereafter had to fit plausibly within its parameters or else implicitly deny the authority of the senate and the religious hierarchy. Hence powerful interests were ranged against those who would dispute such findings, and they constrained aristocratic rivalry to operate according to their terms.[113]

Yet the contribution of these methods of explaining defeats to the continuing political success of *victi* also ought to be a product of the frequency with which they came into play when battles were lost, and here the evidence appears to give reason for pause. Most defeats—in fact the majority—provide no indication that religious errors of any sort were perceived as the principal cause at the time, and thus it is conceivable that such a view of events was the exception rather than the rule at Rome. However, this position is almost certainly incorrect: the lack of evidence for the general scope of the phenomenon is more likely due to the limitations of the sources, which are hardly full for even the gravest military disasters. Yet even here religious causation features prominently.[114]

113. For example, if political rivalries were being played out in the decision to promulgate bills to turn Pompeius and Mancinus (along with the latter's officers) over to the Numantines, the entire shape of that struggle was dictated by the willingness of the senate to accept Mancinus' contention that a violation of Roman *fides* lay at the heart of his failures in Spain. See Rosenstein, *CA* 5 (1986): 244–52.

114. On Drepana, note also the *ludi saeculares* and the introduction of the cult of Dis, Ceres, and Proserpina in 249 as a response to the reverses in Sicily during

Moreover, two minor losses for which details happen to be preserved strongly suggest that in other cases where the consequences were less than dire and little evidence survives beyond a bare notice of the event itself, the senate responded similarly.

The defeats sustained by Ap. Claudius Pulcher in 143 and Q. Fulvius Nobilior in 153 were prosaic affairs. The Republic did not totter; no crisis loomed. Yet here too a search for causes turned up expected kinds of religious errors—failure to perform rites long forgotten or observe restrictions not recognized before. After the Alpine Salassi had repelled Pulcher, the senate ordered the decemvirs to consult the Sibylline books, and they reported an oracle indicating the need for special sacrifices whenever the Romans made war on the Gauls. The senate therefore sent two of the priests north to Claudius to undertake the requisite offerings.[115] Ten years before, Q. Fulvius Nobilior apparently asserted that a religious error had also been responsible for his failures. While commanding in Spain, he had gone into battle on the Volcanalia, and thereafter nothing had gone right. The date of that festival was believed subsequently to be unpropitious for warfare.[116]

Possibly these cases are exceptional. Some defeats may have been more prone to being thought the result of religious problems than others; some *victi* may have more readily ascribed their losses to the anger of the gods. But if these suppositions held true in some cases, then it is difficult to conceive of a reason why the same thinking would not apply for all. Rather, such an analysis seems to have arisen spontaneously among the *patres* themselves, not been imposed on them. Belief in the gods was widespread at Rome during the middle and late Republic among the political elite de-

---

the first Punic war (Cichorius, *Römische Studien*, 1–2, 47–48; Taylor, *AJPh* 55 [1934]: 101–20, at 114); on the crisis in the north late in the second century, note, too, the human sacrifice of 113 (Plut. *Mor.* 284A–C). See discussion in Eckstein, *AJAH* 7 (1982): 71–73; Cornell, "Some Observations on the *Crimen Incesti*," 27–37; on offerings to Ceres and Proserpina in 104, see Obseq. 43; on the religious climate at the time, see Rawson, *Phoenix* 28 (1974): 193–212.

115. Obseq. 21; Dio frg. 74. Claudius' subsequent campaign was successful. Whether the defeat itself was regarded as a *prodigium* or some event in conjunction with it is uncertain, but the belief of the senate that trouble in the *pax deorum* had vitiated Claudius' campaign emerges clearly.

116. App. *Iber.* 45; cf. Sall. *Hist.* 3.50 Maur.

spite individual skeptics. But even these will have kept up appearances for the sake of securing the ascendency of their class.[117] The gods and their kindness toward Rome formed a central element in the Republican ideology of military success.[118] These were the terms in which the senators spoke officially to one another and to the citizens.[119] Tracing the causes of all defeats and every other public misfortune to the same source was merely consonant with that position. In 176 the consul Petilius was killed while leading his men against the Ligurians. The Romans won the fight anyway, but after the battle the senate held an inquiry and determined that errors in auspication and ritual procedure had been responsible for the consul's demise.[120] Petilius naturally played no role in leading the senate to this conclusion, nor did it stem from a need to restore public confidence in the effectiveness of the cult after it had been shaken by a defeat since none had occurred. Clearly resort to a search for a religious error in this case was a result of the almost instinctive tendency of the senate to see any public misfortune in religious terms. Thus even for mundane military failures—notwithstanding the silence of our sources—it seems reasonable to

---

117. Linderski, *PP* 37 (1983): 16–18; Brunt, *Fall of the Roman Republic*, 58–60, 302–3; Jocelyn, *Bul. J. Rylands Lib.* 65 (1982): 158–62.

118. E.g. *SIG*³ 601, lines 13ff.; cf. 611 lines 24f.; Cic. *Har. Resp.* 19; *Nat. D.* 2.8, 3.5; Sall. *Cat.* 12.3; *Hist.* 1.77.3; 3.47.1 Maur.; Livy 5.51.4–52.17; 44.1.11; Hor. *Carm.* 3.6.5. See also Lind, *TAPhA* 103 (1972): 250–52; Liebeschuetz, *Continuity and Change*, 1.

119. Note the settings in which Livy presents such sentiments—official communications of magistrates to the *patres* (5.20.2–3; 8.13.11; 35.6.9; cf. 45.23.1, foreign ambassadors addressing the senate); public declarations between officers and their men (7.13.5; 7.34.6; 24.38.1–2; 26.41.5, 14; 44.1.11). Although all such incidents are not genuine, as a group they certainly represent the weaving of genuine Republican practice into his narrative (cf. Sall. *Hist.* 1.77.3; 3.47.1 Maur.). That these really were the conventions of public discourse in such circumstances seems clear from *BGall.* 5.52, where Caesar, not normally one to involve the gods in his exploits, addresses his men following a setback.

120. Livy 41.18.7–14: the defeat was a case of willful neglect since the senate learned from his *pullarius* afterward that Petilius had knowingly ignored a *vitium* in the auspices before the battle. It was also determined that he erred when carrying out a *sortitio* with his colleague to arrange from which direction each of them was to lead his troops in their joint attack. Linderski, *ANRW* 2.16.3 (1986): 2174–75, has plausibly suggested that this was the *vitium* that Petilius had chosen to ignore. Unfortunately, textual corruption makes its precise nature uncertain, although the general sense is clear. Note also, however, an unrecognized sign: while haranguing his troops before battle, he announced that today he would capture Letum, both the name of the hill he was about to attack and an expression meaning "to die" (Livy 41.18.5; Val. Max. 1.5.9).

assume that their origins were traced back to trouble in the *pax deorum*.

Some evidence is of course pure fantasy—the giant snakes presaging the disastrous German invasions, for example, or the voice that cried "Stay, Mancinus!" as the ill-fated consul was embarking for Spain, or the thunder and lightning that accompanied Crassus' crossing of the Euphrates.[121] The veracity of others is uncertain, as in the case of P. Claudius Pulcher's alleged failure to heed the auspices in 249 or C. Flaminius' similar neglect of religion in 217.[122] But the importance of all such tales lies in the fact that the initiative to invent them sprang from precisely the same impulse that led the senate to command extraordinary efforts to regain the favor of the gods after a defeat. Both were products of an outlook that saw in military failure merely the symptom of a vastly more dangerous break in the ties that bound the Republic to its divine protectors.

Belief in the reality of the *pax deorum* and the conviction that victory was its consequence were too deeply ingrained at Rome, and too crucial as props for the collective authority of its leadership, not to have imbued lost battles with a profound religious significance in the minds of Romans of all ranks. This shift in the focus of public concern from what had occurred on the field of battle to the state of the city's relations with its gods thus represents one of the crucial steps in protecting *victi* against the censure and retribution of an outraged public in the wake of defeat. When the deities were involved, punishing the mortal in command could seem beside the point. Whatever a general's errors, the effects of his actions paled in comparison with the awful consequences of a breakdown in the *pax deorum*. Such a breakdown rendered the efforts of rivals to use a commander's shortcomings against him in subsequent competition petty and irrelevant in the eyes of the pub-

---

121. On snakes, see Gran. Licin. 33.21 C; Obseq. 42. On Mancinus, see Livy *Per.* 55; Obseq. 24; Val. Max. 1.6.7; *De Vir. Ill.* 59.1; Oros. 5.4.9. On Crassus, see Obseq. 64; Plut. *Crass.* 19.1–6; Florus 1.36.3; Dio 40.17.1–19.3. See also above, n. 82.

122. The story of Pulcher's defiance of the auspices is rejected by Walbank *Comm.*, 1:113–14, and more recently by Wiseman, *Cleo's Cosmetics*, 90–92; it is accepted as genuine by Münzer *RE* 3 col. 2858; Bauman, *Crimen Maiestatis*, 27–29; and Cornell, *JRS* 72 (1982): 206. The story of Flaminius' impiety recorded by Livy is also usually rejected (e.g. Scullard, *Roman Politics*, 44 and n. 3) in view of Livy's confusion regarding the place where Flaminius began his campaign (21.63.1–2, 13–15). Cf. Poly. 3.77.1–2, who is followed by most scholars (discussion in Walbank, *Comm.*, 1:410–11).

lic, ensuring that no aristocrat would risk its opprobrium by mounting such an attack.

Thus Roman religion was not, as in the past it has often been assumed to be, merely a passive instrument in the hands of ambitious public men who perverted its tenets in the pursuit of narrow partisan aims. On the contrary, in defeat it constrained those in the political arena to observe the limits it imposed on their conduct. Even skeptics found themselves compelled to accept an interpretation of events based on religious doctrine and the necessity of abiding by its logic both because most of the public and their peers believed in the cult and because their own overriding political interests required the perpetuation of that belief. Provided only that the generals themselves observed its provisions, or at the very least sought confirmation for their decisions in the auspices, they could not be held accountable for the disposition of the gods.

Yet influence did not flow in one direction only. The needs of the competitive system also left their mark on the specific ways in which troubles in the *pax deorum* were believed to arise. It always remained possible in theory to detect the origins of a disaster in small imperfections of ritual or downright incompetence among the priests. But their potential repercussions within a highly contentious elite that shared out responsibility for the cult among its most powerful, and powerfully connected, members made such discoveries too dangerous for all concerned. The need to suppress disruptive forms of rivalry brought other explanations to the fore—undetectable errors for which no one could justifiably be blamed or improprieties willfully committed and then punished by the gods themselves. Not only were the implications of these patterns of religious failure far more benign in terms of the tensions latent within the political arena, but they could even prove beneficial to the corporate interests of the elite in maintaining its authority in the state. On this basis a consensus could arise on the religious causes of defeat that no individual member could contest with any hope of success. For to do so would mean confronting not simply the *victus* himself but the priesthood and the bulk of his peers in the senate as well, all of whom had a strong interest in upholding an interpretation of events highly conducive to their own collective well-being.

3

Defeat and the *Virtus Militum*

The men and women who built the Roman empire were pragmatists as well as believers, people who would never presume that victory was merely a matter of getting all the prayers and sacrifices just right and then waiting for the gods to deliver the enemy into their hands. Although divine aid was essential, alone it was hardly enough to enable the Republic to conquer time and again. Thus it is impossible to imagine that any explanation of defeat encompassing only the gods would have been able to still criticism afterward or enable *victi* to enjoy the continued public support essential to further political success. Neither the senators nor the voters can have failed to recognize that even if some inadvertant error in ritual did disrupt the *pax deorum*, more down-to-earth factors also contributed to the genesis of a defeat, factors coexistent with religious causes and yet having their own impact on the course of events. On this mundane level too, therefore, generals needed ways of mollifying public anger and avoiding blame. For instance, Ti. Sempronius Longus faulted the weather for his failure to come away from the Trebia with a victory against Hannibal;[1] Q. Fulvius Nobilior emphasized the valor of the tribesmen who had beaten him in Spain during his campaigns there in 153;[2] and C. Iulius Caesar could ascribe his second defeat at Dyrrachium to his inferior numbers and the unfavorable site on which he was forced to give battle, among other things.[3] No one could reproach a commander if conditions he was powerless to alter had caused him to lose, and more than one *victus* may have availed himself of this excuse.

However, exculpations based on circumstances beyond one's control alone cannot account for the phenomenon uncovered in

1. Poly. 3.75.1.
2. Poly. 35.4.2.
3. Caes. *BCiv.* 3.72, cf. 73.

chapter 1. Analysis there failed to discern any overall pattern such as would support the notion that a lost battle in any way handicapped a *victus* in subsequent contention for office. Consequently, whatever served to ward off its political ill effects had to work regularly in all cases, not just occasionally in some. Yet whether or not conditions truly had been beyond a general's control might be a matter of considerable debate. As Caelius, weighing the potential domestic repercussions of a defeat in Cilicia, wrote to Cicero in 51, "Any move by the Parthians will mean a major conflict; and your army is hardly capable of defending a single pass. Unfortunately nobody allows for this; a man charged with public responsibility is expected to cope with any emergency, as though every item in complete preparedness had been put as his disposal."[4] In other words, any attempt to excuse failure on the basis of extenuating circumstances could well excite controversy rather than obviate it, and if such disputes had been a regular feature of public life, the record ought to reflect far more evidence of the strife they generated in the curia or the courts. More important, one would expect at least some discernible proportion of *victi* to have come out the worse for them. Hence as a group *victi* ought to have achieved something less than an average rate of electoral success if the effectiveness of these sorts of pretexts in deflecting censure could vary widely. But they do not.[5] Thus although an appreciation of the particular impediments under which generals had labored is not to be discounted as a factor shielding them from criticism for defeats, it had none of the capacity of the *pax deorum* to shape consistently how the Romans understood their fundamental causes and so set firm limits on the extent of subsequent rivalry.

However, one thing on the earthly plane may have attained a nearly equivalent universality in its effect on aristocratic competi-

---

4. Cic. *Fam.* 83 (8.5).1, trans. D. R. Shackleton-Bailey: *nunc, si Parthus movet aliquid, scio non mediocrem fore contentionem. tuus porro exercitus vix unum saltum tueri potest. hanc autem nemo ducet rationem, sed omnia desiderantur ab eo, tamquam nihil denegatum sit ei quo minus quam paratissimus esset, qui publico negotio praepositus est.*

5. It is possible, of course, that although such political battles did curtail the careers of a significant proportion of *victi*, a large enough percentage of the rest nevertheless came through unscathed to make up numbers required to match the average for their undefeated peers. But such a theory would entail assuming also that this latter group somehow managed to have a higher overall rate of political success than undefeated men of the same rank, something difficult to credit.

tion. This was the doctrine that held the quality of the Republic's soldiers to be one of the crucial ingredients in its military success.[6] The Romans were well aware of the obvious truth that the courage, discipline, and determination of their legionaries made an enormous contribution to procuring victories. Caesar many times ascribes success in battle to the *virtus militum*, a phrase that nicely sums up both the physical and mental qualities involved.[7] The observation was certainly as old as hoplite warfare itself and had probably become a commonplace at Rome by the early second century.[8] It represented a convention of public discourse, one of the concepts that informed the ways Romans talked to each other about success or failure in war.[9] The idea frequently makes its appearance in Livy in precisely this guise.[10] Of perhaps greater significance, one often finds it in such settings coupled with references to the kindness of the gods or the fortune of the Roman people, suggesting that together the two sentiments formed what may be termed a public ideology of victory.[11] If so, then one should expect to find the corollary in defeat: a readiness to ascribe failure to the lack of a similar *virtus* among the *milites*.[12] Unhappily, however, the sources do not preserve the abundance of testimony on this point that, comparatively speaking, exists for the gods' role. Yet the extant evidence coupled with the realities of legionary combat not only points unmistakably to a strong and consistent tendency to blame failures on the soldiers but suggests that this tendency formed the terrestrial complement to a rupture in the city's links with its heavenly allies. Together the lack of *virtus* on the part of the troops and a breakdown in the *pax deorum* comprised a way of understanding the causes of defeat that effectively insulated those in command against accusations of negligence or culpability.

6. Cf. Adcock, *Roman Art of War*, 4.
7. Caesar, e.g. *BGall.* 2.8; 5.43; 5.52; *BCiv.* 2.33; 2.41; 3.73. Cf. also Sall. *Iug.* 52.1; 62.1.
8. E.g. Plaut. *Amph.* 191–92.
9. Note the setting of Caesar's remarks in *BGall.* 5.52, a public address to his soldiers, or of Livy 35.6.9, a dispatch from the legate M. Claudius Marcellus to the senate in 193, probably genuine.
10. E.g. Livy 3.62.2, 7.13.5, 7.34.6, 8.13.11, 8.4.6 (in the mouths of Latins in revolt), 24.38.1–2, 26.41.5, 28.25.6, 38.12.3, 40.27.11, cf. 5.20.2–3. Stress on the *virtus militum* is of course also a standard feature in his battle narratives, e.g. 6.30.6, 8.38.4, 29.30.9, 37.30.6. Cf. also Sall. *Cat.* 58.19.
11. For Caesar's speech to his soldiers, see *BGall.* 5.52; for Marcellus' dispatch to the senate, see Livy 35.6.9; for the prefect L. Pinarius' address to his soldiers, see Livy 23.38.1–2; for Africanus' speech to his troops in Spain, see Livy 26.41.5.
12. Cf. Adcock, *Roman Art of War*, 16.

Set-piece battles between formations of soldiers on open ground and at close quarters decided the majority of Rome's conflicts, and the key to success in these lay in the ability of an army to maintain its internal order and maneuver successfully under the pressure of combat.[13] Only a small fraction of the combatants in such battles were directly involved in the fighting at any one time since the range of the weapons involved was limited and each man required a certain amount of open space beside and behind him to wield them effectively.[14] The vast majority of soldiers watched and waited in their rear. As the men in the front line became exhausted or were wounded or killed, those behind them stepped forward to take their places. The same principle operated on a larger scale as well. The maniples and later the cohorts into which the men were organized and which themselves formed the three lines of battle characteristic of a Roman army during the middle and late Republic—the *hastati*, *principes*, and *triarii*—were so arranged as to leave large gaps between the units comprising each line. When the units making up the first line became weary or hard pressed, they could either be relieved by their falling back through the gaps in the second line or reinforced by bringing up units from the *principes* in the same way. The third line was intended primarily to form a reserve to which the first two lines could retreat in case of dire need.[15] The Romans generally prevailed because their legionaries, on the one hand, were able to maintain the integrity of their tactical formations on both the micro and macro levels under the stress of hand-to-hand fighting and, on the other, could themselves press the enemy hard enough to make their opponents break ranks and flee.[16]

---

13. Polybius 13.3.7 could call the Romans old-fashioned in his day for openly declaring war, eschewing ambushes, and fighting at close quarters hand to hand.

14. Poly. 18.30.5–8; cf. Keegan, *Face of Battle*, 104–5, for the concept of a battle's "killing zone."

15. Livy 8.8.1–14. On the operation, see Adcock, *Roman Art of War*, 10–13, and most recently Keppie, *Making of the Roman Army*, 38–39.

16. On this last point, see esp. the important study of Culham, *World Futures* 27 (1989): 191–205. By far the best analysis of combat between armies of heavily armed infantry is Pritchett, *Greek State at War*, 3:1–93, who focuses on Greek phalanges; however, he illustrates the principles involved in such contests by reference to the Roman legions that fought one another at the second battle of Philippi in 42 B.C., as described in App. *BCiv.* 4.128.

For this reason the killing and wounding that occurred at the point where the two armies met were less important to the outcome of a battle than the effect they had on the operation of the carefully organized system of ranks, files, centuries, maniples, and lines that a Roman army presented in combat. Good soldiers possessed the discipline necessary to bear up under the intense physical and mental pressures of close combat, maintain their assigned positions within their particular units, and do what the system required of them.[17] Without training and determination, however, chaos, panic, and flight caused the whole edifice to collapse.

Thus the cardinal virtues in a Roman soldier were to follow orders and stand his ground at all costs. In part these qualities aided self-preservation: heavily armed soldiers were safest in their formations. The moment they turned their backs to flee, they became a disorganized mass of men no longer able mutually to defend one another and instead offered the enemy the least-protected parts of their bodies.[18] But far more important, personal steadfastness preserved the cohesion of the unit and therefore the functioning of the entire system of which it and the men who comprised it were parts. So concerned was the senate to impress on the minds of the soldiers it was dispatching against Hannibal in 216 the need for this kind of unwavering resolution in the upcoming fight that it ordered them all to swear before their officers that they would not break ranks either to flee or out of fear. But the soldiers themselves set no less store by this resolve than the *patres* did: the members of particular units had informally made the same pledge to one another previously.[19] The determination to stand firm under any circumstances seems to have been instilled in the legionaries from early on. Describing the Romans trapped by Hannibal in the defile at Lake Trasimene, Polybius says that they kept up their fight, although they were unable to achieve anything, "because habituation led them to deem it their one, supreme duty not to flee or leave their ranks."

---

17. Note, for example, that Caesar's veterans understood the system so well that they could organize themselves into coherent units by themselves without waiting for orders during a surprise attack (*BGall.* 2.20–22).

18. Keegan, *Face of Battle*, 70.

19. Livy 22.38.2–5.

And so they fell where they stood.[20] The courage not to allow the threat of death to dislodge him from his position in the ranks was the quality most prized in a centurion, and the idealization of this same virtue among the common soldiers endured to the end of the Republic.[21] When Sallust searched for a way to indicate the bravery of the veterans who fought and died with Catiline, he found it in this: "But when the battle was over, then you could truly see how much daring and how much fortitude there had been in the army of Catiline. For almost every man in death covered with his body the position he had held in the fighting."[22] This image of unwavering steadfastness had become a virtual cliché by then.[23] That Roman soldiers would obey orders unquestioningly, even to the point of self-destruction, was simply taken for granted: when Jugurtha ensnared the army of A. Postumius Albinus in 110 and forced it to lay down its arms, Albinus thereafter came in for severe criticism at Rome because he had not elected to battle his way out. But it seems to have occurred to no one that his men might not have been prepared to follow him into an all-but-hopeless fight.[24] A military tribune could display laudable *virtus* for volunteering to lead his troops on a suicide mission, but their willingness to go with him to their deaths wins no similar praise.[25] It was only to be expected.[26] In desperate circumstances surrender was out of the question for veterans.[27] When the situation became truly hopeless, brave soldiers were supposed to kill themselves rather than yield.[28]

The point here is not to assert that Roman soldiers consistently

---

20. Poly. 3.84.7: ἔπεσον οὖν τῶν Ῥωμαίων κατὰ τὸν αὐλῶνα σχεδὸν εἰς μυρίους καὶ πεντακισχιλίους, οὔτ' εἴκειν τοῖς παροῦσιν οὔτε πράττειν οὐδὲν δυνάμενοι, τοῦτο δ' ἐκ τῶν ἐθισμῶν αὐτὸ περὶ πλείστου ποιούμενοι, τὸ μὴ φεύγειν μηδὲ λείπειν τὰς τάξεις. Cf. Livy 24.14.7; Caes. BCiv. 1.44.
21. Poly. 6.24.9; Caes. BCiv. 1.44; 3.28.
22. Sall. *Cat*. 61.1-2: *Sed confecto proelio tum vero cerneres quanta audacia quantaque animi vis fuisset in exercitu Catilinae. Nam fere quem quisque [vivos] pugnando locum ceperat, eum amissa anima corpore tegebat.*
23. E.g. Plaut. *Amph*. 240-41; the image remained a cliché: Lucan, *Phar*. 6.132.
24. Appendix 1.1, no. 72; see below, pp. 135-36.
25. Cato frg. 83 P; other sources in *MRR* 1:207.
26. On the distinction the Romans drew between bravery among the soldiers, which was expected, and individual courage, which was not, see Poly. 6.39.4; cf. Duffy *Military Experience*, 76, cf. 134.
27. Caes. *BGall*. 5.37.
28. E.g. Poly. 3.84.10, cf. Livy 22.6.6; 22.51.5-9.

lived up to these high ideals. In many cases they probably did not. But the expectation that they would hold their positions at all costs, carry out orders to the death, and above all never give up would have made it only natural for the Romans immediately to suspect some deficiency in their training or courage when searching for the reasons why they failed to do so. The best evidence that this is in fact what happened comes from the opening years of the Hannibalic War, one of the longest periods of military impotence the city ever experienced and certainly the best reported. In its struggle to meet this challenge, the senate clearly operated on the premise that much of the blame for the initial failures of the city in the conflict was due to the inferior caliber of its soldiers.

Early in 216, as the fathers made their plans for a final showdown with Hannibal that summer, they ordered the consul Servilius and his colleague to skirmish the troops under their command frequently and vigorously over the remainder of the winter to ensure that they would be ready for the campaign that spring, as "it seemed that not the least reason for their former reverses was the fact that they had fought using newly levied and completely untrained legions."[29] Shortly thereafter one of the two consuls who would conduct that campaign, L. Aemilius Paullus, emphasized the same factors in a speech he made to the troops just before Cannae. He stressed that although many things had contributed to those early defeats, above all the Roman forces then had been raw, ill-trained recruits unused to danger and unfamiliar with the enemy, whereas now the situation was precisely the reverse.[30] Polybius' account of this speech may not reflect what the consul actually said on that occasion, but even if he derived only its tenor from Fabius Pictor or one of his other Roman sources, it exemplifies the kinds of excuses contemporaries in the leadership chose to put for-

---

29. Poly. 3.106.5: τῷ καὶ τὰ πρότερον αὐτοῖς συμπτώματα δοκεῖν οὐχ ἥκιστα γεγονέναι διὰ τὸ νεοσυλλόγοις καὶ τελέως ἀνασκήτοις κεχρῆσθαι τοῖς στρατοπέδοις.
30. Poly. 3.108.6–7: τότε μὲν γὰρ οὔτε τοὺς ἡγεμόνας ἀμφοτέρους οὐδέποτε συνηγωνίσθαι τοῖς στρατοπέδοις, οὔτε ταῖς δυνάμεσι κεχρῆσθαι γεγυμνασμέναις, ἀλλὰ νεοσυλλόγοις κἀοράτοις παντὸς δεινοῦ· τό τε μέγιστον, ἐπὶ τοσοῦτον ἀγνοεῖσθαι παρ' αὐτοῖς πρότερον τὰ κατὰ τοὺς ὑπεναντίους ὥστε σχεδὸν μηδ' ἑωρακότας τοὺς ἀνταγωνιστὰς παρατάττεσθαι καὶ συγκαταβαίνειν εἰς τοὺς ὁλοσχερεῖς κινδύνους, cf. 108.3–10; 109.12. Note also Paullus' concern for the spirits of his troops (Poly. 3.108.3, 109.5).

ward to account for their failures in 218–217.³¹ Certainly Polybius himself accepted this explanation. When he set down Hannibal's assets against the liabilities of the Republic early in the contest, he listed on the Carthaginian side an army continually trained from earliest youth in real combat and noted that the situation among the Roman forces was just the opposite. This assessment strongly suggests that similar rationalizations were prominent in the authors he consulted.³²

Further confirmation of the *patres'* frame of mind can be found in two additional measures they took in anticipation of Cannae. Just in case the winter drilling and skirmishing had not achieved the desired result, the senate decided to double the normal size of its armies in an obvious effort to make up in quantity what the Roman forces had previously lacked in quality.³³ Moreover, as noted above, the senate further resolved on the unprecedented step of requiring all soldiers setting out on this campaign to swear an oath that they would not break ranks. What had formerly been a private vow among the soldiers themselves now became an official act undertaken before representatives of the state.³⁴ Both decisions underscore the senators' deep concern over the steadiness and courage of the soldiers they were sending off to face Hannibal in what they hoped would prove the decisive encounter.

Nearly a century later, when the time came to assess the reasons for Rome's repeated failures in Nearer Spain between 141 and 134, opinion in senatorial circles had changed little. In 136 the consul

---

31. For doubts about authenticity, see Walbank, *Comm.* 1:442. Few however would deny that Fabius or L. Cincius Alimentus was particularly well placed to record the sentiments current among the *patres* at that time. Cf. also Livy 21.39.3; Poly. 3.70.4.

32. Poly. 3.89.5–7. Polybius also lists among the advantages of the Carthaginian army a deep familiarity with its commander and his string of victories in Spain and against Rome, as well as the fact that its only hope of survival lay in conquest. Note too his account of Hannibal's thinking early in the contest: he was eager to join battle with the Romans while their soldiers were still green (3.70.10; cf. Livy 21.53.9).

33. For a discussion of the size of the army, see Poly. 3.107.9; Walbank, *Comm,* 1:339–40.

34. Livy 22.38.2–5, cf. Frontin. *Str.* 4.1.4. The decision to exact the oath was unknown to Polybius or else overlooked by him, but there is no reason to doubt that the senate ordered it sworn on this occasion in the presence of the tribunes of the soldiers.

of the previous year, C. Hostilius Mancinus, came before the senate to exculpate himself for his disastrous retreat from Numantia and defend his humiliating surrender and the treaty that followed. He laid the blame in part on the lazy, unmanageable army he had inherited from his predecessor Pompeius and went on to assert that it had been the cause of the latter's defeats as well.[35] We should probably infer that Mancinus intended the remark also to cover the losses of M. Popillius Laenas, who as consul in 139 had exercised command in the province between Pompeius' and Mancinus' tenures there. Complaints about the quality of the forces that commanders in this theater had had to work with may already have been circulating. It was said that Pompeius arrived in Spain to find all of the veterans discharged as well as other acts of deliberate sabotage by his predecessor. Although there is no indication when the story first surfaced, the period after Pompeius returned to Rome in defeat would be the logical time for such palliatives to have arisen.[36] A *dictum* of P. Scipio Aemilianus in 134 further suggests that Mancinus' contention about the quality of the army in Nearer Spain remained current among the *patres* for some time thereafter. Upon his appointment to take charge of the war with Numantia, Scipio said the war would be a hard one for the Romans: if they had been beaten so many times on account of the enemy's courage, the war would be hard because they would be fighting against such men; but if they had lost so often because of their own cowardice, it would be hard because they would be fighting with such men.[37] Few in the senate can have imagined that the troops serving in Spain had been either courageous or well trained to begin with. Combat there was dangerous and unprofitable, and a general reluctance to serve in that theater led to strife at the levy more than once during this period.[38] None will have been ignorant

---

35. App. *Iber.* 83. Note too that in one account the need of his army for further training motivated Mancinus' decision to begin his retreat from Numantia (*De Vir. Ill.* 59.1).

36. Val. Max. 9.3.7. Cf., however, App. *Iber.* 78, who places the arrival of the recruits after the summer campaign of 140.

37. Plut. *Apoth. Scip. Min.* 15 = *Mor.* 201 A–B, referring possibly to Q. Fulvius Nobilior's excuse (see above, n. 2) and Mancinus'.

38. On problems with the levy in this period, see Schochat, *Recruitment and the Programme of Tiberius Gracchus*, 55–60; on the question of a manpower shortage as their cause, see ibid., 1–76, and Rich, *Historia* 32 (1983): 287–331.

that maintaining discipline and esprit de corps among unwilling soldiers was well-nigh impossible. Scipio himself had to undertake strenuous efforts to restore rigorous discipline when he arrived to take command at Numantia, indicating that Mancinus' assertion had acquired a substantial basis in fact by that time at least.[39]

Scattered testimony ascribes other failures to similar causes. Newly enrolled soldiers, untrained and unfit for service, figure prominently in accounts of two defeats during the social war.[40] Cicero could ascribe the inability of Lucullus to make additional progress in the war against Mithridates to his soldiers' overeagerness for booty. Only this had kept Lucullus from bringing the war to an end.[41] And whereas Caesar never alleged his men lacked courage when he met defeat, he was quite ready to declare that lapses in their discipline had gotten him into trouble.[42] Even so, all this evidence hardly seems sufficient to prove that in all or most cases for which no explicit testimony survives, the Romans commonly put most of the onus of defeat on the soldiers' lack of training, discipline, or courage. Obviously everyone recognized that veteran troops were usually brave and dependable under fire, and a similar acknowledgment of the general unreliability of new recruits was equally commonplace.[43] In any battle the presence or absence of these qualities among the men doing the fighting is of enormous significance for the result. However, the nature of legionary combat put a special premium on them and led the Romans to demand an extraordinary degree of self-control from their legionaries in battle. That expectation in turn made it possible to ascribe a loss to the soldiers' failings in this regard because if they had measured up, they would either have returned victorious or died where they stood. A military ethos founded on the notion that good soldiers

---

39. Astin, *Scipio Aemilianus*, 136.
40. For that of Rutilius, cos. 90, see Oros. 5.18.11, cf. Dio frg. 98.2; for that of Cato, cos. 89, see Dio frg. 100, cf. Sisenna frg. 52 P; Livy *Per.* 75.
41. Cic. *Leg. Man.* 22–23.
42. At Gergovia (*BGall.* 7.47, 52) and at Ilerda (*BCiv.* 1.45); note too the panic of Caesar's men at the enemy's unfamiliar style of attack (*BCiv.* 1.44).
43. On the customary bravery of veterans, note Labienus' revealing taunt to captives from Caesar's legions in 48: *solerentne veterani milites fugere* (*BCiv.* 3.71). Cf. Keegan, *Face of Battle*, 70 (on the relationship between discipline and bravery), 51 (on steadfastness and peer approval). On *tirones*, see Cic. *Fam.* 428 (10.24).3 (Plancus to Cicero); 378 (10.30).1 (Galba to Cicero). Earlier examples include Livy 40.35.10–14; 42.55.3; App. *Iber.* 65.

held their ground at all costs in effect created a double bind for men facing extreme danger in a crisis whereby nothing short of sacrificing their lives could demonstrate that they had done all that was required of them. Thus the mere fact that they had come back alive from a defeat was tantamount to a confession that they had fallen short of their duty in the fight. Those who fled when circumstances left them no other means of surviving became worthy of censure and punishment rather than the leaders who had brought them into that impossible situation in the first place.

After Cannae the senate ordered the legionaries who had escaped the debacle to be culled from the ranks and sent in disgrace to Sicily for the duration of the war.[44] The *patres* made a special point of brigading them with the weaklings from the rest of the Roman forces. They preferred to enroll new troops from among the slaves rather than place the fate of the Republic in the hands of such men again.[45] Although the city faced enormous difficulties during the middle years of the war in finding conscripts to fill its legions, the fathers steadfastly refused to allow the veterans of Cannae to serve in Italy against Hannibal.[46] Moreover, they took whatever opportunities they could to increase their humiliation in a variety of petty ways throughout the remainder of the war.[47] The *patres* certainly intended these actions to spur the rest of the soldiers to fight all the harder and warn those who fell short of their duty to expect no more sympathy from their own people than from the enemy (and probably less). But what exactly was that duty? To die rather than break ranks to survive. There is no hint in the sources that any of the infantry had fled before the last phase of the conflict when the Romans' formation had collapsed and they were being slaughtered mercilessly.[48] The only thing most of these men had done was run away to save their lives when the battle

---

44. Livy 23.25.7–8, cf. 31.2.
45. On weaklings, see Livy 23.25.7–8; on slaves, see 22.57.11–12.
46. On difficulties in recruitment, see Livy 24.18.7, cf. Gabba, *Republican Rome*, 5–6; Brunt, *Italian Manpower* 64–67, 417–420; important criticisms are in Rich, *Historia* 32 (1983): 305–12. On the senate's dealings with the veterans of Cannae, see Livy 23.25.7; 24.18.9; 25.5.5–10, 7.2–4.
47. Livy 24.18.9; 25.7.3–4; 27.11.14. There was a third-century precedent for one of these measures: in 280 the senate ordered the soldiers who had been routed by Pyrrhus at Heraclea to spend the winter under canvas, which was among the indignities inflicted on those serving in *legiones Cannenses* (Frontin. *Str.* 4.1.24).
48. Poly. 3.116.13, cf. 115.1–116.12.

was already lost. Yet solely for that reason the senate deemed them worthy of punishment to serve as an object lesson to others. They made this attitude plain in 212, when the veterans of Cannae sought some remission in their sentence. The fathers remained obdurate, saying that the welfare of the state was not to be entrusted to men "who had deserted their comrades fighting at Cannae," even though by the time these soldiers had done so, most of those comrades were no longer fighting but in fact already dead.[49] Simply because they had elected not to join them, the men of the *legiones Cannenses* were judged guilty of a transgression that warranted the most extreme stigmatization.[50] Good soldiers stood their ground, and when things got tough, they died where they stood. There was no other option. However, the surviving consul, C. Terentius Varro, was thanked for not having despaired of the state—although he too had fled from the field when all had come to ruin around him, and he might fairly have been criticized for his decision to give battle against the advice of his more experienced colleague.[51]

Throughout the remainder of the war the fathers applied the same punishment to other legions who, with varying justification, had run away from a defeat, seemingly blind to the situations into which each had been led.[52] They made a similar point in their categorical refusal to consider ransoming those who, when certain destruction loomed, had surrendered to Hannibal.[53] Nothing excused flight from the ranks or capitulation; extenuating circum-

---

49. Livy 25.7.3: *qui ad Cannas commilitones suos pugnantes deseruissent*; cf. 5.10–7.4.

50. The fact that the senate had exacted an oath from these men not to break ranks undoubtedly increased the magnitude of their transgression in the eyes of the fathers.

51. Poly. 3.110.1–4, cf. 116.13; Livy 22.44.4–45.8; Plut. *Fab.* 14–15; App. *Hann.* 18.

52. The survivors of Cn. Fulvius Flaccus' defeat and Cn. Fulvius Centumalus' were all punished by being sent to Sicily to serve with the *legiones Cannenses*: Livy 26.1.9–10; 27.8.13, despite the fact that the circumstances of the flight in each case were different. Flaccus' men allegedly did not even withstand the first charge of the enemy but broke and ran before contact was made: Livy 25.21.8, cf. 5; 26.2.1–2; see further below, chap. 4, pp. 128–29. Centumalus' soldiers, however, had fought long and hard against Hannibal's forces and were only overcome when attacked by cavalry from the rear: Livy 27.1.4–15. On the veracity of Flaccus' defeat, see appendix 3.

53. Livy 22.60.6–61.3, although the city's financial straits at the time were also an important consideration for the fathers.

stances were irrelevant. In adopting this stance they were merely undertaking in the case of entire armies what individual commanders did when specific units gave way before the enemy.[54] However, invariably finding fault with the legions themselves when they failed to stand firm offered a means of rationalizing defeat that could work much to their commander's advantage, particularly when he could be charged with mistakes himself. For example, M. Claudius Marcellus ascribed a loss to Hannibal at Herdonia in 209 to his men's cowardice, according to Livy, and bitterly reproached them afterward for their terrified flight from the field.[55] Although Livy's narrative highlights the role of panic among the ranks during the collapse of the Roman lines, in truth the origins of this repulse seem to have been more complex. The Romans withstood the enemy attack for two hours until an allied contingent on one wing began to drop back in the face of sustained pressure from its opponents. Marcellus ordered a legion to come forward to relieve it. Livy reports that the legion moved into position too slowly; meanwhile the wavering allies fell back in fright, the rest of the army became disordered, and a rout ensued. But Plutarch indicates that a good portion of the responsibility may have belonged to Marcellus himself: the very act of shifting new forces up into the front line at the critical moment had thrown it into turmoil.[56] Yet the belief that soldiers who knew their duty did not flee under any circumstances was so completely ingrained in his troops that afterward they reportedly even blamed themselves.[57] In this they seem to have merely reflected the sentiments of the public at large. When a personal enemy sought to rouse popular anger at the defeat and proposed to abrogate his command, Marcellus defended his operations with spectacular success.[58]

---

54. On decimation generally, see Poly. 6.38.1–4; for specific examples, see Livy 2.59.11; Dion. Hal. 9.50.7; Suet. *Aug.* 24.2; Frontin. *Str.* 4.1.34–37; Dio 48.42; Vell. Pat. 2.78.3; Plut. *Crass.* 10.2; App. *BCiv.* 1.118; Dio 49.38; App. *Ill.* 26. On other punishments, see Poly. 6.37.9–13; Frontin. *Str.* 2.8.11, cf. 4.1.29, Livy 10.36.6–8; Frontin. *Str.* 6.1.23, cf. Val. Max. 2.7.10; Vell. Pat. 2.5. See also Keegan, *Face of Battle*, 70, on the fundamental principle in warfare of making the consequences of flight from the ranks more terrifying than standing and fighting.
55. Livy 27.13.1–7, esp. 2; cf. Plut. *Marc.* 25.5.
56. Livy 27.12.17; Plut. *Marc.* 25.4.
57. Note Livy's portrayal of the soldiers' response, 27.13.8.
58. Marcellus was elected consul for the following year (Livy 27.20.10–21.4).

This military ethos not only supplied a ready-made defense in case of criticism but could actually shape the nature of the criticism itself and define the issues in any partisan contest that might grow out of it. Rarely does a general's choice of the time or place for an engagement appear to have been raised in a public controversy, or his plans of battle, or a decision to order one thing done rather than another while the fighting was taking place.[59] Charges of battles undertaken rashly sometimes occur; if these are not simply the product of literary convention, they may conceal specific complaints about commanders' decisions.[60] But such charges never led to any sort of political fracas. In 218, after P. Cornelius Scipio's defeat on the Ticinus, opinion at Rome was divided as to its cause: some held the consul's rashness responsible; others blamed the treachery of the Celts.[61] Given a choice between finding the cause of a defeat in the character of a general or that of the men he led, the latter view apparently prevailed: the senate sent Scipio off to Spain in the following year to command what would become virtually an independent war. Whatever concerns the defeat had raised about his judgment were insufficiently strong to cause doubts in the *patres'* minds about the wisdom of this decision.[62]

---

59. Marcellus is a rare exception, and even here the issue may have had more to do with his decision to retire to winter quarters after the battle than with responsibility for the defeat itself: see below, chap. 4, p. 139. The only clear case is L. Cornelius Merula, cos. 193, whom his legate Marcellus criticized for bringing up the reserves too slowly to prevent Roman losses and not giving the signal quickly enough to allow an effective pursuit (Livy 35.6.8–7.1, cf. 4.1–5.14). But the battle resulted in a victory for Rome, not a defeat; the quality of the soldiers could hardly be impugned. Only the *virtus militum*, it was claimed, had saved the day (Livy 35.6.9). The charges still may have been politically damaging, however, since Merula left Marcellus in charge of the army when he returned to Rome to claim a triumph. Because that move foreclosed the possibility of hearing his critic, two tribunes refused to allow the senate to pass a decree concerning the triumph (Livy 35.8.1–9). For criticisms of Cn. Manlius Vulso's generalship in 187 when he also sought a triumph, see Livy 38.45.10–46.5.

60. See above, chap. 1, pp. 10–11; Caes. BGall. 5.52; on *temeritas* as a Livian topos, see Walsh, *Livy*, 71–72; in regard to 218–216 B.C., see Will, *Historia* 32 (1983): 173–82.

61. Poly. 3.68.9.

62. For sources, see appendix 1.1, no. 25. Note also that M. Minucius Rufus, dict. 217, whose overboldness (Poly 3.105.8), rashness (Livy 22.28.2), or vanity (Plut. *Fab.* 10.2–5) was blamed for his near disaster against Hannibal, served with the army at Cannae, where he certainly sat on the consuls' *consilium* (appendix 1.1, no. 62); the inexperience and stubbornness (Poly. 3.110.3–4) or rashness (Livy 22.44.5–7) of one of these, M. Terentius Varro, was held responsible for that disaster, yet he enjoyed two further commands as a promagistrate (appendix 1.1, no. 85).

Plutarch relates that after Pyrrhus' victory over the Romans at Heracleia in 280, C. Fabricius opined that the fault lay with Laevinus, the consul, rather than with the army, but the senate apparently felt otherwise: it left Laevinus in command and ordered the soldiers who had been routed to spend the winter under canvas. That arrangement seems to indicate that those who had been asserting that the blame for reversal rested with the soldiers had prevailed in the dispute.[63]

In another case where defeat gave rise to controversy, the quality of the soldiers likewise came to dominate the debate. In 212 the army of the praetor Cn. Fulvius Flaccus dissolved at the onset of a Carthaginian attack, and in the following year its commander faced trial on account of the defeat.[64] In his defense, as Livy presents it, Flaccus both asserted the propriety of his own conduct and heaped blame on that of the soldiers: he had done everything a good general should; they had run away from the enemy.[65] Significantly, the prosecutor did not even contest Flaccus' assertion that the soldiers had been unruly and contumacious; he only charged that responsibility for this behavior lay with their commander. Neither did he deny that the legionaries had fled, only that the impulse to do so had come from them: their leader, he maintained, had been the first to run.[66] The defendant's allegations about the state of his forces were never at issue during the trial. The mere fact that they had been put to flight demonstrated their indiscipline and damned them irreparably. The senate sent them to Sicily for the duration. Despite the revelation in the course of the trial that Flaccus himself was indeed guilty of cowardice and that this really had precipitated

---

63. *Pyrrh.* 18.1; Frontin. *Str.* 4.1.24. On Degrassi's hypothesis that Laevinus may have been forced to abdicate, see appendix 1.1, no. 90. This is not to say, however, that the sources preserve no indication of specific criticisms leveled against a commander's actions: note, e.g., Poly. 1.50.1–52.3 on P. Claudius Pulcher, appendix 1.1, no. 20; Poly. 3.72.1–6 on Ti. Sempronius Longus, no. 78; Gran. Licin. 33.6–11 C.; Dio frg. 91 on P. Servilius Caepio, no. 81. The first and last named men in fact suffered prosecution in connection with their defeats. Yet their mistakes in command had far less to do with bringing these about than religious transgressions or moral failures: on Pulcher, see above, chap. 1, p. 79; on Caepio, see below, chap. 4, pp. 124–28.

64. For sources, see appendix 1.1, no. 35. On the trial, see further below, pp. 128–30.

65. Livy 26.3.1–4. Livy's account of the battle repeatedly stresses the soldiers' indiscipline and refusal to heed their officers' commands: 25.20.6; 21.1; 21.5–10.

66. Livy 25.2.7–16.

his soldiers' terror, the fathers still held them worthy of punishment, and so they served out the remainder of the war in disgrace with the survivors of Cannae.[67] All the prosecutor could do was attempt to incorporate these "facts" into his case and turn them against the defendant.

The Roman military ethos thus made it possible to find fault with the quality of soldiers every time they ran, which must not have been uncommon. In hand-to-hand combat at close quarters soldiers usually had no other means of extracting themselves from the fray once the battle turned decisively against them. The only other escape from a pitched battle was an orderly withdrawal when a commander sounded the retreat, and there was little reason for that to occur save when fears that the men were about to break ranks and flee advised retiring from the field. Thus either flight from battle or an order to withdraw could place the principal blame on the soldiers themselves. Had they possessed the proper discipline and courage, none doubted that they would have stood firm until they prevailed or fell. The invariable application of such an analysis, whether justified or not, furnished generals with an explanation for failure that avoided all questions about their own conduct of operations by localizing its causes among the rank and file.

The evidence does not reveal how many *victi* availed themselves of this excuse, but that should not surprise us given its limited extent in the case of most defeats. Yet perhaps the question should not be how many did so but instead how many will have had to? Among the *patres* the culpability of soldiers was self-evident any time they ran, and the public largely seems to have shared that belief. At a time when the citizenry was being asked to make enormous sacrifices to sustain the Roman effort against Hannibal, it never seems to have questioned the need to keep the *legiones Cannenses* in Sicily where, except during 213 and 212, they contributed little to the fight against Carthage until they redeemed themselves in the invasion of Africa.[68] Thus the very pervasiveness of the belief may well have precluded most criticism of the commander's man-

---

67. Livy 26.1.9–10.
68. Indeed, in 212 the senate expressly forbade the soldiers from serving in Italy (Livy 25.7.4).

agement of a battle whenever his men wound up fleeing the field. But as is evident in the prosecution of Flaccus, there was still a way to cast the blame on the general in such circumstances by asserting that through his negligence he had corrupted the discipline of his troops. It was a powerful charge and one highly effective for inciting senatorial indignation. In 204, as the storm over the Pleminius affair broke at Rome, the enemies of Scipio Africanus further enraged the fathers against him by charging that he had allowed discipline in his army to collapse entirely.[69] But in practical terms the corporate nature of responsibility for the legions' condition blunted the effect of such accusations.

Roman soldiers were, of course, not born with the ability to hold their positions at all costs; that kind of self-control and courage was the fruit of long, careful training and hence could not be the product of a single man's efforts. It had to be a collective task. As a practical matter, therefore, responsibility for discipline devolved onto subordinates on a day-to-day basis. During the Republic military tribunes did much of this work. At the most elementary level the tribunes selected the men who would serve in their legions, and in camp their duties were extensive as well.[70] Thus when an army's indiscipline or poor performance in battle gave rise to concern, precisely who was to blame could become a matter of some dispute. In 170 the senate dispatched legates to investigate the condition of the legions in Macedonia after their dismal showing against the enemy. The envoys reported back that leaves of absence too freely given had drastically reduced Roman forces—for which the consul blamed his tribunes, and they the consul.[71] In battle the

---

69. Livy. 29.19.3-4, 11-13. Scipio of course had not sustained a rout demonstrating the indiscipline of his army and so could defend himself by proving that his forces were in top condition (Livy 29.22.1-3).

70. On selection of the recruits, see Poly. 6.20.1-7; but cf. Brunt, *Italian Manpower*, 625-34, who argues that the tribunes did not select the actual soldiers who would make up the army, only those who would serve in their individual legions, chosen from a pool sent to Rome by local officials in the countryside. That practice placed responsibility for the caliber of the men in the ranks at an even greater remove from the general and diffused it among an even wider group of men. On the military tribunes' responsibility for discipline, see Poly. 6.37.7-8 and, in general, 34.1-41.21. See further Suolahti, *Junior Officers*, 43-51. We have very little information regarding the specifics of how a Roman army was trained, but it seems fair to assume that here too the junior officers played a prominent role, along with the centurions.

71. Livy 43.11.9-10.

presence of the military tribunes and of the *legati* was an important means of ensuring that the soldiers did their duty and that courage in the ranks was recognized and rewarded.[72] But the crucial figures in keeping the soldiers ordered and standing firm in the fighting were the centurions and standard-bearers. The men who occupied these posts formed the structure within which the men they commanded were contained. If they remained in place, then everyone else did too. Good centurions were believed to be men not so much daring as steady—"men who will hold their ground when worsted and hard-pressed and be ready to die at their posts."[73] Standard-bearers too were selected for outstanding physical qualities and spirit.[74] Thus when discipline collapsed and a unit ran, suspicion naturally fell on these men, and they became a particular focus of punishment.[75]

Responsibility for a rout, then, could conceivably lodge at a number of points along the chain of command. Yet officers above the rank of centurion were almost never punished. Of course, they were in a completely different relationship to the ordinary soldiers than centurions and standard-bearers. They controlled units in battle but do not appear to have had a role in how well they fought or maintained their position comparable to that of the latter.[76] Perhaps as important, however, military tribunes, prefects, quaestors, and legates all came from the aristocracy—if not always the cream of the nobility, at least families on the fringes.[77] Their rank made

---

72. Caes. *BCiv.* 1.67; *BGall.* 1.52; cf. Poly. 6.22.3.

73. Poly. 6.24.9: Βούλονται δ' εἶναι τοὺς ταξιάρχους οὐχ οὕτως θρασεῖς καὶ φιλοκινδύνους ὡς ἡγεμονικοὺς καὶ στασίμους καὶ βαθεῖς μᾶλλον ταῖς ψυχαῖς, οὐδ' ἐξ ἀκεραίου προσπίπτειν ἢ κατάρχεσθαι τῆς μάχης, ἐπικρατουμένους δὲ καὶ πιεζομένους ὑπομένειν καὶ ἀποθνήσκειν ὑπὲρ τῆς χώρας.

74. Poly. 6.24.6: οὗτοι δὲ καθ' ἑκάστην σπεῖραν ἐκ τῶν καταλειπομένων ἐξέλεξαν αὐτοὶ δύο τοὺς ἀκμαιοτάτους καὶ γενναιοτάτους ἄνδρας σημαιαφόρους.

75. E.g. in 209 Marcellus degraded centurions whose maniples had lost their standards (Livy 27.13.9). Sulla stigmatized centurions along with their men when both had given way before the enemy (Frontin. *Str.* 4.1.27). Their punishment was mild compared to what Augustus meted out: centurions guilty of leaving their posts were put to death (Suet. *Aug.* 24.2); cf. Augustus' contemporary Calvinus (Vell. Pat. 2.78.3; Dio 48.42.2). Standard-bearers could also become the scapegoats for a panicked flight: see, e.g., Caes. *BCiv.* 3.74; cf. App. *BCiv.* 3.62–63.

76. Cf. Kromayer-Veith, *Heerwesen*, 317–18; Suolahti, *Junior Officers* 48–49; Harmand *L'armée*, 355–57.

77. For the family backgrounds of the military tribunes, see Suolahti, *Junior Officers*, esp. 140–45, 275–79; for legates, see Schleussner, *Legaten der römische Republik*, 223–40.

summary punishment of them far more difficult than of centurions or common soldiers. But their wider links within the aristocracy also were important in preventing responsibility for a defeat from becoming a political issue. Because maintaining discipline in an army involved the joint efforts of the group of aristocrats who made up its officers, blame for the poor discipline that had rendered the soldiers incapable of standing up to the enemy might plausibly be laid at their door. But criticisms of that sort impinged upon the interests of a substantial number of other aristocrats too—the families and friends of those affected by such charges. Furthermore, the voters elected new tribunes and quaestors annually. Legates also apparently tended to serve only as long as the general who appointed them, so that in a political establishment where one-year terms of office were the norm and lengthy prorogations rare, there was a fairly rapid turnover within the command structure of the legions.[78] However, at least from the late third century onward, armies usually were maintained for several years, so that over the course of time a sizable number of men within the aristocracy took a hand in the running of one. This situation, in turn, created a powerful reluctance within the political class to open the question of just who had been responsible for the poor condition of the soldiers when a defeat was traced to this source, for the corporate character of military command made it politically difficult to hold any single person accountable without implicating many others as well and so involving the interests of a wide spectrum within the elite. Senators therefore had good reason to limit their inquiries in this regard and instead turn their attention solely to the performance of the soldiers themselves.

The dissipative effects of collective responsibility here clearly parallel those uncovered in connection with maintenance of the *pax deorum*. The fact that actual responsibility for securing each of the vital prerequisites for military success—the support of the gods and the discipline of the soldiers—was shared out among a group of powerful, or at least well-connected, men made it difficult politically to raise the question of who was to blame when defeat

---

78. On length of prorogations in the second century, see Brunt, *Fall of the Roman Republic*, 44.

revealed something amiss in either area. Within a tightly knit aristocracy, even one that displayed a high degree of competitiveness within its ranks, it was simply not possible to get, as it were, a clear shot at a *victus*. Charges of personal negligence or incompetence could spread much too widely and unpredictably to gather extensive support among the political elite, even if some were inclined to make them. Instead, self-interest helped foster the belief that the primary burden for the performance of the legions in battle reposed outside the boundaries of the aristocracy, on the legionaries themselves.

———|———

Disorder and panic characterized almost any defeat on land, as some or all of the troops broke ranks and fled under enemy pressure. Yet the expectation that Roman soldiers ought to hold their assigned positions at all costs under any conditions appears to have remained constant and rigid. There is no evidence that the Romans relaxed their military ethos to make allowances for extenuating circumstances or to make room for compassion when soldiers in desperation abandoned their posts in a crisis to save their lives. As a practical matter, it is unlikely that every rout was followed by the degradation of the entire army, as happened during the second Punic war, although it is probable that individual units that had given way, and in particular their noncommissioned officers, regularly found themselves stigmatized in some fashion. But the important point is less the frequency of punishment in such cases than the attitude from which it stemmed. When the men fighting in the ranks fell short of expectations, they, rather than the general or the officers, became the focus of blame—even though the latter may have led them into battle insufficiently trained, or against unfavorable odds, or on disadvantageous terrain, or poorly deployed, and so made their failure to stand firm against the enemy onslaught in large measure inevitable. Certainly it is not always obvious that the soldiers were censured because their inadequacies were believed to have caused the loss, as opposed to simply because they had fled. But the connection between victory and the integrity of an army's formations under the pressure of combat is so direct that it is doubtful the Romans would have drawn any meaningful distinction between the collapse of order in the ranks and the reason for their defeat.

Likewise, because direct ascription of failures to such causes is not extensive in the sources, it is not possible to build a compelling argument that this type of rationalization occurred in every defeat based on an accumulation of ancient *testimonia*. However, the nature of legionary combat, coupled with the prevalence of conventional assumptions about the level of discipline and self-sacrifice that could be expected from legionaries, makes it highly probable that the double bind that resulted colored perceptions in the majority of cases. Thus although proof is not possible, it is reasonable to believe that the Romans attributed their defeats to the soldiers' indiscipline, cowardice, or lack of experience frequently enough to have made this a principal factor in bringing about the results uncovered in chapter 1, as was their tendency to see in the same phenomenon a demonstration that the gods had withheld their cooperation. The two represent not so much alternative as complementary explanations for failure to a people who viewed both as operating simultaneously on independent levels of reality and each as essential for military success.

Of course, the cultures of most states that have built empires have stressed discipline and courage in their armies, just as all certainly believe that victory indicates the efficacy of their prayers in gaining the support of their gods. Neither conviction is unique to Rome. What demands attention in the case of the Republic, first, is the clear parallelism in the Roman view of the fundamental ingredients for military success. Just as precision in the execution of ritual was crucial to inducing the gods to cooperate, so the operation of a legionary army in combat depended above all on every man in the ranks executing his battle drill precisely. In both cases the stress was on the *disciplina* necessary to carry out the critical operations exactly. The Romans' understanding of what was crucial to the success of an army in combat thus mirrored in its essentials their conception of what was required to maintain the *pax deorum*. Second, this mentality played a critical role in aristocratic rivalry. In each of its aspects it served as an effective buffer between a military defeat and its potential repercussions in the political arena because both were able to offer serious obstacles to making generals accountable for their defeats. The more success was held to depend on flawless execution of drill or ritual, the greater the likelihood that when failures occurred, the decisive events would be seen as having taken place either at Rome, in connection with the city's cult, or on the battlefield, when the two armies were locked in close combat. From this perspective the fight had not really been a general's to lose in the first place. Although he might make mistakes anywhere between these two points, the Romans simply did not accord them the same critical importance as those involving the gods or the soldiers. Conventional assumptions about the causes of failure and success in war thus suppressed the tendency to raise the issue of a *victus'* responsibility for a defeat and thereby served to limit the extent of political competition in the aftermath.

4

The Aristocratic Ethos and the Preservation of Status

The gods and the soldiers could shield a general from blame, but that protection would not have been enough to ensure his survival in the public arena. Strictly speaking, the problem was not one of escaping accountability for a defeat but one of protecting a political career from its domestic repercussions. Although the one was germane to the other, it was not inevitable that a *victus* would go on to win high office simply because he had somehow been judged not culpable for a disaster on the battlefield (although of course had the contrary been the case, it would certainly have meant personal ruin). Defeat could engender an irrational animus that an opponent might focus against him in subsequent rivalry. If *victi* as a group were to enjoy no better or worse a rate of success than that of their undefeated peers, then in order to strip lost battles of all consequence in future struggles for office, something had to keep the mere fact of having presided over a defeat from becoming a source of opprobrium. Avoiding recrimination was not enough, in and of itself, to bring that about.

A key step, therefore, lay in the ability to limit aristocratic competition in such cases solely to moral issues. The causes of the defeat itself were never in doubt and so could not become a source of controversy. Certainty on that point left a general's own conduct at the center of public attention. What counted above all else in the eyes of the Romans was not generalship in a technical sense but leadership in a moral one—how well or poorly a man's actions had reflected those qualities expected of a commander in defeat. The ideals and values comprising what may be termed the Roman aristocratic ethos laid down clear-cut standards that a war leader facing adversity was expected to meet and against which his conduct could therefore be judged. His performance on this score, not the outcome of his battle, became the critical factor determining the public response.

This emphasis on personal deportment is most evident in the few cases where a *victus* failed to measure up to what the ethos demanded, and rivals capitalized on the anger he had thereby aroused to mount a prosecution against him. The complaints that lay at the center of these proceedings are overwhelmingly moral in character. They are little concerned with the broad questions of how the defeat had come about and who or what was responsible. They center instead on the far more narrow issues of the general's own behavior in the crisis and whether the required standards had been met. Contracting the focus in this way severely restricted the scope for aristocratic competition. Only if a *victus* had fallen short did a political issue exist and with it the opportunity for *inimici* to exploit it in court. Moral, not military, failure is the common thread connecting this small number of prosecutions, which strongly suggests that meeting expected standards was what allowed the majority of defeated generals to escape trial altogether. Given the high degree of competitiveness within aristocratic culture, there is no reason to think that opponents would have failed to raise these same sorts of charges against the vast bulk of *victi* except in the absence of a similar perception of personal disgrace.

As in the courts, so in the *comitia*. The existence of such generally accepted criteria of conduct furnished *victi* with a way of presenting themselves as successes despite their failures, and the availability of that recourse was of fundamental importance in limiting the political consequences. The fact that even in defeat their *virtus* could win respect or even high praise drove a wedge in the mind of the public between a lost battle and what it said about a general. Defeat implied nothing about his abilities or, more important, his character, thus limiting its potential for harm back in the competitive arena at Rome. As long as the expectations of the public had been met, no grounds for criticism existed and hence no issue for critics to exploit in subsequent rivalry. *Victi* would continue to enjoy electoral triumphs because the bases of their political strength—such things as their ancestry, connections, personal popularity, achievements, and especially a reputation for courage and moral worthiness—remained intact. Furthermore, and of equal importance, the power to obtain this protection reposed principally in the hands of the *victi* themselves, not among the soldiers or with the fortunes of war. Although commanders had little ability to shape the broad course of events once the fighting started, they did have the capacity to control their own actions. By making plain what was expected of them, the aristocratic ethos thus gave to generals in the midst of a crisis the ability to determine its impact on their future careers. They therefore possessed the means to guard the one thing that really mattered—their standing among their peers in the race for status and prestige.

———|———

The aristocratic ethos at Rome was both multifaceted and complex but emphasized two qualities pertaining directly to a general's conduct in defeat. T. Quinctius Flamininus summed them up this way in 197 as he lectured the Aetolians on proper deportment in war: "Gentlemen ought to be stern and hot-blooded in combat, noble and high-minded if worsted, but moderate, mild, and benevolent when they conquer."[1] These last elements were certainly uppermost in the proconsul's mind, for his victory at Cynoscephalae had put him in a position to dictate terms for a settlement in Greece; however, the first and especially the second parts of his formulation clearly reflect an awareness that there was a proper stance for a Roman aristocrat in defeat.[2] Perhaps the most impressive monument to this ideal is the remarkable transformation of C. Flaminius' final hours in the historical tradition. Working from sources both contemporary and highly critical of the consul, Polybius paints him as distressed and largely inert while the fighting swirled around him and the tribunes and centurions took what steps they could to meet the emergency at Lake Trasimene. But in Livy's telling more than a century later the portrait is dramatically different: the consul is conspicuous in the thick of the fray, struggling courageously and lending his aid wherever the fighting is

---

1. Poly. 18.37.7: πολεμοῦντας γὰρ δεῖ τοὺς ἀγαθοὺς ἄνδρας βαρεῖς εἶναι καὶ θυμικούς, ἡττωμένους δὲ γενναίους καὶ μεγαλόφρονας, νικῶντάς γε μὴν μετρίους καὶ πραεῖς καὶ φιλανθρώπους; cf. Gelzer, *Hermes* 68 (1933): 165 (= *KS* 3.90), who thinks the remark probably authentic. Note also Poly. 3.75.8.

2. On Flamininus' position following Cynoscephalae, see Eckstein, *Senate and General*, 285–297. On the Romans' alleged moderation in victory, see the references collected by Gruen, *Hellenistic World*, 346 n. 156; Gelzer, *Hermes* 68 (1933): 165–66 (= *KS* 3.90–91).

hottest until at last he is cut down in single combat.³ The change is not likely to have been the result of writers in the interval becoming generally more sympathetic to Flaminius. He emerges elsewhere in Livy's narrative as the same thoroughgoing demagogue and opponent of the nobility that Polybius encountered in the accounts he consulted. Rather, the amelioration occurred because the annalists were compelled to recognize that Flaminius was a Roman aristocrat notwithstanding his origins.⁴ Whatever else they may have thought about him, the historians knew how their audiences expected a man of his rank to die, and so they obliged by remolding the accounts of his conduct they received to reflect the required standards.⁵ His rehabilitation occurred precisely in terms of his stance in the face of disaster. Gone is the overwhelmed and helpless sufferer, replaced by a warrior unbowed in the crisis and stubbornly resisting to the end. The idealization clearly manifests in concrete terms precisely the qualities Flamininus commended to the Aetolians.

Thus a general was expected to display courage and self-control when things were falling apart all around him—a willingness to fight hard, take risks, and, if necessary, meet death fighting bravely. M. Caelius Rufus politely assumed in one letter to Cicero during his stint as governor of Cilicia that that not-very-bellicose *imperator* might find himself in the thick of it were he forced to do battle against the strong Parthian contingent invading Syria.⁶ The remark is more than mere empty flattery of a vain man's martial delusions. Generals died in battle frequently enough during the last two and a half centuries of the Republic to indicate that crisis often led commanders to put themselves in harm's way, and those

---

3. Poly. 3.84.6; Livy 22.6.2–4; Plut. *Fab.* 3.3; cf. Jannsen, *Mnemosyne* 59 (1926): 189–94. On Flaminius' career generally and its representation in the sources, see Gelzer, *Hermes* (1933): 152–53 (= *KS* 3.76–77).

4. He was, of course, a *novus homo*, but by 217 he had been consul once already and censor as well, and these achievements put him solidly within the political elite of the city.

5. And who is to say that the image the historians created abuses the truth? Flaminius had at least once before evinced a discomforting readiness to insist that his peers adhere in their private financial dealings to the strictures appropriate to men of their station, in his sponsorship of the *lex Claudia* (Poly. 21.63.3–4). It is, moreover, suggestive of mendacity in Polybius' sources that the haplessness he ascribes to him and the initiative of the tribunes in the crisis echo the allegations made by the same author in connection with Flaminius' battle against the Insubri during his first consulate (Poly. 2.33.6–9).

6. Cic. *Fam.* 87 (8.10).1.

who survived took pains to advertise the fact.[7] Caesar chose to present himself on more than one occasion striding up into the front lines to check his wavering men.[8] Sulla apparently had likewise recorded his declaration at one point that he would stay and fight on alone if his troops fled to shame them into standing their ground.[9] The image had an immediate resonance for contemporaries until the very end of the Republic because the palpable courage it represented mattered in the race for prestige and status.[10]

We have more than one instance of a general entering the fray to help turn the tide of battle by leading an attack or endeavoring to shore up a critical point.[11] Inasmuch as he brought his personal bodyguard with him, a commander's presence in the line of battle

---

7. Any assessment of frequency must necessarily be tentative, owing to the incompleteness of the sources, but the following is a chronological list of commanders killed in battle between 300 and 49 B.C. (sources may be found in *MRR* under the appropriate year unless otherwise noted; cf. also Harris, *War and Imperialism*, 40): P. Decius Mus, cos. 295; L. Caecilius Metellus Denter, pr. 283 (on the date, however, see Morgan, *CQ* 66 [1972]: 304–25); P. Decius Mus, cos. 279; Q. Fabius Maximus Gurges, cos. 265; C. Atilius Regulus, cos. 225; C. Flaminius, cos. 217; C. Centenius, propr. 217; L. Aemilius Paullus, cos. 216; L. Postumius Albinus, pr. 216, cos.-elect, 215; Ti. Sempronius Gracchus, procos. 212; M. Centenius Paenula, special command, 212 (Livy 25.19.9–17); P. Cornelius Scipio, procos. 211; Cn. Cornelius Scipio, procos. 211; Cn. Fulvius Centumalus, procos. 210; M. Claudius Marcellus, cos. 208; T. Quinctius Crispinus, cos. 208; C. Atinius, propr. 186; Q. Petilius, cos. 176; P. Iuventius Thalna, propr.(?) 148; C. Vetilius, pr. 147; P. Licinius Crassus Mucianus, procos. 130; Sex. Pompeius, pr. 119; L. Calpurnius Piso Frugi, pr. 112; L. Cassius Longinus, cos. 107; M. Aurelius Scaurus, leg. 105; L. Postumius, pr. 90; P. Rutilius Lupus, cos. 90; Q. Servilius Caepio, procos. 90; T. Didius, leg. 90; L. Porcius Cato, cos. 89; L. Thorius Balbus, leg. 79; M. Domitius Calvinus, procos. 79; L. Cossinius, pr. 73; L. Aurunculeius Cotta, leg. 54; C. Scribonius Curio, propr. 49.

8. E.g. *BGall.* 2.25; *BCiv.* 3.69. Cf. Vell. Pat. 2.5.3–4; Suet. *Iul.* 62; Plut. *Caes.* 56.2; Frontin. *Str.* 2.8.13.

9. On the events of 86 at Orchomenos, see Plut. *Sull.* 21.2; App. *Mith.* 49; Frontin. *Stra.* 2.8.12. The story probably originated in his own memoirs. Note also the same gesture during his march on Rome in 88: App. *BCiv.* 1.58, probably from the same source. Cf. M. Atilius Regulus in 294 (Livy 10.36.6–15, cf. Frontin. *Str.* 2.8.11; Frontin. *Str.* 4.1.29, probably from Fabius Pictor: Livy 10.37.13) and M. Aemilius Lepidus, tr. mil. in 190 at Magnesia (Livy 37.43.1–4).

10. Cf. the young P. Cornelius Scipio Nasica's self-advertisement of his exploits in 168, in Plut. *Aem.* 15.3–16.2, and the youthful Ser. Sulpicius Galba's of his in 43, in Cic. *Fam.* 378 (10.30). One would expect such personal testimonials to have been a common practice among men of that age in view of Polybius' remark about the importance of a reputation for courage to an ambitious aristocrat (Poly. 31.29.1, cf. Diod. 31.27.8), although it is clear that age and prior achievement were no impediment to similar self-aggrandizement (Plut. *Cat. Mai.* 14.2–4).

11. In addition to the cases mentioned above, note also C. Calpurnius Piso (Livy 39.31.7); Sulla (Plut. *Sull.* 29.5); Pompey (Plut. *Sert.* 21.2; App. *BCiv.* 1.58; and Sallust's portrait of Catiline's last stand (*Cat.* 60.4). Cf. Harris, *War and Imperialism*, 39; Campbell, *Emperor and the Roman Army*, 59–60.

perhaps made no small contribution to the physical task of winning a victory.[12] Far more important, however, was the emotional charge his presence brought to the soldiers. Generals in battle most frequently appear just behind the front lines, encouraging their men, allowing themselves to be seen sharing their dangers, and thus spurring them on to greater efforts.[13] That was where Scipio Africanus was during the assault on New Carthage in 209.[14] Even as late as the second battle of Philippi both Octavian and Brutus were racing about along the battle line, "exciting the men by their ardour, exhorting the toilers to toil on, and relieving those who were exhausted."[15] In the eyes of peers and citizens who believed that victory or defeat was fundamentally a result of the soldiers' determination to stand their ground and prevail or die, the most important thing a general could do was bolster their spirits and enhance their resolve in the contest. A general's visibility and personal deportment therefore had a direct, material relevance to the legionaries' own performance.[16]

This influence was particularly felt in a crisis, when by setting an example of bravery for his men, a general could shame them

---

12. On the bodyguard, see Poly. 6.31.3, cf. Walbank, *Comm.*, 1.714, 2.647; Harris, *War and Imperialism*, 39.

13. On the crucial role in all armies of leadership by example and the need for generals to be perceived as sharing risks, see Keegan, *Mask of Command*, 329–38.

14. Poly. 10.13.1; Livy 26.44.7–8, and esp. Walbank's comment, *Comm.*, 2.214.

15. App. *BCiv.* 4.128 (Loeb trans.): οἱ στρατηγοὶ δὲ σφᾶς, περιθέοντες καὶ ὁρώμενοι πανταχοῦ, ταῖς τε ὁρμαῖς ἀνέφερον καὶ παρεκάλουν πονοῦντας ἔτι προσπονῆσαι καὶ τοὺς κεκμηκότας ἐνήλλασσον, ὥστε ὁ θυμὸς αἰεὶ τοῖς ἐπὶ τοῦ μετώπου καινὸς ἦν. Cf. Caesar's approval of Cotta's performance while his men were under attack during their retreat: *in appellandis cohortandisque militibus imperatoris . . . officia praestabat: BGall.* 5.33. Note also P. Valerius Laevinus at Heracleia in 280 (Frontin. *Str.* 2.4.9, cf. Plut. *Pyrrh.* 17.2); M. Claudius Marcellus in 222 (sources in *MRR* 1.233); P. Cornelius Scipio at the Ticinus in 218 (Livy 21.46.5–10, cf. Poly. 10.3.4–5); C. Calpurnius Piso in Spain in 185 (Livy 39.31.4–9); Q. Petilius Spurinus against the Ligurians in 176 (Livy 41.18.11); Pompey on the Sucro in 75 (Plut. *Pomp.* 19.2–3; App. *Iber.* 110); C. Scribonius Curio in Africa in 49 (Caes. *BCiv.* 2.34); T. Labienus in Africa in 46 (*Bell. Afr.* 16); Hirtius and Pansa at Mutina (sources in *MRR* 2:335); Sulla (Plut. *Sull.* 29.7); Caesar (above, n. 8); Aemilius Paullus (below, pp. 122–23); Flaminius (above, pp. 116–17).

16. Note the reaction of Caesar's troops to the news that their *imperator* was in danger: *BGall.* 2.26. Cf. the remarks of Keegan (*Face of Battle*, 179, 188–90) on what made the British regiments at Waterloo stand firm under hours of intense bombardment: he finds the example of courage and honor set by their officers to have been a crucial factor, although of course the way honor and courage were to be demonstrated by an aristocrat in the era of gunpowder was quite different from the conventions of Rome in the middle and late Republic.

into greater efforts. That was clearly what Sulla and Caesar hoped to do by their dramatic interventions in the fray as the tide was turning against them. But perhaps the best evidence comes from a case where there can be no suspicion that events were touched up in later memoirs by the principal himself. In 176 the forces of Q. Petilius Spurinus were thrown back during an assault on a body of Ligurians dug in on a hill and began to waver toward flight. Petilius rode out in front of the standards to rally his men, where he was killed by an enemy spear. Petilius had deliberately exposed himself to danger, in effect daring his men to leave him to face the enemy alone—the ultimate disgrace. As it was, even though his troops recovered their resolve and went on to overcome the enemy, the senate held them culpable for the death of their consul and docked them a year's service and pay.[17] Certainly there were limits to how far a general was expected to go with such efforts. Deliberate suicide was not necessarily called for. As Livy has Cn. Fulvius Flaccus ask rhetorically during his trial by way of exculpating his conduct at Herdonia, was he expected to throw his life away for no reason when his men were fleeing the field in defeat? Clearly the answer ought to have been no.[18] But the most damning accusation against Flaccus was not that he had fled but that he had been the first to do so. He had done nothing whatsoever to stem the tide of battle. By contrast, when the forces of A. Manlius Vulso were chased from their camp in a surprise attack and fled in panic, Vulso himself ran too, but only after having tried in vain to stop them by every form of command and entreaty. Although the rout provoked panic at Rome and bitter complaints against Vulso himself, he never faced trial.[19] He had done everything he could to recall the soldiers to their duty and promote resistance.

As a consequence of this demand for unwavering determination

---

17. Livy 41.18.11–13; Val. Max. 2.7.15; Frontin. *Str.* 4.1.46. Petilius himself could not have burnished the account, and the family was thereafter of so little importance that the tale is hardly likely to have suffered from excessive enhancement in subsequent funeral elogia and on other such occasions, as was perhaps true with the greater *gentes* (Cic. *Brut.* 62; Livy 27.27.13; and, generally, *RE* 12.1 col. 992–94).

18. Livy 26.3.2–3; see further below.

19. Livy 41.2.8, cf. 41.1.1–2.13. On panic and complaints, see Livy 41.5.1–2; 6.1–3; 7.4–10; cf. 10.13. Note, however, that Vulso recaptured his camp and with his colleague won a subsequent victory (Livy 3.1–4.8; 10.1–4).

in a defeat, few *victi* are recorded as having allowed themselves to be captured alive in combat.[20] Sallust, always alive to the posture true *virtus* required, put it this way when he wrote Catiline's speech to his followers as they prepared to make their final stand against their pursuers: "But if fortune envies your *virtus*, take care not to die unavenged, and do not be captured and slaughtered like beasts, but rather, fighting like men, leave the enemy a bloody and mournful victory."[21] The sentiment derives in good measure from a rhetorical topos, of course; it was a cliché by that time.[22] But it became one at Rome, as elsewhere, precisely because the posture it signified represented the standard aristocrats were expected to meet. Catiline himself lived up to those high words; he perished far out in front of his own lines, surrounded by enemy dead.[23] The Romans had a highly effective means of making vivid the equation between surrender and degradation in the ritual slaughter they inflicted on the enemy war leaders they had taken prisoner as part of their own victory celebrations.[24] Nothing could make plainer for Roman generals the possible consequences of preferring capture to death when they lost.[25] The attitude was a venerable one among the Roman upper class. L. Postumius Albinus died resisting capture with all his might in 216.[26] When L. Hostilius Mancinus realized his troop of cavalry would not be able to outrun the Numidian horsemen who had surprised them, he rallied his men for a sui-

---

20. Scipio Asina (appendix 1.1, no. 26), an apparent exception, was in fact trapped with very few men by the enemy and either compelled to surrender or taken prisoner during a parlay; on Regulus, see below, n. 25; on Aurelius Scaurus, see below, n. 30.
21. Sall. *Cat.* 58.21: *quod si virtuti vostrae fortuna inviderit, cavete inulti animam amittatis, neu capti potius sicuti pecora trucidemini, quam virorum more pugnantes cruentam atque luctuosam victoriam hostibus relinquatis.*
22. Xen. *An.* 3.2.2f.; Poly. 3.63.9; cf. Vretska, *De Catilinae Coniuratione*, 671–72.
23. Sall. *Cat.* 61.4–6. Cf. the death of Cn. Fulvius Centumalus, procos. 210 (Livy 27.1.12).
24. See Dar.-Sag. 5:489.
25. Note too the tales concerning the fate of the proconsul M. Atilius Regulus, whom the Carthaginians took prisoner in 255 and then tortured to death after he refused to do their bidding. For sources, see *MRR* 1.209–10; for discussion, see *RE* 2 cols. 2088–92, and De Sanctis, *Storia*, 3.1²: 154–56, who reject the traditional accounts; *contra*, however, see Frank, *CPh* 21 (1926): 311–14. It matters less that the story is probably untrue than that it was told and repeated. The Romans found it satisfying, for it confirmed not only what they believed to be true of the Carthaginian character, but what tradition taught them about their options in defeat.
26. Livy 23.24.11.

cidal charge against the enemy.[27] P. Licinius Crassus Mucianus' end was much celebrated: in the confusion following the defeat of his army by Aristonicus, he was caught by a Thracian mercenary. To avoid falling into enemy hands, he stabbed his captor in the eye with his riding crop and so enraged the man that he killed Crassus reflexively.[28] To die resisting desperately was thus not only to avoid the shame of capture but possibly even to achieve a certain measure of *gloria* as well.[29]

Yet even eluding capture did not necessarily mean avoiding disgrace; survival itself could be unacceptable under certain conditions. An overwhelming defeat appears to have raised the expectation that the man in command simply would not return alive. According to one version of events, M. Aurelius Scaurus could have escaped the slaughter of his legions in 105, but he preferred death: his sense of honor would not allow him to survive unharmed when he had lost his army.[30] Caesar likewise could present his propraetor, C. Scribonius Curio, as proclaiming that he would never return to Caesar after having lost the forces entrusted to him and then rushing forth to seek death in the melee.[31] The same deliberate resolve to perish with his men rather than return without them also features prominently in Livy's highly wrought portrait of L. Aemilius Paullus at Cannae. The consul had given his all in

---

27. Livy 22.15.9–10. Cf. M. Centenius Paenula in 210 (Livy 25.19.8–17). The son of this Mancinus became praetor in 180 and consul in 170, the first of that family to achieve eminence. One wonders what role, if any, his father's heroism in death contributed to his son's elevation.

28. Val. Max. 3.2.12; Flor. 1.35.4–5, cf. Livy *Per.* 59; Asc. 25 C; Vell. 2.4.1.

29. Cf. Cic. *Sest.* 48: *innumerabiles alii partim adipiscendae laudis, partim vitandae turpitudinis causa mortem in variis bellis aequissimis animis oppetissent*; see also Earl, *Moral and Political Traditions*, 32; cf. idem, *Sallust*, 23. Note too the image of heroic self-sacrifice to bring about victory represented by the *devotio* of P. Decius Mus, cos. 340, and his son, P. Decius Mus, cos. 295: for sources, see MRR 1:134, 177. On the ceremony itself, see Latte, *Römische Religionsgeschichte*, 125–26; 203–4.

30. Gran. Licin. 33.1–5 C. Livy recorded a different version of Scaurus' end focusing on a different manifestation of courage and heroism (*Per.* 67; Oros. 5.16.2; cf. Valerius Antias, frg. 63 P). The important point here, however, is not to decide which account contains the truth of the matter but to take note of how contemporary and later writers idealized Scaurus' posture in defeat and so contributed to the ongoing process of defining aristocratic models of conduct; cf. Griffin, JRS 67 (1977): 17–26, on the phenomenon of life imitating art imitating life in the late Republic. On the ideal of an unbowed attitude in defeat, the central feature of Scaurus' portrayal in the Livian tradition, see below, n. 78. Note also P. Valerius Falto (Zonar. 8.18) and M. Centenius Paenula (Livy 25.19.16).

31. Caes. *BCiv.* 2.42.

the battle, fighting fiercely throughout, and finally, when all was lost, he replied to those who would have him flee, "Let me die amid this slaughter of my soldiers."[32] That statement unmistakably evinced the nobility and courage demanded at such a moment.[33] The criticism leveled against Varro for having survived the debacle certainly grew out of the pointed contrast his detractors could draw between his colleague's death fighting furiously in the thick of the battle and his own failure to measure up to the same ideal.[34] The greater the extent of the disaster, it seems, the more extreme the gesture that was required to prove one's *virtus*. In a calamity like Cannae, only death could signal the greatness of spirit that decorum exacted, even if one had to do the job oneself.[35]

In some ways, therefore, dying in the midst of calamity could seem attractive to a defeated general. He might achieve a measure of glory to enhance his memory and increase the honor of his family, whereas the very fact that he had come back alive could become a potential source of danger if questions were raised about how he had managed to survive when so many others had died. Thus the senate's famous decree of thanks to Varro after Cannae was necessary to put an end to criticism of his conduct and rehabilitate him for further service in the war.[36] Even Cicero was acutely aware

---

32. Livy 22.49.11: *Me in hac strage militum meorum patere exspirare*.
33. Note also the refusal of Cn. Octavius, cos. 87, to flee when Cinna and Marius captured Rome. Instead, according to Appian, he withdrew to the Janiculum with the remnants of his forces and, in the full regalia of his office, there awaited death (App. *BCiv*. 1.71); cf. Plut. *Mar*. 42.5, which places him on the rostra, probably incorrectly.
34. On Paullus' death, see Poly. 3.116.1-4, 9; Livy 22.49.1-12, cf. 50.7; Vell. Pat. 1.9.3; Plut. *Fab*. 16.5-8; Plut. *Aem*. 2.2; App. *Hann*. 23-24; Frontin. *Str*. 4.5.5. Criticisms of Varro; see Poly. 3.116.13 (probably from Fabius Pictor: Walbank, *Comm*. 1:448); App. *Hann*. 25; Plut. *Aem*. 2.3; Oros. 5.5.8. On the portrait of Varro in the sources, see Will, *Historia* 32 (1983): 173-82.
35. Cf. Cicero's picture of Crassus' end at Carrhae: *ne videret victorem vivus inimicum, eadem sibi manu vitam exhausisse, qua mortem saepe hostibus obtulisset* (*Sest*. 48). This passage is a particularly revealing instance of idealizing a general's conduct in defeat in view of the far more sordid version of Crassus' demise in the narrative sources (Livy *Per*. 106; Plut. *Crass*. 31.1-6; Dio 40.27.1-3). But Cicero was speaking directly to the Roman public, and he knew the standard of conduct the citizenry expected from its leaders in such circumstances. On Cicero's personal motives in manipulating this ideal, see further below.
36. Sources are in appendix 1.1, no. 85; see further below, pp. 139-40. Nevertheless, according to one tradition, Varro preserved an attitude of contrition and disgrace thereafter. He let his hair and beard grow long and refused to eat reclining (Frontin. *Str*. 4.5.6).

of the trouble accusations of self-serving flight in a desperate situation could spawn. To be sure, he never lost a battle of the sort we are concerned with here, but he did cast the options open to him in the final phase of his struggle with Clodius in 59–58 in terms of taking up arms and the likelihood of death or withdrawal into exile.[37] He chose the latter course. Following his triumphant return he was at pains to justify his conduct two years earlier and in particular to answer critics who declared that he ought to have met death fighting.[38] He insisted his decision had not come because he was afraid to die, but out of patriotism and concern for the state. No one could call him a coward.[39] The relevance to the predicament of a *victus* is clear: survival under the wrong circumstances led to disgrace and hence political vulnerability. The prefect T. Turpilius Silanus had the singular misfortune to be the only man left alive when the inhabitants of Vaga massacred the town's Roman garrison during the Jugurthine War. How he got out unscathed Sallust was unable to explain, but, that author continued, "he appeared base and contemptible because he had valued his wretched life more highly in the crisis than his good name."[40] Brought before Q. Metellus Numidicus to account for his escape, he could not do so satisfactorily, and the consul ordered him put to death.[41] Both the general and the historian presumed Turpilius must have done something shameful to survive, and his failure to prove otherwise warranted the supreme penalty.[42]

The threat that arose when a general fell short of expectations on this score is most strikingly revealed in the trial of Q. Servilius

---

37. Cic. *Sest*. 39–40, 43–44; *Dom*. 63.
38. Cic. *Sest*. 45: *Unum enim* [var. in other eds.] *mihi restabat illud, quod forsitan non nemo vir fortis et acris animi magnique dixerit*: "*Restitisses, repugnasses, mortem pugnans oppetisses.*"
39. Cic. *Sest*. 47–49, cf. 36; *Dom*. 63–64, 95.
40. Sall. *Iug*. 67.3: *quia illi in tanto malo turpis vita integra fama potior fuit, inprobis intestabilisque videtur.*
41. Sall. *Iug*. 69.4, cf. Plut. *Mar*. 8.1–2; App. *Num*. 3.
42. Whatever pressure the legate Marius applied to secure Turpilius' execution could only be brought to bear because of the strong conviction among those in Metellus' *concilium* that survival in such circumstances equaled dishonorable conduct, stemming from a consensus on this point among aristocrats generally (Plut. *Mar*. 8.2). On the politics involved, see Badian, *Foreign Clientelae*, 196–97; Gruen, *Roman Politics*, 152–54; on doubts about Marius' involvement, see Passerini, *Ath*., n.s. 12 (1934): 24–25.

Caepio, one of the ill-fated commanders at Arausio in 105. We know very little about the proceedings themselves beyond the fact that they were a violent affair and that some years later, in 94, his accuser, C. Norbanus, himself faced charges of *maiestas* in connection with the events.[43] M. Antonius defended Norbanus successfully on that occasion in a famous speech, of which Cicero preserves a summary. After upholding the right of the Roman people to undertake a *seditio*, Antonius focused his whole speech on a denunciation of Caepio's flight and a lament for the destruction of his army, rekindling among his listeners their grief at the loss of friends and relatives.[44] It is not certain that these were the principal themes in Norbanus' case against Caepio nine years before, but on balance the likelihood seems strong. If Antonius believed the flight of Caepio and the destruction of the army would be effective in moving the jurors to side with Norbanus, then it is a fair surmise that they were among the main issues that Norbanus himself had raised against Caepio since by his appeal to them Antonius intended to reawaken old animosities. There is no reason to assume that what aroused the jurors' hostility in 94 would not have done the same among the voters in 103.[45] But even if the accusation does not represent the burden of Norbanus' case against Caepio, its political impact is nonetheless demonstrated clearly in the outcome of the trial in 94: Norbanus was acquitted.[46] Whatever crimes he

---

43. On the *seditio Norbani*, see Cic. *De Or.* 2.197; *MRR* 1:564; appendix 1.1, no. 81.

44. Cic. *De Or.* 2.199, esp.: *Tum omnem orationem traduxi [Antonius] et converti in increpandam Caepionis fugam, in deplorandum interitum exercitus: sic et eorum dolorem, qui lugebant suos, oratione refricabam*; cf. 2.124, 200, 203.

45. Caepio had of course altered the composition of the juries of the criminal courts during his consulship to replace equites with senators (sources are in *MRR* 1:533, cf. 3:194). Antonius expected the memory of that measure would increase hostility among the equestrian jurors in 94 (*Orat.* 2.199–200). But although anger on this score surely fueled the antipathies of his audience, it hardly constituted their prime source, as the tenor of Antonius' speech demonstrates.

46. Gruen, *Historia* 15 (1966): 45–46 (cf. *Roman Politics*, 195–96), views this verdict, along with several others in cases around the same time, as a demonstration of the equestrian jurors' disinterest in involving themselves in the partisan rivalries he sees being played out in the trial. Disinterested in factional politics the jurors may have been, but certainly this indifference was not the main, or even an important, reason for their verdict. Such a view places the event in far too limited a perspective. Everything we know about this case, especially from Cicero's report of Antonius' speech, indicates that it, like the one brought against Q. Servilius Cae-

had committed in the course of prosecuting Caepio were largely outweighed in the jurors' eyes by the enormity of Caepio's own conduct in connection with the defeat. It stands to reason, therefore, that if Caepio's flight and the destruction of the army were central to Antonius' case on Norbanus' behalf, something about them was open to criticism. The material presented here strongly suggests that simply surviving a catastrophe of this magnitude without a clear demonstration of personal bravery in the fight was tantamount to a proof of cowardice and sufficient to call down the wrath of the public.[47]

Thus certainly in Norbanus' trial and probably in Caepio's the standards of conduct imposed by the aristocratic ethos were vital in determining the political implications of the defeat. The attack against Caepio did not come about simply because of factional intrigue or the hysteria generated by the disaster, important as those

---

pio, the son of the consul of 106 at about the same time, asked the equestrians to pass judgment on the violent events of a decade before. Their verdicts put an unmistakable seal of approval on the punishment Norbanus inflicted on Caepio senior for his actions in connection with the Arausio disaster as well as for his son's resistance to Saturninus' demagoguery notwithstanding the violence of which each had been guilty. Both had been justified; neither diminished the majesty of Rome. Elaborate speculation about the factional alignments revealed by these cases has obscured their real meaning in the larger context of Roman politics. See also Badian, *Studies*, 34–70, on the trials of Caepio and Norbanus and further prosopographical musings.

47. The depth of hostility against Caepio is also evident in the fact that he was not allowed to withdraw into exile after the verdict against him but was hauled off to prison to await execution. He was only saved by the intervention of a friendly tribune (Val. Max. 4.7.3, cf. 6.9.13); on the custom of allowing exile, see Poly. 6.14.9; on imprisonment preliminary to execution, see Mommsen, *Röm. Strafr.*, 960–62. Caepio's imprisonment may only have been owing to the fact of his having been fined as a result of the trial and held in prison to guarantee its payment (Lengel, *Hermes* 66 [1931]: 303), but this would have been highly unusual and seems therefore far from probable. It is sometimes also believed that Cn. Mallius, who also suffered a defeat by the Cimbri in conjunction with Caepio's, stood trial as well (Gruen, *Roman Politics*, 165). No source so states, however, and Cic. *De. Or.* 2.125 need not refer to a speech in his defense, only to a lament for Mallius' fate in another context. The sources tell us only that he was *ob eandem causam quam et Caepio L. Saturnini rogatione e civitate plebiscito eiectus* (Gran. Lic. 33.24 C), and this statement might plausibly be taken to mean that he elected to withdraw from Rome rather than face a trial in which violence similar to that which marred Caepio's would render his defense otiose, and that afterward a bill confirmed this self-imposed sentence of exile (Lengle *Hermes* 66 [1931]: 312–13; contra Gabba, *Ath.*, n.s. 29 (1951): 22 n. 4, is not convincing). Furthermore, Mallius too may have survived the debacle by running away, exposing him to public wrath equally with Caepio.

factors may have been.⁴⁸ Political *inimicitia* and public anguish were constants following serious losses. Rather, Caepio opened himself to his enemies' attempt to direct public anger against him by seeming to prefer to save his life by flight while his men were being cut to pieces. It is striking that, as Cicero preserves his speech, there is little indication that Antonius taxed Caepio principally with actually causing the disaster, although he would not have lacked grounds for such a charge: Caepio had refused to join forces with the consul Mallius when the latter urged this course; he was determined instead that credit for the victory should belong to himself alone. An attempt at reconciliation left the two men more hostile than before. When the Cimbri sought terms of peace, Caepio's response convinced them that they had no alternative but war.⁴⁹ If Antonius touched on these transgressions, he apparently made so little of them that Cicero thought them not worth mentioning.⁵⁰

Nor was it the case that nothing more than the severe shock and outrage in the aftermath of a disaster of such magnitude had made

---

48. On factional alignments, see above, n. 46; on *inimicitiae*, see Epstein, *Personal Enmity*, 16.

49. Valerius Antias frg. 63 P (= Oros. 5.16.2); Gran. Lic. 33.6-11 C.; Dio 27 frg. 91.1-3; cf. Livy *Per*. 67. These transgressions are commonly believed to have been the central issues in his trial (Gruen, *Roman Politics*, 161-65; Epstein, *Personal Enmity*, 16). However, Caepio was legally in the right in refusing cooperation: he could act as he thought best within his *provincia* and was in no sense Mallius' subordinate. Caepio may have met such charges with the plea that the fortunes of war had brought about the loss of his army, not his own actions (*Rhet. Her.* 1.24; cf. Cic. *Brut.* 135; Lengle, *Hermes* 66 [1931]: 307-8).

50. Cf., however, Cic. *De Or*. 2.164, which, if it actually comes from Antonius' defense of Norbanus, shows that at some point he argued that *si maiestas amplitudo ac dignitas civitatis, is eam minuit qui exercitum hostibus populi Romani tradidit, non qui eum qui id fecisset, populi Romani potestati tradidit*. This statement may indicate that Antonius' speech included the accusation that Caepio's decisions in command had caused the destruction of his army, but it is more in keeping with the thrust of Cicero's summary of the speech at 2.199 to see it as a reference to the effect his flight had on his men, causing resistance to crumble among the rank and file when it became generally known that their commander had fled. Cf. the result of Cn. Fulvius Flaccus' flight and its role in the proceedings undertaken against him, discussed immediately below. Val. Max. 4.7.3 suggests that Caepio was imprisoned because it appeared that it was his fault his army was destroyed, but that may be nothing more than Valerius' own inference. Yet even if we assume that Caepio's decision to put the interests of the state behind the selfish pursuit of his personal feud against Mallius formed a principal theme in the case against him, his action involves much the same sort of moral turpitude as does his flight to save his own life instead of sacrificing it in a final, desperate attempt to turn the tide of battle. Cf. Cic. *Fam*. 395 (10.18).2, Plancus to Cicero, for an appraisal of the likely response of the public to such a choice on the part of a commander.

Caepio vulnerable. These factors contributed but were not crucial. M. Iunius Silanus underwent prosecution in the year following the debacle, when passions were, if anything, running higher, and he stood accused of being the cause of all the current misfortunes of the Republic. He was acquitted by a wide margin.[51] It was not simply the loss of his army that set Caepio's case apart; the critical difference was his failure to display the self-sacrifice and personal valor expected of a man of his station. That failure transformed what might have been an unhappy, but politically benign, episode into a personal catastrophe.[52] The centrality of this transgression is underscored by its power to shape the outcome of rivalry almost a decade later. Despite the strength of the case against Norbanus— the indisputable violence that had attended his prosecution of Caepio and his disregard for a tribunician veto of the proceedings— Antonius was able to use the proconsul's own moral failure to blunt the assault launched against his client.[53]

Even when defeat was not grave enough to bring the fate of the Republic into doubt, conformity to the ethos defined the issues around which rivalry took shape in its wake. In 212 the army of the praetor Cn. Fulvius Flaccus dissolved at the onset of a Carthaginian attack, and in the following year its commander faced trial on account of the defeat.[54] The complaints raised against him did not center on his management of the battle and its role in bringing about the defeat. That the soldiers themselves were responsible was never in doubt. In his defense, as Livy presents it, Flaccus both asserted the propriety of his own conduct and heaped blame

---

51. Appendix 1.1, no. 44, see further above, pp. 47–48.
52. The charge of cowardice in the face of defeat came at a time when the moral worthiness of the senatorial class to lead was generally being questioned: cf. the speech of Marius in 107 as given by Sallust, *Iug.* 85. Such allegations may have considerably increased the impact of the charges against Caepio.
53. Cf. Cic. *de Or.* 2.197. Note also that when the son of M. Aemilius Scaurus, *princeps senatus*, fled the Germans' victorious charge while serving as a legate under the consul Catulus in 102, his father sent word that he would rather have seen his son dead in battle than charged with a disgraceful flight and ordered the young man never to come into his presence again. Shame drove the son to suicide (Val. Max. 5.8.4; Frontin. *Str.* 4.1.13; *De Vir. Ill.* 72.10). Scaurus himself may have had little choice; he had been present at Caepio's trial, apparently as one of his defenders, and seeming to condone Caepio's cowardice may have made it imperative for Scaurus to condemn the same behavior on the part of his son to protect his own position.
54. Sources for the battle are in appendix 1.1, no. 35. De Sanctis and Brunt both reject this episode as a doublet of the defeat of Cn. Fulvius Centumalis, pr. 210, but incorrectly; see appendix 3.

on that of his men: he had done everything a good general should; they had run away from the enemy.[55] The prosecutor concurred. He accepted the defendant's assertion that the soldiers had been unruly and contumacious but charged that they had become so by contagion from their commander's turpitude. Nor did he deny that the legionaries had fled, only that the impulse to do so arose from among themselves: their leader had been the first to run. He could only blame Flaccus for the defeat, in other words, by imputing it to flaws in his personal character and to the effect these had had on his men.[56]

However, the complexion of the trial changed dramatically once the charge of cowardice could be substantiated. When witnesses came forward to testify that not only had Flaccus been the first to run, but his flight had indeed precipitated a general rout among his men, public indignation became acute.[57] Popular outrage brought the defendant's life suddenly into jeopardy as the *contio* hearing the case began to shout for the death penalty. His accuser obliged by substituting a charge of *perduellio* for the fine originally proposed. Worse, the revelation damned Flaccus in the eyes of his peers. The other tribunes refused his pleas to block the new charges, and an appeal to the senate from his eminent brother Quintus, consul for the third time the year before and now in command of the siege at Capua, for permission to return to Rome to attend the trial was turned down flat. Revulsion at his cravenness had put this scion of one of the most eminent and powerful *gentes* of the era outside the pale, and he, seeing the handwriting on the wall, slunk off into exile.[58]

The issues of culpability and moral failure are not easy to disentangle in this affair, even assuming that Livy reports accurately

---

55. Livy 26.3.1–4. Livy's account of the battle repeatedly stresses the soldiers' indiscipline and refusal to heed their officers' commands (25.20.6, 21.1, 5–10). See further above, pp. 106–7.

56. Livy 26.2.7–16. Losing one's army was never accounted a crime at Rome. The closest one gets to such a charge is in a comment by the second-century A.D. jurist Scaevola on the *lex Iulia Maiestatis* (*Dig.* 48.4.4) regarding leading an army intentionally into an ambush or some other form of betrayal. Such actions may have been explicitly included within the scope of Caesar's law, possibly on the model of Saturninus' legislation. I owe this reference to Michael Alexander, in a private communication.

57. Livy 26.3.5: *testibus datis . . . iurati permulti dicerent fugae pavorisque initium a praetore ortum, ab eo desertos milites cum haud vanum timorem ducis crederent terga dedisse.* Cf. 2.12, 16.

58. Livy 26.3.6–12.

the substance of what was said and done at the trial.[59] But the point is surely that given the role of the gods and the importance of the soldiers themselves in determining the outcome of a battle, what mattered to the Romans was the personal conduct of a general as opposed to his management of the army as a whole. In a case such as that made against Flaccus, culpability could only really be expressed in moral terms because in a crisis it was as an exemplar rather than as a manager that a general made his greatest contribution.

Consequently, more is involved in the prosecutions of Caepio and Flaccus than merely two cowards who were caught and punished. Theirs are two of the few cases in which the political repercussions of a defeat were fatal to a general's career: their cravenness exposed them to the wrath of the citizens and their peers. That fact argues strongly that the right posture in defeat worked equally to shield the bulk of *victi* from public ire and partisan attack. On one level the protection such a stance offered resulted simply from the important contribution a general's display of courage could make to the outcome of a battle, as we have seen. But such displays are merely conventional in face-to-face combat. Under such circumstances war leaders are expected to exhibit great bravery and thereby inspire their men to fight harder, to be avatars of the qualities required of the group.[60] On a deeper level the peculiarly Roman feature of this convention was its political ramifications. Its utility did not cease once the fighting had stopped but instead continued to exert a powerful influence in the competitive arena back at Rome. This potency arose not simply because it could there be said that a *victus* had done his utmost to turn the tide of battle and snatch victory from the jaws of defeat, so that no grounds for complaint against his performance existed on that score. Rather, the key to the political significance of the convention lay in the fact that the courage he had displayed reconfirmed his aristocratic status.

Generals who deliberately put themselves in danger during the

---

59. If not, it is still instructive concerning the lines along which Livy and his sources thought such an affair ought to have been played out.

60. See in this regard Keegan's analysis of Alexander's generalship (*Mask of Command*, 60–91) and the remark of Paul Fussell: "The whole trick for the officer is to seem what you would be, and the formula for dealing with fear is ultimately rhetorical and theatrical: regardless of your actual feelings, you must simulate a carriage which will affect your audience as fearless, in the hope that you will be imitated, or at least not be the occasion for spreading panic" (*Wartime*, 274).

heat of battle, who refused to surrender or even survive when all was lost, displayed a superior form of courage and self-discipline to that of their men, for theirs was the product of an individual decision, not something expected of them because they were part of a group. It was precisely this readiness to face extreme danger when no necessity compelled it that was acknowledged as the supreme manifestation of personal courage at Rome and that won decorations for valor, not the bravery of soldiers in the line of battle.[61] And it was distinction in valor that represented one of the great avenues for winning fame and building a political career. During the middle Republic a reputation for courage was virtually an indispensable prerequisite for success in public life.[62] When the dictator appointed in 216 to revise the role of the senate, M. Fabius Buteo, made his *lectio*, he selected first the former curule officeholders not yet enrolled, next ex-plebeian aediles, tribunes of the plebes, and quaestors, and finally those who had spoils taken from the enemy affixed to their walls or a civic crown.[63] The expectation is clearly that men in the last-named category would under ordinary circumstances move into the other two as a matter of course. Fabius simply accelerated the normal sequence of political advancement to fill up the ranks of the senate depleted by the carnage of the opening years of the Hannibalic War. The normal pattern is reflected in the *cursus* of M. Claudius Marcellus, consul in 222 and thrice thereafter: victories in single combat brought him spoils; saving his brother's life won him a civic crown. The reputation that followed boosted him to a curule aedileship, after which a consulate might seem virtually certain.[64]

By the late Republic the aristocratic ethos had evolved considerably, and a far wider range of behavior served to demonstrate

---

61. Poly. 6.39.4. On monomachia during the Republic, see Oakley, CQ 35 (1985): 392–410.
62. Poly. 31.29.1.
63. Livy 23.23.5–6.
64. Plut. *Marc.* 2.1–2. On the frequency with which curule aediles rose to the consulship, see Develin, *Practice*, 92–96; cf. *Patterns in Office-Holding*, 23–24. Note too that among the ten highest goods attained by L. Caecilius Metellus, cos. 251 and 247, *primarius bellator* occupied the initial position; with *optimus orator* it served as entrée and foundation for the rest: Q. Caecilius Metellus, ORF[4] 2; on the identity of L. Metellus, see ORF[4] 535 and the works cited there. Cato the Elder was certainly well aware of that fact; according to his biographer, although as a young man he devoted much time to pleading cases in court, his principal concern was to gain high repute as a warrior (Plut. *Cat. Mai.* 1.5–6; cf. Astin, *Cato the Censor*, 6–7).

elite status.⁶⁵ Yet even down to the close of the first century personal bravery still counted for much, and one's prowess as a warrior continued to be considered a strong claim to membership in the ruling class of Rome.⁶⁶ Cicero in Cilicia could proclaim a willingness to face any and all dangers in the line of duty.⁶⁷ Perhaps this affirmation should be considered merely a matter of form, but the fact that he felt convention demanded it indicates that it still mattered to those he addressed that a general commanding the Republic's forces express himself in those terms. As late as 18 B.C. a man being purged from the senate by Augustus could bare his chest in the curia to display his scars and enumerate his campaigns by way of validating his claim to a place within its ranks.⁶⁸ *Virtus* supplied a principal element within the ideological underpinnings of senatorial dominance, and one of its most basic manifestations was as personal courage.⁶⁹ Consequently generals who displayed exceptional, deliberate bravery in the crisis of battle not only contributed materially to efforts to salvage a victory from the midst of impending defeat, but, more important, they placed themselves firmly within the moral tradition that defined the aristocracy and thereby protected themselves against prosecutions or other attacks intended to strip them of that status. They proved themselves worthy of the stature they already enjoyed—perhaps even enhanced it—and so neutralized the impact of their defeats on their chances for future political success. Defeat became politically dangerous only when, as in the cases of Caepio and Flaccus, it revealed that such pretensions to moral superiority were fraudulent.

---

65. Note, e.g., the "five greatest goods" that a consensus of historians in the later second century B.C. believed P. Licinius Crassus Mucianus had attained: Sempronius Asellio frg. 8 P (= Gell. *NA* 1.13.10). But note also how he died: above, p. 122.
66. Nicolet, *World of the Citizen*, 136–37; on the role of personal valor in the elevation of *equites* to the ranks of the senate, see idem, "Armée et société à Rome," 117–156.
67. Cic. *Fam.* 104 (15.1).4.
68. Dio 54.14.3; cf. the political authority that M. Servilius Pulex Geminus asserted such scars conferred on him when he addressed the *populus* in 167 (Livy 45.39.14–19; Plut. *Aem.* 31.2). Note also the coins of his descendants, C. and M. Servilius, moneyers in 127 and c. 100, which commemorate their ancestor's exploits in battle (Crawford, *Roman Republican Coinage*, 289, 328–29).
69. Harris, *War and Imperialism*, 20.

However, courage was demonstrated not only by a general's performance in the battle itself; equally important was his steadfastness afterward. Like his soldiers in the battle, a *victus* was still expected to stand his ground at all costs once it was over and the enemy had won. Polybius explained to his Greek readers the Romans' peculiar ancestral custom of appearing at their most stubborn and severe whenever they were beaten.[70] At such times they never softened their bargaining position; rather, they were most to be feared at moments of real danger.[71] Down to the end of the Republic it remained a point of honor even among defeated generals to refuse negotiations with an armed enemy.[72] The nobility and high-mindedness that Flamininus held up to the Aetolians in 197 as the characteristics a gentleman ought to display in defeat thus acquired a specific and concrete manifestation once the fighting was over; hence *victi* were under considerable pressure to adopt a hard-line stance in negotiating with victorious opponents to demonstrate the necessary courage and resolve.[73] This could lead to patent absurdities.

After beating the Romans under P. Licinius Crassus' leadership in 171, the Macedonian king Perseus sent envoys to seek a negotiated settlement of the conflict. Crassus, however, with the backing of his *consilium*, elected to return as stern a reply as possible, commanding the king to surrender unconditionally and leave the fate of Macedon to the discretion of the senate. Diplomatically the Roman position was utter folly—the enemy found it difficult to be certain whether it was the height of arrogance or a bargaining ploy.[74] To be sure, peace on the terms the king was offering may not have accurately reflected the Roman perception of the balance of power between the two sides. But the specific terms of Crassus' response arose less out of a calculated realpolitik than out of the imperatives conventional expectations about proper conduct in defeat had imposed on him. Exhibiting flexibility and an openness to compromise would have been viewed as a disgrace back at Rome. Rather, the moral stance demanded after a loss dictated that his

---

70. Poly. 27.8.8; cf. Livy 42.62.11.
71. Poly. 21.17.1 with Livy 37.45.12 and Walbank, *Comm.*, 3:109; Poly. 3.75.8.
72. Caes. *BGall.* 5.36.3; cf. Sall. *Cat.* 34.1.
73. Poly. 18.37.7.
74. Poly. 27.8.1–11; cf. Livy 42.62.1–15.

negotiating position be exactly the same as if he had won a resounding victory.[75]

Fortunately for Crassus, his loss was not serious, and success soon followed.[76] But for others in predicaments far worse, the need to preserve the required stance could lead them to make their situations truly desperate. Rebellious Gauls besieged the forces of Caesar's legate Q. Tullius Cicero in their cantonments over the winter of 54/3. After surrounding his camp, they offered to allow the Romans to depart unharmed, but the nature of Cicero's reply was a foregone conclusion: "It was not the custom of the Roman people to accept terms from an armed enemy. If they wished to lay down their arms, he would intercede for them if they wished to send envoys to Caesar; he trusted that, in view of his justice, they would obtain what they wanted."[77] The Gauls must have been mightily confused at a demand for their surrender; they seemed to hold all the high cards: the Romans were facing the possibility of a long siege and uncertain prospects of rescue. Certainly Cicero may have suspected that the enemy's promise of safe conduct was a fraud; he may have hoped for Caesar's speedy succor. Yet even so, it is the form of his reply that is arresting. He could have opened talks in a play for time. He could have feigned acceptance and invented reasons for delay. But instead he chose to behave as if he had the Gauls exactly where he wanted them—at his mercy.

Cicero knew what honor required of a leader in a tough spot and acted accordingly. He also must have been aware that had he not, he would have faced the judgment of his peers and countrymen. Contemporaries would remember whether he had backed down from a posture of superiority and escaped by allowing the

---

75. As it was, Crassus was reluctant to relocate his camp so as to place a stream between him and the enemy because he feared the disgrace of an apparent confession of fear (Livy 42.60.3–4). Sensitivity on such points of honor persisted to the end of the Republic; cf. Caelius' fears that a decision by Cicero to retreat in the face of an overwhelming Parthian force would damage his reputation, for the public tended not to appreciate the necessities facing a commander (Cic. *Fam.* 87 [8.10].1, quoted above, chap. 3, n. 4).

76. Crassus was fined after his year in command, but for cruelty toward the allies, not his military failures (Zonar. 9.22; cf. Livy 43.4.5–8).

77. Caes. *BGall.* 5.41: *Cicero ad haec unum modo respondit: non esse consuetudinem populi Romani accipere ab hoste armato condicionem: si ab armis discedere velint, se adiutore utantur legatosque ad Caesarem mittant; sperare pro eius iustitia, quae petierint, impetraturos.*

enemy to dictate the terms of egress. A man of his station could not afford the stigma of having done anything unworthy in order to survive.[78] So he stood firm and resorted to desperate expedients in order to extricate himself and his men.

Ultimately his patience was rewarded: Caesar came to the rescue and the *imperator* warmly praised his legate's energy and determination.[79] Other of Caesar's officers faced choices fully as desperate as Cicero's that winter, but their resolve was less firm: they accepted the enemy offer to allow the Romans to march away in safety. The judgment Caesar places in the mouths of tribunes and centurions who urged the officers to endure a siege stands as a general censure of all who would take this course: "What is more foolish or more disgraceful than to make decisions about life and death on the advice of an enemy?"[80] As if to illustrate its dangers, the enemy promptly violated its word and slaughtered the Romans virtually to a man.[81]

Yet the political dangers of truckling to a victorious enemy were hardly less acute than the military ones. When *victi* faced a stark choice between accommodating the harsh realities confronting them or persisting in the moral posture their ethos required, there can be no doubt how they were expected to choose. The public placed a far greater value on holding firm, refusing to accept defeat, and defending the honor of the city than on sparing the lives of its soldiers. Sp. Postumius Albinus, the consul of 110, left his brother Aulus in charge of his army in Africa while he returned to Rome to conduct elections, and Aulus had promptly allowed himself to be lured into a trap by the Numidian king Jugurtha. His army was surprised in a night attack, driven from its camp, and

---

78. Cf. the favorable judgment passed on M. Aurelius Scaurus when he confronted the Cimbri and Teutones at a parlay in 105 following his defeat: *nihil indignum viro Romano qui tantis honoribus fructu[s] aut fecit aut dixit* (Gran. Licin. 33.1–5 C). More important, note that the stance attributed to him in the Livian tradition also clearly derives from the ideal of an unbowed attitude in defeat: although his army had been beaten, Scaurus attempted to dissuade the enemy from invading Italy on the grounds that the Romans could never be conquered (Livy *Per*. 67).

79. On the siege and rescue, see Caes. *BGall*. 5.39–51; for Caesar's praise of Cicero, see *BGall*. 5.52.

80. Caes. *BGall*. 5.28.6: *postremo, quid esse levius aut turpius quam auctore hoste de summis rebus capere consilium?* Cf. 5.52 and J. Szidat, *Caesars diplomatische Tätigkeit im Gallischen Krieg*, 79–82.

81. On the siege and destruction of these forces, see *BGall*. 5.26–37.

surrounded on a nearby hill. On the following day Aulus agreed to terms laid down by the king: surrender of arms, passing beneath the yoke, a treaty of peace dictated by the victors.[82] Public anger exploded when news of these events reached Rome. Although his forces had been trapped, were in disarray, and faced certain destruction if resistance continued, Aulus ought to have held firm and battled his way out: "All were hostile to Aulus," Sallust reports, "and especially those who had often been outstanding in war, because although he had had his weapons, he had sought safety by disgrace rather than by fighting."[83]

Death was never too high a price to put on the honor of Rome, and the aristocratic ethos demanded that generals themselves pay it unflinchingly when called on to do so. But to sacrifice the lives of their men on the same altar was something else again, something that took real moral courage (albeit completely misguided in modern eyes). Yet generals who balked at this step provoked a disastrous political backlash. Aulus' surrender ultimately gave rise to the *quaestio Mamiliana*, before which his brother, as the magistrate formally responsible for his actions, was condemned.[84] Far more grim was the fate of C. Hostilius Mancinus, consul in 137. After the Numantines had trapped his army and compelled him to lay down his arms, surrender his baggage, and swear to a treaty of peace, he and his officers argued strenuously before the senate for ratification of the pact. They emphasized the hard realities they had faced in making their decision and the number of men it had saved.[85] That fact understandably pleased the friends and relatives of the soldiers, and the terms of the treaty itself do not seem to have significantly weakened the Roman position in Spain.[86] The senate had actually agreed to a less advantageous peace there three

---

82. Sources on the defeat are in appendix 1.1, no. 72.
83. Sall. *Iug.* 39.1: *Aulo omnes infesti, ac maxime qui bello saepe praeclari fuerant, quod armatus dedecore potius quam manu salutem quaesiverat.*
84. On the Mamilian *quaestio* generally and the politics involved, see Gruen, *Roman Politics*, 142–51; on Spurius' conviction, see Cic. *Brut.* 128.
85. Dio frg. 79.2.
86. Mancinus' quaestor, Ti. Sempronius Gracchus, enjoyed great popularity among the relatives of the survivors as a result of his efforts to bring negotiations between the Romans and the Numantines to a successful conclusion and so preserve the soldiers' lives (Plut. *Ti. Gracch.* 7.1). Mancinus' friends could urge the fact that the agreement left the Roman possessions in Spain intact in support of the treaty (Dio. frg. 79.2; cf. Astin, *Scipio Aemilianus*, 151).

years before.[87] Nonetheless, Mancinus' decision met with severe criticism from public and *patres* alike. The details of the pact were beside the point; Mancinus' surrender was the central issue, and neither diplomatic advantages nor the lives of his men could compensate for the ignominy it represented. He ought to have had the courage to cut his way out, even at the price of annihilating his entire army. Ultimately the assembly voted to hand Mancinus over to the enemy as a means of voiding the pact he had made, tantamount to a sentence of death.[88]

The situation of the legate C. Popillius Laenas thirty years later was even more tragic. He assumed command of what was left of the army of L. Cassius Longinus, consul in 107, after it had been driven into its camp following a crushing defeat by the Tigrini in Gaul and the death of its general. The enemy offered terms, and Popillius elected to save the survivors by accepting them. When he returned to Rome, he was brought up on charges of treason and condemned.[89] In this instance the sole question under scrutiny was the character of the legate's dealings with the enemy. Popillius could hardly be saddled with responsibility for the defeat itself. Whatever blame there might have been on that score rested squarely on the shoulders of the consul, now dead. Nor did the conclusion of a treaty intrude to cloud the picture: Popillius had made none. The single issue inciting revulsion against him was the price he had paid for the lives of his men. So stark was Popillius' dilemma between honor and necessity that his predicament actually became a standard debating topic for rhetoricians a genera-

---

87. In fact that treaty followed a serious defeat. But there is no indication that the commander who made it, Q. Fabius Maximus Servilianus, was forced to surrender or ever encountered any trouble back at Rome because he had made it. The first overtures concerning a settlement had come from the enemy, and Servilianus could present the results of the battle as having induced the enemy to approach him seeking a peace, which he had judged it in the interests of the Republic to grant. A treaty on those terms was perfectly acceptable, and it was duly ratified at Rome; for sources, see appendix 1.1., no. 33. On the factors leading the senate to accept a settlement of the war, see Astin, *Scipio Aemilianus*, 142–43. The fathers ordered the treaty abrogated soon thereafter (App. *Iber.* 70, cf. Livy *Oxy. Per.* 54; Diod. 33.1.4).
88. On the reaction in Rome, see Cic. *De Or.* 1.181, *Har. Resp.* 43; *Brut.* 102; Plut. *Ti. Gracch.* 7.1–3; App. *Iber.* 80, 83. Sources on the defeat and the bill to surrender Mancinus are in appendix 1.1, no. 41.
89. Caes. *BGall.* 1.7.4, 12.5–7; Livy *Per.* 65; App. *Gall.* 13; *Rhet. Her.* 1.25; Cic. *Leg.* 3.36; Oros. 5.15.23–24.

tion later.⁹⁰ Victory or death were the only acceptable ways out of the bind in which he found himself, and his failure to take the sole course honor allowed not only disgraced Popillius himself and Rome but laid him open to attack from his political opponents.

Thus one might say the aristocratic ethos demanded above all that a general manifest a refusal to accept defeat. That defiance motivated the heroics of commanders like Petilius or Sulla, who risked their lives when their men wavered and dared them to leave their leaders to fight on alone. It was most emphatically what Aulus Albinus, Mancinus, and Popillius had failed to do in choosing to surrender. The army's passing under the yoke and handing over of its weapons clearly symbolized their acceptance of the enemy victory and their own refusal to fight on. Most *victi* never found themselves in situations in which they were called upon to make similar choices, but the imperatives the ethos imposed on them remained the same. The optimal response to a reverse was simply to go on the attack once again and, if possible, win a resounding victory. Many did just that.⁹¹ Sp. Postumius Albinus, who did not, was nevertheless well aware of how important it was politically to renew the struggle in Africa. He raced back to his province in 110 eager to take the offensive against Jugurtha once more in order to ease the hostility his brother's surrender had engendered.⁹² Even the annalists knew that picking oneself up and taking another crack at the enemy was the way a proper Roman general ought to respond to an initial reverse: they invented a second, successful battle for that exemplary *imperator* M. Claudius Marcellus after Hannibal had beaten his army in 209.⁹³

Conversely, the appearance of having left the field to the enemy

---

90. *Rhet. Her.* 4.34, cf. 1.25; Cic. *Inv. Rhet.* 2.72–73.

91. E.g. Q. Fabius Maximus Gurges, cos. 292; P. Cornelius Rufinus and C. Iunius Brutus, coss. 277; P. Sempronius Tudetanus, cos. 204; M. Claudius Marcellus, cos. 196 (see appendix 1.1, no. 19); L. Aemilius Paullus, procos. 190; C. Calpurnius Piso, L. Quinctius Crispinus, promags. 185; A. Manlius Vulso, cos. 178; L. Mummius, pr. 153; Ap. Claudius Pulcher, cos. 143; Q. Lutatius Catulus, cos. 102; C. Sentius, propr. 92; L. Iulius Caesar, cos. 90; L. Licinius Murena, propr. 83–81; Q. Caecilius Metellus Pius, procos. 79–72; Cn. Pompeius, procos. 76–72; M. Aurelius Cotta, cos. 74, procos. 73–70. Sources are in *MRR* under the appropriate years.

92. Sall. *Iug.* 39.5; but the condition of his army kept Albinus in camp. Note also P. Valerius Falto, cos. 238, who after an initial defeat at the hands of the Gauls renewed the war when fresh troops arrived, determined to conquer by his own efforts or die, for he preferred death to living in disgrace (Zonar. 8.18).

93. See appendix 1.1, no. 18.

altogether involved serious political danger. The same M. Claudius Marcellus who won this fictive second battle against Hannibal in reality withdrew his forces into winter quarters after his authentic first defeat despite the fact that it was still the middle of the campaigning season. That move sparked a public outcry in the city orchestrated by an *inimicus* in the tribunate strong enough to compel the proconsul to return and defend himself against a bill to abrogate his command.[94] For C. Plautius Hypsaeus, a similar decision proved disastrous. His defeat in Farther Spain in 146 was notable not so much for the extent of the losses as for his pusillanimousness afterward: he fled into winter quarters in the towns in the middle of summer and refused to march out against the enemy for the rest of the year. That decision left his opponent Viriathus free to pillage Rome's allies at will. Plautius faced trial and condemnation in the following year. He had failed to defend the friends of the Republic, but more than that, he had abandoned the contest altogether and covered himself with shame.[95]

But perhaps the episode that does the most to illuminate how the reaction of the public to a general depended on its perception of his commitment to continue the fight is the celebrated reception accorded Varro after Cannae. Following the battle he had made his way to Canusium and there made every effort to rally the survivors and form them into some semblance of an army.[96] His actions demonstrated unmistakably that notwithstanding the magnitude of the catastrophe that was then engulfing the Republic, he was not pre-

---

94. Appendix 1.1, no. 18. Clearly Marcellus had some explaining to do, which he managed with extraordinary success: he was unanimously elected consul for the fifth time on the heels of his appearance before the assembly. Nothing is known of what he said on this occasion, unfortunately, but it was always possible to blame the soldiers, as Marcellus did after the battle (Livy 27.13.1–10; Plut. *Marc.* 25.5–6). Moreover, one could frequently justify staying on the defensive in the name of restoring the discipline and spirits of the army; cf. A. Hostilius Mancinus, cos. 170 (Livy 44.1.5–6); his son, C. Hostilius Mancinus, cos. 137 (*De Vir. Ill.* 59.1). Livy presents the tribune's complaints against Marcellus as centering on charges of a conspiracy among the senators to prolong the war unnecessarily. This presentation is largely tendentious, however: see the same theme in the annalistic accounts of the complaints Varro and others made against the handling of the war by the senate early in the conflict (Livy 22.25.3–11; 34.3–11; 38.6–7; Plut. *Fab.* 8.4; 14.2).

95. Appendix 1.1, no. 67. On disgrace at failing to protect friends, see Caes. *BGall.* 7.10; at being forced to keep to one's camp, see Caes. *BCiv.* 3.24, 3.37; Livy 40.27.10. Cf. Gruen, *Roman Politics*, 29, who rightly emphasizes anger at Plautius' cowardice as the reason for his condemnation.

96. Livy 22.54.1–2, 6, 22.56.1–2, 23.14.2; App. *Han.* 26; Dio frg. 57.29.

pared to give up the fight or consider its cause lost. And it was to this resolve that his countrymen responded: when the consul returned to Rome, a crowd of senators and common citizens went en masse to meet him and offer their thanks *quod de re publica non desperasset*, a gesture unique in the city's history.[97] That willingness to fight on even in the face of seemingly hopeless odds is clearly in accord with the refusal to accept defeat that is central to the aristocratic ethos, as this demonstration of approval for his conduct unmistakably acknowledged. Inasmuch as it paralleled the senate's own determination, Varro was still fulfilling the principal duty of a consul in defeat to exercise leadership by example. His position was somewhat ambiguous, however, and a certain amount of rehabilitation therefore became necessary. Varro had elected to escape death on the battlefield rather than refuse to survive the calamity at all, in contrast to his colleague Paullus. On that score, then, some might harshly criticize him for failing to measure up to the highest standard of aristocratic conduct in defeat.[98] The public gesture of support was necessary to stamp his decision as a manifestation not of cowardice but of that very same ideal: he had survived to carry on the struggle despite the apparent hopelessness of Rome's plight—an act of extraordinary courage in such desperate circumstances.[99] Ultimately, heroic valor in the heat of battle and stubborn perseverance in the face of adversity were simply two methods of striking the same posture in defeat.

The five or possibly six men tried following defeats on charges of extortion in the provinces (*de rebus repetundis*) form a distinct problem and require separate treatment. The question that needs to be answered concerns the role anger at their defeats played in these proceedings: to what extent did the formal charges serve as a vehicle to channel public hostility against them, so that in effect condemnation for extortion became a form of punishment for their losses? To assume that this was so might seem easy and natural.

---

97. Livy 22.61.14, cf. 25.6.7; Val. Max. 3.4.4; Plut. *Fab.* 18.4–5; Frontin. *Str.* 4.5.6; Sil. Ital. *Pun.* 10.615–39; *Schol. in Juv. ad Sat.* 11.200; cf. Münzer, *RE* 5.1A col. 688.
98. See above, n. 34.
99. Cf. Frontin. *Str.* 4.5.6; Flor. 1.22.17.

Consider the case of C. Porcius Cato, who sustained a severe reverse at the hands of the Scordisci in Thrace in 114 and suffered prosecution on charges of extortion at some point between his return and 110, probably in 113.[100] It has been suggested that the one was the result of the other and that "righteous wrath" secured his condemnation.[101] Yet information is extremely scanty concerning the trial, and *post hoc propter hoc* logic is no more than an argument from silence. No source explicitly connects Cato's defeat with the trial that followed. Charges may have centered on acts of official misconduct toward allies of Rome, and what little is known of the case seems to lend support. The fine assessed against the defendant was ludicrously small—HS 8,000 (or possibly no more than HS 4,000). Not unreasonably, the hand of Cato's powerful friends has been seen at work here.[102] Yet if so, then their effectiveness in shielding Cato is highly revealing. How great could public indignation have been if the jurors were persuaded to mete out punishment amounting to no more than a slap on the wrist? It seems far more plausible to assume that Cato was tried for some minor abuse against provincials while abroad, that proof was furnished to the jurors' satisfaction, and that they elected to view it as falling within the scope of activities proscribed by law. The minimal fine accords well with this view: he was mulcted for the damages he had caused the plaintiffs, not out of vengeance against him for his defeat.[103]

Any conclusions regarding the relationship between the defeat Cn. Papirius Carbo suffered while consul in 113 and the prosecution he sustained must be regarded as even more speculative. Carbo attacked the Cimbri by surprise, suffered a disastrous defeat, and lost a large part of his army.[104] At some point he was brought to trial, and although the charge is nowhere specified, *repetundae* and *perduellio* both have been suggested.[105] The date like-

---

100. Sources are in appendix 1.1, no. 71.
101. Gruen, *Roman Politics*, 127, cf. 126.
102. Gruen, *Roman Politics*, 127.
103. Badian, *Roman Imperialism*, 50. The fact that Cato was still on the public scene three years later when he faced prosecution before the *quaestio Mamiliana* demonstrates that no stigma attached to his conviction; see appendix 1.1, no. 71.
104. Sources are in appendix 1.1, no. 65.
105. On *repetundae*, see Gruen, *Roman Politics*, 306, although he is more cautious at 131; Tyrell and Pruser, *Correspondence of Cicero*, suggest *perduellio* at *Fam.* 9.21.3, as does Malcovati, "Ad Cic. Fam. 9,21,3," 218.

wise is a matter of conjecture and to some extent hangs on the question of the outcome of the trial. Commonly it has been supposed that Carbo was condemned. Hence the trial must follow his consulship, and the accusation and condemnation fall into place as the consequence of his terrible defeat. But the evidence for conviction is tenuous in the extreme, and acquittal is a far more likely verdict.

The case for condemnation is supported only by Cicero's obscure remark that Carbo *accusatus . . . sutorio atramento absolutus putatur*.[106] The phrase has been interpreted to mean that Carbo drank a copper sulphate solution in anticipation of certain condemnation.[107] However, this view ought to be rejected. No parallel exists for *sutorio atramento absolutus* in this sense. Furthermore, it would have been an extraordinary coincidence if Gaius as well as his brother Gnaeus, both consulars, had each taken his own life in connection with a criminal prosecution, and one would expect Cicero to have remarked on the fact either here or elsewhere. The older view should be preferred, that the phrase somehow refers to a corrupt verdict.[108] If so, then the trial itself may not have followed his consulate, and all connection with the defeat he suffered in it evaporates. The trial may have involved charges arising out of a term as governor of Asia Minor in 116 or shortly thereafter.[109] The case can offer little dependable evidence on the relationship, if any, between defeat and a prosecution before the extortion court.

Testimony is a little better concerning two governors active in Sicily during the slave revolt there at the end of the second century. It is important to note that neither suffered a major defeat. L. Licinius Lucullus won a victory against the slaves in the open field in 103 and then laid siege to their stronghold; his attack met with mixed success, and he retired having had the worst of it.[110] His successor, C. Servilius, probably suffered no real defeat at all in 102.[111] Both, however, underwent trial for extortion and were con-

---

106. Cic. *Fam.* 188 (9.21).3.
107. Most recently by Malcovati, "Ad Cic. Fam. 9,21,3," 216–20, accepted by Tyrell and Pruser, *Correspondence of Cicero*, and Gruen, *Roman Politics*, 131.
108. Shackleton-Bailey, *Cicero Epistulae ad Familiares*, 2:330.
109. Münzer, *RE* 18.3 col. 1022–23; Holleaux, *RA* 8, ser. 5 (1918): 234–35.
110. Appendix 1.1, no. 46.
111. Appendix 1.1, no. 80.

demned.¹¹² In view of the minor nature of their setbacks we cannot rule out the possibility that their trials, like Cato's, arose mainly out of wrongs inflicted on provincials rather than out of an effort to find a pretext to punish them for their losses. But be that as it may, Diodorus preserves some indication of the complaints made against their conduct, assuming his evidence is reliable.¹¹³ The thrust of these complaints concerns ineffectiveness in command as opposed to defeat per se. After noting Lucullus' failure against the rebel stronghold and the boost it gave their morale, Diodorus continues by remarking that he accomplished nothing of what was necessary, perhaps having been bribed or perhaps out of indolence, on account of which he was brought to trial and punished.¹¹⁴ A second excerpt offers a bit of information that accords well with this passage. There Diodorus reports that Lucullus was criticized for seeming to increase the war, presumably because he was taking no effective steps to stop it; whereupon Lucullus, assuming that if his successor likewise failed, his own performance would appear that much better, dismissed his army and burned his camp and supplies.¹¹⁵ Servilius, according to Diodorus, merely accomplished nothing worthy of note, on account of which he, like Lucullus, was exiled. Yet we also learn that Servilius had allowed the enemy to overrun the countryside without hindrance, even to the point of their putting some cities under siege.¹¹⁶

Defeat does not loom large in all this, except in so far as it might be considered symptomatic of the two men's ineffectiveness in stamping out the revolt. Certainly, in view of the crisis in the north during these years, being perceived as having done too little—and that badly—to ease the situation in Sicily will have appeared far more egregious a failing than under ordinary circumstances.¹¹⁷ Moreover, the fact both Lucullus and Servilius had faced only con-

---

112. On the charges and their political aspects as well as the identity of Lucullus' accuser, see Münzer, *RE* 2A col. 1762-63; Van Ooteghem, *L. Licinius Lucullus*, 14-15; Gruen, *Roman Politics*, 176-78; Epstein, *Personal Enmity*, 65, 115.
113. On the nature of the excerpts comprising Diodorus' book 36, see Rubinsohn, *Athenaeum* 60 (1982): 437-39.
114. Diod. 36.8.5.
115. Diod. 36.9.2.
116. Diod. 36.9.1.
117. Rubinsohn, *Ath.*, n.s. 60 (1982): 449-51.

temptible rebellious slaves undoubtedly made their helplessness against them all the more disgraceful.[118] Yet it is significant in that regard that P. Licinius Nerva, who led the war against the slaves in 104 previous to Lucullus, sustained a far more serious defeat than either of his successors yet suffered no prosecution thereafter.[119] Clearly it was not simply the fact of a defeat, even against servile opponents, even in the context of the German invasion, that brought about the condemnations of Lucullus and Servilius. Perhaps, then, these prosecutions ought to be viewed as arising out of a context of moral failure as well. The charge against Servilius is strongly reminiscent of that brought against C. Plautius Hypsaeus in 146—abandoning the open country to the enemy and refusing to protect Rome's allies.[120] And perhaps Lucullus' inertness following his loss, more than the loss itself, was what counted most heavily against him. Certainly if accusations that he had deliberately handicapped Servilius' efforts against the enemy played a role in Lucullus' trial, they will have done nothing to enhance his image as a man who refused to accept defeat (at least in any way that redounded to his credit). Thus the behavior of these two *victi* after their losses and the states of mind it reflected, rather than military failure alone, may represent the key factor in securing their condemnations. The latter was certainly relevant but not sufficient in itself.

The element of moral failure becomes even more pronounced in the trial of M. Antonius Hibrida, the consul of 63. During his proconsulate in Thrace from 62 until 60, his depredations against subject and neighboring tribes provoked attacks in response, and he was twice seriously defeated. Late in 60 he was recalled and put on trial the following year.[121] The charge is somewhat murky: extortion receives support in the sources, although *maiestas* or *vis* remain possibilities.[122] Likewise the factors impelling the prosecution were complex. Dio Cassius in a confused passage seems to say that events in Thrace were responsible for securing Antonius' convic-

---

118. Cf. Plut. *Crass.* 9.6; App. *BCiv.* 118.
119. Appendix 1.1, no. 49.
120. Appendix 1.1, no. 67, and see above, p. 139.
121. Sources are in appendix 1.1, no. 4.
122. *Schol. Bob.* 94 St.; cf. Gruen, *Latomus* 32 (1973): 301–10, at 307–9.

tion, although the formal charges involved complicity in the Catilinarian conspiracy.[123] That analysis has been strongly disputed and the contrary maintained: whereas his dismal record abroad supplied the pretext, in fact old partisan scores were being settled in the trial, and new political agendas were being advanced as well.[124] But whether as pretext or substance, it seems clear that Antonius' failures in Thrace played a significant role in his political demise. What, then, sets these apart from the defeats other *victi* sustained? The best answer seems to be the charge that in them Antonius revealed himself as a coward and a drunk.

When the Dardanians advanced against him, Antonius purposely retired with the cavalry and left his infantry to bear the brunt of their attack. In a battle against the Bastarnae Dio says flatly that he ran away.[125] One might argue that Dio's words are not to be pressed here, that one should take them as referring to a rout of the entire army, not to Antonius himself. But one other fragment of evidence seems to go against that interpretation. A passage preserved from the speech of one of his accusers, M. Caelius Rufus, portrays Antonius as asleep in an alcoholic stupor surrounded by his harem during an enemy attack. The women made a desperate effort to awaken him, but Antonius, still groggy, only responded by trying to embrace them, and once awake, he was too drunk to function effectively in command. The fragment ends with him being tossed between his concubines and the centurions, presumably in an attempt to bring him to his senses.[126] Although certainty is not possible, the likelihood is strong that this passage refers to the battle against the Bastarnae: it was apparently a surprise attack since they were bringing aid to an Istrian tribe Antonius was trying to plunder, whereas Antonius himself was long gone when the Dardanians made their assault. A terrified flight would have served as a fitting climax to the comedy Caelius described.[127] Of

---

123. Dio 38.10.3.
124. Gruen, *Latomus* 32 (1973): 301–10; cf. Epstein, *Personal Enmity*, 122.
125. Dio. 38.10.1–3.
126. M. Caelius Rufus, ORF⁴ 17 (= Quint. *Inst.* 4.2.123–4), cf. 18.
127. Alternatively, of course, the episode could have occurred some years earlier in Antonius' career and have been one of the charges that led to his expulsion from the senate in 70: sources are in *MRR* 2:127. But such an explanation appears to multiply hypotheses needlessly, inviting application of Ockham's razor.

course, accusations of moral turpitude were the common stuff of political invective during the late Republic. Caelius himself would come in for a healthy dose when he faced trial in 56. But the prevalence of that practice does not prove the charges untrue: Antonius already had a reputation as a dissolute wastrel and had been expelled from the senate on that account.[128] Nor, more important, does it diminish their significance as evidence of what a prosecutor thought would rouse *invidia* against a *victus* among the judges in this trial. Immorality and a failure to display the courage demanded under the aristocratic ethos thus seem to have played a pivotal role in the proceedings, as in the case of Cn. Fulvius Flaccus.[129] They mediated between the partisan forces lying behind the prosecution and the extensive public hostility that his enemies needed to foster against Antonius to secure his condemnation.[130]

The moral issue was equally crucial in the trial of Q. Pompeius but led to the opposite result. He was brought up on charges of extortion following a series of failures against the Numantines during 141–140. Yet his conduct in their aftermath seems to have done most to stir up political trouble. He was eager to win credit for ending the war despite his losses and so came to terms with the enemy. But with the arrival of his successor, the deal began to unravel. The Numantines asserted that Pompeius had entered into a formal treaty of peace with them; he, on the contrary, insisted he had received their unconditional surrender. Unhappily for him, testimony from the members of his own *consilium* supported the Numantines and proved an acute embarrassment to his pretensions. The whole affair was packed off to Rome and a senatorial inquiry that decided to continue the war.[131] Subsequently he faced not only charges of extortion but efforts in 136 to pass legislation requiring that he be handed over to the Numantines along with Mancinus to invalidate the treaties each had struck with them.[132]

---

128. *Comm. Petit.* 8; Sall. *Cat.* 21.3; Asc. 83, 84, 88, 93 C.
129. See above, pp. 128–29.
130. Note also that charges of immorality and cowardice help explain why Antonius' rehabilitation under his nephew the triumvir included a censorship in 42. Undertaking the supervision of public morality that the office entailed restored some of the damage done to his good name. Although some may have received the news with derision, open mockery will have been dangerous and rare.
131. Full sources are in appendix 1.1, no. 69.
132. For discussion of the date, see Rosenstein, *CA* 5 (1986): 246 n. 52.

Yet from both ordeals Pompeius emerged unscathed. Again, it is possible that his trial may have had little to do with his defeats or his agreement with the enemy.[133] Yet even if it did, the result indicates that his enemies had not succeeded in arousing widespread antagonism against either his defeats or his dealings in Spain.

The protection he enjoyed may be traced to his posture in defeat. Throughout, Pompeius steadfastly maintained that the enemy had performed a full and formal *deditio in fidem*, in spite of everyone else connected with the event asserting the opposite. In part this insistence arose out of a need to secure senatorial support for ratification of his agreement since absolute victory was the *patres'* sine qua non for ending the war in Nearer Spain.[134] Yet his stance was also calculated to demonstrate that, like P. Licinius Crassus or Q. Cicero, he had persisted in treating the victors as vanquished despite his position of military inferiority. Anything else would have been viewed as disgraceful, and Pompeius knew it.[135] The difference in his case was simply the Numantines' weariness with the war, which led them to trust Pompeius' assurances of lenient treatment if only they surrendered. It was an arrangement few other *victi* could hope to convince their victorious adversaries to accept. But once the Numantines did, they allowed Pompeius to seize the

---

133. Richardson, *JRS* 77 (1987): 1–12 (cf. idem, *Hispaniae*, 137–40), has argued that the *lex Calpurnia* establishing the *quaestio de repetundis* did not cover crimes by magistrates against provincials. If he is correct, Pompeius' trial had nothing to do with events in Spain; it may indeed have preceded or followed those events by a considerable interval. Yet Richardson's arguments are not conclusive. In any case, politics seems to have played a role in securing his acquittal: the jurors, rather surprisingly, refused to credit the testimony of the four eminent consulars who gave evidence against him (Cic. *Font.* 23; Val. Max. 8.5.1, cf. Gruen, *Roman Politics*, 36–37; Epstein, *Personal Enmity*, 99, 105, for discussion).

134. See Richardson, *Hispaniae*, 144–150.

135. Note especially Pompeius' insistence on the Numantines' *deditio* because, as he told them, "he knew of no other terms worthy of the Romans": ὁ δὲ (Πομπήιος) ἐς μὲν τὸ φανερὸν ἐκέλευεν αὐτοὺς Ῥωμαίοις ἐπιτρέπειν (οὐ γὰρ εἰδέναι συνθήκας ἑτέρας Ῥωμαίων ἀξίας); note also his alleged awareness that the treaty he had made was "shameful," αἰσχράς (App. *Iber.* 79). If, as Richardson suggests (*Hispaniae*, 144–45), the "advisors" who arrived from Rome late in 140 (App. *Iber.* 78) were in fact a ten-man legation from the senate to oversee a settlement of the war, this may mean not only that he had misrepresented the military situation in his dispatches home but also that he had already begun discussions with the Numantines concerning a settlement. Coming to terms after a defeat was what led to political danger, and the knowledge that he had done this supplies the reason Pompeius began to fear prosecution and a motive for his efforts in public to get the Numantines to surrender (App. *Iber.* 78).

moral high ground and keep his actions free of any taint. That stance made him proof against his enemies' attacks, as verdicts from the jurors on the extortion court in 138 and the voters in the assembly in 136 confirmed.

———|———

What evidence can be gleaned concerning *victi* tried *de repetundis* therefore indicates that here too the focus of attention was their personal conduct in defeat. Violating the conventions of the aristocratic ethos unleashed an angry political reaction in these cases, and this conclusion strongly reinforces the impression that for the rest security from a similar fate came with adherence to the dictates of the code. Its role as a trigger in unleashing aristocratic rivalry emerges forcefully. Whatever indignation and passion a lost battle might have engendered among the elite or the populace at large remained inaccessible to a *victus' inimici* or other interested parties eager to exploit such sentiments unless they could raise the cry of moral failure or disgrace and tie it convincingly to his actions. Yet precisely because of the ethos conventions of deportment could protect as well as injure a *victus*. They made it possible for him to demonstrate to the satisfaction of all that he had behaved in a manner above reproach.

Efforts in this direction can occasionally be detected in the posture of someone like Pompeius, struggling gamely to maintain the image of having received a *deditio*. But the most impressive monument to a *victus'* efforts to manipulate his conduct to meet the expectations of the code is the performance of C. Hostilius Mancinus. Once it became clear that the senate would not agree to ratification of his treaty but would instead propose legislation to hand its author over to the Numantines, he put on an unprecedented display of personal bravery in the midst of this political disaster by coming before the assembly to urge *passage* of the bill. The senate had determined that although Mancinus' agreement was not legally binding since the people had never voted to ratify it, nonetheless it had placed a strong moral claim on the Romans' *fides*. Hence it could not be ignored without in some way neutralizing the religious consequences this would involve. Mancinus therefore had to be sacrificed to free the Republic from these obligations. He turned sacrifice into self-sacrifice: he offered to give his life willingly in this cause.¹³⁶

The effectiveness of this step in reversing public hostility toward him was virtually complete. He was duly handed over to the Numantines, who refused to accept him. Mancinus then returned to Rome and attempted to reenter the senate. He was prevented by a tribune who contended that the act of being handed over to the enemy had deprived Mancinus of his citizenship. The issue was debated before the *patres*, who found merit in the tribune's assertion. Yet far from indicating the vindictiveness of the senate, the controversy merely stemmed from a continuing concern for legal and religious form evident throughout this affair. To solve the problem, Mancinus was made the subject of a special law granting him citizenship once again. What is more, he later gained election to a second praetorship, which restored to him a place in the senate and honorable rank as well.¹³⁷

There is no trace of hostility toward Mancinus on the part of his peers or the people in these events. The bill to renew his citizenship would not have passed easily in the teeth of senatorial opposition or continued ill will among the voters. If anything, the reverse is indicated: election as praetor once again meant he had won a considerable following among the senators and first-class voters. The change in his political fortunes is striking in view of the revulsion that greeted his return following his capitulation, and it can only be ascribed to the fact that he had adopted, albeit belatedly, precisely the stance of exceptional self-sacrifice the aristocratic code required from men of his class in defeat.¹³⁸ Although the bill to surrender him represented a political, not a military, reverse, Mancinus by his gesture cast it in the latter terms. He insisted that since it grew out of his predicament at Numantia, the

---

136. Mancinus' own *fides* was at stake as well. He had guaranteed the treaty with his oath, and his stance here manifestly demonstrated his commitment to keeping his pledge. He would offer his life in atonement for its violation. No less could be expected of an aristocrat where personal honor as well as patriotism were concerned. For sources, see appendix 1.1, no. 41; for discussion, see Rosenstein, *CA* 5 (1986): 244–51.
137. On the debate, see Cic. *De Or.* 1.181, 238; 2.137; *Caecin.* 98, *Top.* 37; *Dig.* 49.15.4, 50.7.17. On the citizenship bill and second praetorship, see *Dig.* 50.7.17; *De. Vir. Ill.* 59.4. Mancinus might even have gone further but for the fact that iteration of the consulate was forbidden after c. 151.
138. On the reaction at Rome, see above, n. 88.

public judge him here by the standards appropriate there. The gesture was perhaps all the more welcome inasmuch as it did not require the soldiers trapped with him in Spain to die in order to demonstrate his courage and vindicate the honor of the city. Mancinus himself was quick to exploit the popularity his action had won. Not only did he immediately attempt to return to his rightful place in the senate and later run for public office, but he had a statue made depicting himself just as he had been when he was handed over, bound and naked, to the Numantines.[139] The statue clearly aimed to memorialize the extraordinary *virtus* he had displayed in offering to die in order to sustain the refusal of Rome to accept defeat. He had covered himself in glory and, having survived, intended to lay claim to its fruits by advertising that fact.

Mancinus' case, however, is clearly special. He was struggling to regain his good name after the egregious disgrace of electing to lay down his arms to survive. His exceptional success here was rewarded with a dramatic comeback in the political arena. Yet most *victi* did not go on to subsequent electoral triumphs, only about the same percentage as was normal among their undefeated peers. Of these, it is certainly possible that some, perhaps even many, may have performed some striking feat of bravery or determination in their defeats to distinguish themselves and so enable them to rise to heights they would not otherwise have achieved. But for that to have been the case, an equal number who under normal circumstances would have reached consulates or censorships will have had to have disgraced themselves sufficiently in their defeats to deny them these positions. Only in that way—the latters' failures canceling out the formers' successes—will a statistically average result have been possible. Clearly, given the limits of the evidence, this hypothesis cannot be ruled out completely. But probability seems to tell against it.[140] Rather, the effect of the ethos was defensive, protecting the political status quo as it existed previous to these men's defeats. Most of those initially strong enough

---

139. Plin. *HN* 34.18.
140. It should be noted, however, that the percentage of consular *victi* not prosecuted and exiled who went on to a censorship is slightly higher than was normal among all consulars, about 27 percent (see above, chap. 1, p. 18). Possibly, therefore, this anomaly is to be explained by the opportunity a defeat offered a general for a display of heroics whence to garner glory.

to gain higher office continued to be so afterward. Defeat neither eroded the basis of their support nor aroused additional antagonism against them.

Conversely, failure to measure up to the dictates of the code gave opponents a pretext to direct the passions and outcry that defeat engendered against a *victus*. Those who came under fire for their behavior did not suffer condemnation for immorality per se—that was never formally a crime under the Republic—but for its effect when manifested by someone in a position of military leadership. In some cases their behavior had a direct role in bringing about a defeat or a deterioration in the military situation, as when Flaccus' cowardice caused his men to flee or Plautius' refusal to leave the safety of camp allowed the enemy to overrun the countryside.[141] But in others, like Caepio's or Antonius', a direct connection is more problematic. Malfeasance was less the issue in such trials than fitness to lead. Just as great *virtus* was deemed to qualify men to govern and enable them to benefit the state, so moral inferiority constituted grounds for censure and even expulsion from the senate.[142] *Victi* who could be shown to have violated the canons of aristocratic conduct in their defeats thus were judged to have forfeited their claim to a place among the governing elite. At stake in most of these trials was the question of whether or not the defendant would remain within the political community or withdraw into exile.[143] Viewed from this perspective, such condemnation represented in effect a process of purging a senator who had revealed himself to be incapable of bearing one of the primary moral burdens of leadership. In military commanders failings of this kind were tantamount to treason because of the general's role as an exemplar for his men. His own courage and refusal to accept defeat served as a model for theirs. Such failures also posed a

---

141. P. Claudius Pulcher's refusal to heed the auspices falls into this category as well (see above chap. 2, p. 79).

142. On *virtus* and the *res publica*, see Mitchell, *Hermathena* 136 (1984): 23; Earl, *Sallust*, 18–27, cf. idem, *Moral and Political Traditions*, 20–24. On expulsion from the senate and the social role of the censors' *regimen morum*, see Astin, *JRS* 78 (1988): 32–33.

143. There are two exceptions. P. Claudius Pulcher was fined, but his first trial was on capital charges and, had it resulted in a guilty verdict, would have led to his exile. Porcina was fined, but here the issue was willful disobedience of a direct injunction from the senate not to expand the war in Spain (Richardson, *Hispaniae*, 150–51).

threat to his peers in the senate since they might raise doubts in the mind of the public about the ability of the aristocracy as a whole to measure up to the same standards. Thus such purges amounted to both a collective reaffirmation of the community's demand that its leaders live up to the conventions the *victus* had betrayed and a demonstration by their leaders of their own allegiance to those norms. *Victi* who met expectations, however, deserved praise for their success and earned the right to continue in their accustomed prominence. Their lost battles cast no doubt on their title to lead.

5

Conclusions and Implications

In the preceding chapters I have identified evidence for a surprising degree of restraint in political competition at Rome and then sought to understand what made this restraint possible within a system that otherwise encouraged a continuous, intense struggle for status and power among the ruling elite of the Republic. A *victus'* immunity from the public's hostility in the wake of defeat derived ultimately from beliefs and assumptions both widespread and deeply held among it: the certain conviction that the city's bonds with its heavenly protectors were vital in procuring its victories; insistence, for the same reason, on iron discipline and bravery among the legionaries under any and all circumstances; and a readiness to accord honor and deference to generals who met the demands of the aristocratic ethos in defeat. Ordinary Romans and aristocrats alike will have subscribed to these tenets, and even if some among the latter entertained doubts or were inclined to skepticism, still, the solid, practical advantages that they along with the rest of their class derived from seeing them perpetuated among the public at large will have made them hesitate to question their veracity openly in political debate. We are now in a position to assess the precise mechanisms by means of which this complex of ideas resulted in the continued political success of the *imperatores victi*.

Three things seem particularly important. Certainly the most crucial was the timocratic structure of the *comitia centuriata*. As argued in chapter 1, wealthier voters had no intrinsic reason to be better disposed than poorer ones to the subsequent aspirations of defeated generals. Military service was required of both—more so, in fact, of voters in the first class—and one might logically expect that given a choice, they would rather serve under winners than losers. But the finding that beliefs about the causes of defeat and expectations regarding the conduct of an aristocrat in adversity played the key role puts the practical implications of the structure of this assembly in a different light. The evidence for these attitudes derives largely from the senatorial class. Acts of the curia regularly give them expression; most of what few explicit articulations we have come from its members. There is no reason to assume that the outlook of ordinary Romans was substantially different. A consensus shared between them and their rulers on these points as well as many others formed an essential basis for the latter's political dominance. Yet it is only reasonable to expect that the nearer a citizen stood to the senatorial class in economic and social background, the more likely he was to share its outlook, and such men were enrolled in the equestrian and first-class centuries along with the senators themselves. Their votes, of course, carried a preponderant influence in the selection of consuls and censors. They also enjoyed a decisive voice in capital trials. Furthermore, older citizens, generally speaking, were those least likely to break with traditional ideas and embrace new ways of seeing the world. As is well known, all classes of centuries were divided into an equal number of *iuniores* and *seniores*, an arrangement that afforded the votes of the elder citizens far greater weight than their numbers warranted. Thus the structure of the assembly, by tilting the balance of power toward the views of the rich and the old, tended to ensure that a conservative view of the world similar to that of the ruling elite governed the choices of the *comitia* precisely in those areas where military defeat was most likely to become an issue in political rivalry—the selection of new generals and the question of punishing those who had failed.

Second, those most likely to refrain from criticizing a *victus* who had demonstrated courage and maintained an unbowed stance in the face of defeat were other aristocrats. For such men, *virtus* represented both an important means of defining and legitimizing their elite status in the community as well as a claim to public office. Hence they were far more likely to offer praise than censure, for in honoring a defeated general's *virtus*, in effect they demanded that others offer a similar deference to their own. The immediate, personal stake that each of them had in perpetuating the political implications of this ideology constituted a firm basis on which to sustain what in chapter 1 was termed a gentlemen's agreement or sense of noblesse oblige to refrain from raising an opponent's defeats against him. This consensus in turn had practical results at the polls. An angry public needed leaders in order to exercise its latent power. Rome was not Athens: the freedom of the *populus* to wield its undeniably decisive theoretical authority was in fact largely confined to an ability to select among the options offered it. If no real choice was presented, the voters could do little to alter the situation.[1] In particular, their capacity to articulate their sentiments was in most cases limited to the words of a magistrate or those he allowed to speak at a *contio*. Thus the refusal of the aristocracy to raise the issue of a *victus'* failure stifled whatever rumblings of dissatisfaction existed among the public and so kept them from swelling into widespread outcry. Even assuming an aristocrat broke with his peers and openly criticized an opponent's conduct of a war, as long as a consensus prevailed within the rest of the senatorial class on this point, he would find it difficult to persuade the public to follow his lead, for in all but a handful of cases the voters heeded the collective *auctoritas* of their rulers.[2]

Third, the complex of beliefs and expectations traced in the previous chapters also helped facilitate continued cooperation between *victi* and other members of the elite. This mutual assistance, too, was vital to their continued political success. Over the past thirty years a series of devastating critiques of what may be called the factional model has profoundly altered our understanding of the dynamics of political behavior in the middle and late Republic, and it is now clear that a great deal of basic work must be done before we can reconstruct a picture of competition within the ruling class.[3] Yet even if past hypotheses of armies of obedient clients, *amicitia* as the building block of factions, and permanent parties spanning generations into which all members of the ruling class are to be neatly sorted must at last be jettisoned altogether, it is difficult to see how we can rule out completely a role for political groups of some type—combinations of ambitious men working together to advance their individual interests and often linked by some personal bond, whether of kinship, obligation, or even af-

---

1. On this crucial point, see the important papers by North, *Past and Present* 126 (1990), 3–21; idem, *CP* 85 (1990), forthcoming.
2. This was particularly true of those in the equestrian and first-class centuries, where a *victus'* future success was determined, yet not much less so in the plebeian assembly. If the consensus within the aristocracy broke down, however, real choice then became possible.
3. See above, chap. 1 n. 141.

fection. Roman political culture simply did not produce atomistic behavior. If, then, a *victus* would need the commendations and support of others among his peers in his quest for the votes he needed to gain further offices, it is clear that this help would only be forthcoming if they perceived that association with him was in no sense likely to become a liability to their own advancement but rather could become an asset. An outlook that not only absolved him of blame for his defeat but even allowed him to become admirable in the eyes of his fellow citizens went a long way toward making his support desirable to potential allies.

This is not to claim, of course, that the assumptions and ideals that operated through these mechanisms caused *victi* overall to become more likely to win offices than they had been before, only that they kept them from becoming any less so by virtue of having lost a battle. The point to stress is that they helped establish limits that kept highly competitive aristocrats from exploiting the passions a defeat could engender in their rivalries with one another. What the limits also protected, therefore, was the value of the usual factors governing the outcome of such contests. Ser. Sulpicius Galba's exceptional accomplishments as an orator could become an important source of public support for his political aspirations in no small measure because the limits rendered the fact of his incompetence as a general irrelevant to the struggle for office. Likewise the juristic brilliance of a M'. Manilius, the popularity of a Q. Pompeius, or the consular ascendants of many *victi* could serve to commend them to the voters only because the battles they had lost did not negate the advantages such assets represented in political contests.[4] As we shall see, guaranteeing their validity had profound and far-reaching consequences for the character of aristocratic competition itself and helps explain how a state of affairs that seems to have run counter to the natural tendency of rivalry could be perpetuated over the course of centuries.

---

4. Galba, see Cic. *Brut.* 82, 295; *De Or.* 1.58; other sources are in *RE* 7A 766–67. On Manilius, see Cic. *Rep.* 3.17; *De Or.* 1.212; Gell. *NA* 17.7.3; Pompon. *Dig.* 1.2.2.39. On Pompeius, see Rutilius Rufus, frg. 7P, cf. Plut. *Apoth. Scip. Min.* 8 (= *Mor.* 200 C); Cic. *Amic.* 77; *Brut.* 96; Vell. Pat. 2.1.5.

Up to this point I have offered an analysis couched largely in static terms, yet in fact things rarely stand still. Therefore, it is essential to address the question of change over time and attempt to understand what vicissitudes these limits underwent in the course of the period covered by this study. In the light of the conclusions reached in the preceding chapters, however, the question cannot simply be whether the treatment of defeated generals varied at all between the fourth and first centuries. It is also essential to consider whether the larger trends in the course of the development of the Republic altered the underlying complex of ideas that shaped the way men thought about defeat or made their choices in the political arena.

If any faith can be placed in Livy's narrative of events in the fifth century, the point at which these restraints originated can be surmised with some precision. He records a number of instances during that era in which not only did defeats become issues in current political struggles, but the generals deemed negligent or culpable in them thereby faced prosecution and fines. Thus the failure of T. Menenius Lanatus, cos. 477, to prevent the slaughter of the Fabii at the Cremera formed the basis for the capital charges laid against him. These he seems to have escaped, but he sustained a heavy fine nonetheless and died shortly thereafter.[5] The mood of the public remained hostile to *victi*, however, and Sp. Servilius Structus' defeat in the following year led to criminal charges against him also, though he escaped condemnation.[6] An attempt at prosecution likewise reportedly followed Ap. Claudius Sabinus' failures in 471.[7] Livy relates that a generation later T. Quinctius Cincinnatus Poenus and M. Postumius Albinus Regillensis both stood trial for failures at Veii in 426 as military tribunes with consular power following a defeat suffered by the consul in 423, C. Sempronius Atra-

---

5. Livy 2.51.1–2, 52.3–5; Dion. Hal. 9.23.1–2, 27.1–5; Dio frg. 21.3. Ogilvie, *Commentary on Livy*, 366–69, however, doubts the historicity of this episode.
6. Livy 2.51.7–8, 52.6–7; Dion. Hal. 9.26.4–9, 28.1–33.3
7. On the battle, see Livy 2.58.4–59.11; Dion. Hal. 9.50.3; Val. Max. 9.3.5; Frontin. *Str.* 4.1.34; App. *Ital.* 7; Zonar. 2.7.17; on the trial, see Livy 2.61.1–9; Dion. Hal. 9.54.1–6. The outcome of the trial is unclear: Livy, Dionysius of Halicarnassus, and Zonaras all report Claudius died of an illness or suicide before he could be tried, but he was consul again in 451 and one of the *decemviri* of 451–50: Ogilvie, *Commentary on Livy*, 386.

tinus. Postumius was compelled to pay a fine, but Quinctius escaped punishment. Livy also records criticisms leveled against Sempronius and three years later a trial resulting in a fine.[8] In 402 the military tribunes with consular power L. Verginius Esquilinus and M'. Sergius Fidenas were compelled to abdicate and fined besides following a reverse at the siege of Veii.[9]

None of these events inspires much confidence in its veracity, but taken together they do lend some support to the notion that during the fifth century defeat often had serious political repercussions for the generals involved.[10] This was particularly so owing to the Struggle of the Orders, which formed the background to most political conflicts of the period. Tribunes of the plebs reportedly served as accusers in all these cases and sought to exploit public anger at a defeat in their battles against the patricians. Yet thereafter prosecutions on similar charges are strikingly absent until 249 and the trial of P. Claudius Pulcher for the consequences at Drepana of his memorable act of impiety.[11] Clearly something had occurred in the meantime to change the way the Romans responded to defeat. Political rivalry certainly did not come to an end; the Struggle of the Orders did not find its final resolution until the fourth century drew to a close. And the Republic did not stop losing battles. Rather, an abrupt shift in outlook appears to have taken place between the fifth and fourth centuries, and that shift strongly suggests that a single, pivotal event intervened to alter fundamentally how the citizens and their leaders perceived the causes of defeat. The best candidate for such a jolt occurred in 390 with the massive reverse suffered at the Allia and the sack of Rome immediately following. As argued above, this disaster gave rise to the

---

8. On the defeat at Veii, see Livy 4.31.2–4; on the trial of the military tribunes, see 4.41.4, 10–11. On Sempronius' defeat, see Livy 4.37.6–8; on his trial, see 4.44.1–10, cf. 4.42.3; Val. Max. 6.5.2.

9. Livy 5.8.4–9.1, 11.4–12.2.

10. However, defeat was not necessarily fatal either to the generals themselves or to their political careers: note that Claudius and Postumius both won elections subsequently, Claudius as consul in 451 and Postumius as military tribune with consular power for 403.

11. On any account this absence is arresting, for even if one holds the trials before 390 to be no more than annalistic fabrications, the question arises why the annalists should have ceased inventing similar prosecutions in the fourth century.

first authentic determination by the senate on record that religious errors had been responsible for a defeat.[12] It is perhaps also credible that the fathers became acutely aware in its aftermath that the battle had been lost when their soldiers, unable to withstand the Gallic onslaught, broke ranks and fled.[13] Poor generalship, in other words, did not account for this loss.[14] The trauma appears to have brought about a consensus at Rome for the first time that the gods and the legionaries were principally to blame for a military defeat.

Some in the senate may have regarded such explanations as a convenient means of defeating what had previously been an effective line of attack for their opponents among the tribunes of the plebs. Others, however, will have embraced them on broader grounds, both because they seemed valid and hence struck the *patres* as far more satisfying intellectually and because they tended to support the political status quo in the ways already outlined. In the ideology of a ruling class the two often go hand in hand.[15] As plebeians made their way into the senate and eventually reached the highest circles of the political elite, they also came to accept them for most of the same reasons. Thereafter these explanations were applied regularly until they became conventional. Once generals came to be seen as not responsible for causing defeats, primary stress could be placed on their exemplary role in a crisis: to display *virtus* to inspire the troops and thereby to acquire *gloria*.

The obvious place to look for the beginning of a change might seem to be the cluster of trials that took place in the latter half of the second century: Plautius in 146, Pompeius in 139, Mancinus in 136, and Porcina in the same year; Cato in 114, possibly Carbo the year after, and Postumius Albinus in 110; Popillius Laenas in 107 and Silanus in 104; Caepio, Lucullus, and perhaps Mallius in 103

---

12. See above, chap. 2 pp. 67–68, 73–74.
13. Cf. Livy 5.38.5–7; Diod. 14.114.4–5; Dion. Hal. 13.12; Plut. *Cam.* 18.4–7. This awareness may also be reflected in tactical changes introduced after the Gallic defeat—the development of the manipular formation and an order of battle based on age and experience rather than census rating (Homo, *CAH* 7:568; Salmon, *Samnium*, 105–7). However, the date at which these innovations were made remains unclear: Adcock, *CAH* 7:596, 601, places them significantly later, at the time of the Samnite wars.
14. To be sure, however, criticisms of the commanders are not lacking in the sources: see Livy 5.37.3, 38.1.
15. Cf. Linderski, *PP* 37 (1982): 18–19 n. 14.

and Servilius in 102.[16] Yet as argued in the preceding chapter, these men did not face prosecution simply for losing battles but principally because they had failed to manifest the conduct expected of them under the aristocratic ethos. Their trials, far from indicating that a fundamental change was taking place in this area, instead demonstrate that the consensus on the central importance of *virtus* and an unbowed attitude in defeat still obtained. Certainly there is no evidence of an ideological split on this point. Critics of the aristocracy never denied that moral excellence ought to define the leaders of the Republic. Rather, the reverse is true: frequent charges of senatorial hypocrisy and corruption suggest that the point of the *populares'* critique was not that the customary sources of legitimacy were no longer valid but that their opponents in the governing elite no longer possessed them.[17] It appears that as the second century drew to a close, *victi* were becoming less willing or able to conform to the patterns of behavior required to protect them from the wrath of the public, just as the populace under the tutelage of the *populares* was becoming more insistent on traditional standards of conduct in their leaders. Efforts to punish moral failure among unsuccessful Roman generals thus comprised one element within a much broader attack on the senate's title to rule, whereas the sudden propensity of *victi* to have such lapses itself arose out of the increasing military difficulties the Republic faced at the time and perhaps also reflected a growing unwillingness among the aristocracy always to act strictly according to its ancestral ethos.

In the same way the old belief in the *pax deorum* as the fundamental cause of victory and defeat remained intact throughout this period. Neither the senate nor the public at large appears to have abandoned its faith in the gods or in the cult that secured their support.[18] Mancinus in 136 was able to convince the *patres* that their error in renewing the war in Spain without first having neutralized

---

16. Brunt, *Fall of the Roman Republic*, 78. For sources on these trials, see appendix 1.1, nos. 67, 69, 41, 3, 71, 65, 74, 44, 81, 51, 46, 80; on Popillius Laenas, see above, chap. 4, n. 88.
17. A proper exploration of this theme would take us too far afield in this context, but note C. Gracchus' charges against his peers: ORF⁴ 44 (= Gell. NA 11.10.2–6). Of course, Sallust made much of it in his treatment of the Jugurthine War.
18. See in general Rawson, *JRS* 63 (1973): 161–74; idem, *Phoenix* 28 (1974): 193–212.

the religious constraints imposed on them by Pompeius' agreement had in large part been responsible for his failures there. The prosecution of Scaurus in 104 demonstrates that precision in the sacrifices was still considered a prerequisite of military success. To be sure, Domitius, his accuser, was challenging the usual tendency to understand these mistakes as occurring in ways that were undetectable and hence inescapable. That framework played a crucial role in suppressing recrimination in the wake of defeat, and a successful attack on it would have breached one of the fundamental limits on the political impact of defeat. Yet Scaurus was acquitted, albeit narrowly. More important, similar accusations of religious malfeasance did not subsequently become a regular means of pursuing rivalries following military failures. The trial was unique in this regard. It is also likely that the Romans continued to locate the principal human causes of defeat among the legionaries rather than in the men who led them. Once again Mancinus at the beginning of this period laid heavy stress on the inferior quality of the men he had commanded when explaining his defeat to the fathers. And once again, at its conclusion, the military reforms undertaken in the wake of the Arausio disaster suggest that the state of the army was held principally to blame for a defeat.[19]

It might appear that harbingers of a change in these basic attitudes arrive in the aftermath of the social war. In 68 Cicero set out an analysis of the religious causes of victory that seems fundamentally at odds with the principles of the *pax deorum*. In his speech urging the voters to award a special command against Mithridates to Pompey, Cicero sought to portray him as someone specially favored by the gods, possessed of a *fortuna* that set him apart from the common run of men but linked him to all the great commanders of bygone days.[20] Other conquerors too were beginning to portray themselves as enjoying some special connection to the heavenly powers from which their successes derived.[21] The implications of such a shift in the religious ideology of victory might have had

19. On the reforms, see Last, *CAH* 9:146–47; Carney, *Marius*, 32–33.
20. Cic. *Leg. Man.* 47–48.
21. On *fortuna/felicitas* in the military ideology of the middle and late Republic, see Combès, *Imperator*, 208–22; Weinstock, *Divus Julius*, 112–15; Keaveney, *Sulla* 40, cf. idem, *Studies in Latin Literature*, 3.46–50. On the complex problem of the origins and development of the two concepts and their relation to one another, see Erkell, *Augustus, Felicitas, Fortuna*; Zieske, *Felicitas*; Wistrand, *Felicitas Imperatoria*.

a profound effect on the ability of the system to shield *victi* in defeat; for the corollary to victory as the special product of a general's unique relationship to the gods is a vision of defeat as deriving from the same source—their hatred of a particular person or some innate bad luck.

Yet change in the thought-world of a culture rarely occurs as a short, decisive break with the past; continuities are strong, and apparently contradictory modes of thought often seem to coexist easily for considerable periods of time. This case is no exception, for although a stress on personal *fortuna* or *felicitas* was becoming increasingly prominent in the political propaganda of some figures, it did not lead to a complete cessation of earlier beliefs in which the state of the *pax deorum* played the central role in victory or defeat. There were still prominent men at Rome who could envision Crassus' great disaster at Carrhae as the result of disobedience of the auspices, and Cicero himself was quick to point out the political dangers that failure would entail for a commander who acted in defiance of a Sibylline oracle. Generally speaking, the whole elaborate machinery of public cult continued to function throughout the late Republic and commanded respect. If some ambitious public figures sought to manipulate its elements for partisan ends, they did so mainly because they understood that traditional religious beliefs enjoyed strong support among the public at large as well as most of their peers and so had the power to become important factors in political conflict.

Thus what might appear to have been incompatible ideas about the religious basis for victory or defeat seem to have existed side by side in the late Republic. Perhaps if the Republic had endured for several more generations, a belief that defeat was the result of a general's personal *infelicitas* or bad luck would have gradually supplanted the view of it as the product of errors in ritual or in responding to signs from the gods. But not necessarily: ideas about the gods' role in war were becoming increasingly complex, and this is not the only scenario imaginable. A clever politician might have found it possible to play newer, private ideas about *fortuna* or *felicitas* off against the older, more traditional public consensus on the importance of the *pax deorum*. For instance, although Pompey's unique link with the gods may have justified entrusting him with a special command against Mithridates, it is not difficult to believe that if he had failed miserably in that task, his friends would have begun to hunt for a *prodigium* that had gone unexpiated or some previously unsuspected flaw in the rituals at Rome. The end result of any clash between these two very different perspectives on victory and defeat, in other words, might have been a new synthesis rather than the replacement of one set of ideas with another. As previously noted, the aristocracy had powerful reasons to cling to its belief that the *pax deorum* was central to success in war. As long as this class continued to hold power at Rome, there is every likelihood that its members would have continued to believe what helped to sustain their collective ascendancy, and such beliefs, in turn, would have continued to protect *victi* from the political backlash of their defeats.

One might also imagine that a growing sense of a corporate identity and an increasing awareness of their own interests would have led the soldiers to refuse to shoulder much of the blame for defeats any longer and that this refusal could have threatened *victi*. Yet most legionaries in the period remained conscripts drawn from the impoverished rural classes, whose principal interest upon discharge was limited to land.[22] The creation of a professional class of soldiers was primarily an achievement of the Principate. Yet even allowing for an enhanced sense of their common advantage among the men in the ranks, such an awareness is unlikely to have had much of an effect on the ability of the system to protect the political futures of defeated generals. As the Republic's armies came to be drawn more and more from the poor and the landless, the soldiers themselves became increasingly less likely to vote in the equestrian or first-class centuries, where the struggles for office were usually decided. Much the same point is relevant to evidence for a progressive estrangement between a considerable segment of the populace and the senate in the late Republic. A growing impoverishment accompanied this trend, and criticism of senatorial rule generally found its best reception among the poor and the landless. Thus the tendency of alienation from the senatorial outlook to take place in conjunction with economic deterioration robbed the phenomenon of any ability to influence the outcomes of con-

---

22. On the origins and aspirations of the soldiers in this period, see Brunt, *Fall of the Roman Republic*, 240–80.

sular or censorial elections. Those segments of the populace most likely no longer to see matters in the same light as the senatorial class were the same ones losing power within the *comitia centuriata*.

Rather, the fundamental change in the nature of the limits protecting *victi*, like so many other profound changes in the rules of the political game, was ushered in by the death of the Republic and the opening of the Principate. Once *honores* were disposed of at the whim of a single man rather than by the votes of the people and the endorsements of their leaders, imperial ideology and the interests of the emperor replaced civic ideology and the advantage of the aristocratic class as the decisive factors governing how struggles to obtain them were to be waged. Limits on aristocratic competition did not disappear with Augustus, but they now became the products of a set of needs and constraints in many respects far different from those that had obtained before.

———|———

Thus the ability of the limits that shielded *imperatores victi* to endure ultimately lay in the contributions they made to the larger interests of the Republic and the aristocracy that ruled it as well as to the stability of the competitive system that nourished them both. The short-term advantages are obvious immediately. Perhaps the Romans' most noteworthy trait as warriors was sheer determination and persistence against their enemies, particularly in the face of adversity. The resolve of the senate to continue the struggle against Hannibal after Cannae is only the most celebrated example. More than half a century earlier, and after two crushing defeats at Pyrrhus' hands, the fathers spurned all offers of peace.[23] Likewise throughout the middle of the second century they steadfastly insisted that nothing short of a complete victory would constitute an acceptable end to the war in Spain despite repeated demonstrations of their armies' inability to win one.[24] Yet precisely at such moments Roman determination might be most susceptible to irresolution and doubt. According to legend, the *patres* wavered and

---

23. Sources are found most conveniently in *MRR* 1:192–93; full discussion is in Lefkowitz, *HSCP* 64 (1959): 147–77; Garoufalias, *Pyrrhus*, 79–83, 85–88, 193–98.
24. Astin, *Scipio Aemilianus*, 137–60; Richardson, *Hispaniae*, 140–48.

inclined toward accommodation with Pyrrhus in 279 until Ap. Claudius Caecus steeled their resolve to continue the fight.[25] In the 140s and 130s a succession of commanders in Spain hoped to get their senatorial colleagues to accept a good deal less than absolute victory there.

In a crisis, suppressing wrangling over who was responsible and whether punishment was called for kept domestic strife from exacerbating the situation and helped unite the Republic and its political elite to meet such challenges when they arose. Partisan contests did not cloud the issue or create tensions; all could concur and coalesce to do what had to be done. Restoring the *pax deorum* and improving the quality of the legions drew the upper class together in this common effort because of the collective nature of these tasks. The political conflicts that occasionally did break out over the issue of punishment actually served to encourage this consensus, for generally they occurred only when a *victus* had in some way broken ranks with his peers. The disasters of Pompeius, Mancinus, Postumius, and others became causes célèbres because these generals appeared to have given up in the aftermath of their defeats, either by outright surrender or through some other act that seemed to accept the irreversibility of the enemy's success. Punishing, or threatening to punish, those who had dared to dissent galvanized both the leadership and the commons in a renewed commitment to press on with the struggle. The ensuing political battles over their fates thus worked to purge all traces of doubt about the prospect of ultimate victory.

The limits conferred an operational advantage as well. The knowledge that the domestic consequences of failure were not likely to endanger themselves, their families, or their careers gave generals the confidence to prosecute their wars as they saw fit without worrying about public opinion back home. The contrast with Athens under the democracy is illuminating. At Syracuse Nicias proclaimed his reluctance to cut his losses and withdraw from the city, despite the difficulties of his army's situation, because he feared being brought to trial for the failure of the siege. The frequency with which military setbacks led to condemnation at Athens must have meant that decisions in the field were constantly

25. Cic. *Sen.* 16; *Brut.* 55; Livy *Per.* 13; Plut. *Pyrrh.* 19.1; App. *Sam.* frg. 10.2.

overshadowed by concern over the likely political consequences if these turned out to be wrong.[26] Roman generals did not operate under the same constraints. In 217 Q. Fabius Maximus could refuse to concern himself with how his highly unpopular and seemingly fruitless strategy of delay and attrition against Hannibal was being received back at Rome. Certainly his handling of the war led to political turmoil, but none of this affected Fabius vitally.[27] Fears of private disaster following on the heels of public misfortune never made *imperatores* hesitate to take risks or reluctant to conduct their campaigns as they believed the military situation required.

The practice was also useful to the broader interests of the whole aristocracy. Placing the onus of blame on one member of an oligarchy as narrow, inbred, and jealous of personal and family *dignitas* as Rome's was certain to be divisive in the highest degree. The humiliation touched many and might ignite bitter feuding, yet cohesiveness was vital to collective dominance. More serious still, defeat afforded a way for one or a few ambitious politicians to use popular anger in its wake to undermine the collective authority of the senate. Championing the right of the *populus* to pass judgment on a losing general emphasized its claim to primacy in the conduct of the *res publica* and, concomitantly, gained power for those who proclaimed themselves the people's spokesmen and guides. That development would have struck at one of the cornerstones of aristocratic rule. Once again it may be instructive to compare the case at Athens, where the fact that generals regularly came before the citizens, either sitting as juries or as boards of examiners to scrutinize the accounts of public officials, highlighted the supremacy of the demos in the management of the affairs of the polis.

The greatest benefits accrued in the long run, however, and affected the system of competition itself. Aristotle observes in the *Politics* that one of the ills to which aristocracies and oligarchies in

---

26. Thuc. 7.48.2–5. Nicias of course had other reasons for wishing to remain in place and prolong the siege, and his wishes encountered strong opposition from his colleagues. However, the important point is his ability to use fear of prosecution as a pretext to justify an operational decision. Thucydides offers no indication that the other generals questioned the likelihood that a plan of action that entailed confessing their failure in the siege could bring about the most serious political consequences (cf. 7.49.2). Note also the hesitancy of Chabrias to press home his advantage after his victory at Naxos in 376 (Diod. 15.35.1).

27. Poly. 3.103; Livy 22.25–26.

Greece often fell prey was the concentration of privilege and power in the hands of a smaller group within their ranks—the formation of an oligarchy within an oligarchy, as it were. When this happened, the jealousy of those excluded and their anger at being denied the offices and honors they considered their due fractured the upper class, and stasis was the result.[28] This model is of interest in understanding some phases of the history of the Republic—one thinks immediately of the Catilinarian conspiracy, for instance—but in the present context it is helpful because it makes obvious the fact that the Roman aristocracy for the most part avoided the threat to its cohesiveness that this danger entailed. Far from shrinking, the circle of privilege steadily—albeit slowly—expanded as new men and members of families not previously among the front ranks of the aristocracy competed for and won the city's highest offices, thereby entering the highest echelons of the senate.[29]

To bring about this gradual expansion, however, the system had to ensure a fairly wide distribution of those offices within the political class—both among those who might claim them as their ancestral prerogative as well as among men of more recent origins whose achievements and abilities had made them forces to be reckoned with. This is not to say that such positions were awarded indiscriminately or that descent was ever irrelevant, only that some means had to be in place to prevent a few individuals from monopolizing them to the exclusion of other members of the upper class who might feel entitled to share in the *honores*.[30] Making sure that a large enough number of different persons enjoyed the fruits of political success gave everyone within the aristocracy a reason to support the system and allowed each to believe that eventually he would in some way benefit—if not directly, then by securing the advantage of a kinsman or political ally. It also helped encourage cooperation and coalition building: knowing that a candidate would hold an office only once or perhaps twice in his career made it easy for other ambitious men to support his aspirations now in

28. Arist. *Pol.* 1306b22ff., cf. 1305b1ff.
29. The point is well illustrated by Hopkins and Burton, *Death and Renewal*, 55–69.
30. Cf. the remarks of Develin, *Patterns in Office-Holding*, 36, who detects an "understanding" among the patrician *gentes* during the fourth through the early second centuries as to how often each of them would place one of its members in the consulate.

return for his help in contests to come, confident that they were unlikely to be strengthening a potential rival in that struggle. Moreover, since the opportunities to gain the wealth and glory that military success furnished Republican aristocrats were generally linked to public office, getting one's share of the spoils depended on securing one's own or one's friends' political success. The profits of empire were one more foundation of the aristocratic consensus; hence the more people who could win a praetorship or consulate, the wider the group such riches united.[31]

However, the number of offices at stake in the contests was severely limited. If the rules of the game had ensured the continual success of the same few men and thus diminished or denied to the rest what they might consider their fair share, the result would have set the stage for conflict of a kind the system could not tolerate. Those who saw themselves as the losers under such an arrangement would thereby have lost any incentive to continue to compete within the customary guidelines, and that spelled trouble, for "no oligarchy could survive if its members refused to abide by the rules."[32] Furthermore, placing the highest offices of the Republic in the hands of many different men also helped sustain the institutional power of the senate. Were a few highly capable and successful leaders to monopolize the consulship, they would have had exclusive access to the wealth, the glory, and hence the political capital to be derived from military leadership and victory. The censorship and the vast influence to shape the very composition of the body politic it conferred would also have remained the prerogative solely of these same men. Down that road lay domination and a dangerous challenge to the collective authority of the senate.[33]

Therefore, various measures were in place to guarantee the necessary diversity among those who held *imperium*. Of these, the greatest significance attaches to restrictions on the repetition of office. According to Livy, the first step in this direction occurred in 342 when a *lex Genucia* forbade holding the same magistracy twice within ten years.[34] Scholars have long recognized the problems that

---

31. Cf. North, *JRS* 71 (1981): 6.
32. Syme, *Roman Revolution*, 57–58.
33. Cf. Brunt, *Fall of the Roman Republic*, 43.
34. Livy 7.42.2; 10.13.8; Zonar. 7.25.

the evidence of the consular *fasti* raises for Livy's account. They contain a host of exceptions to this purported rule, and, not surprisingly, various solutions to the problem have been proposed.[35] For the present purposes, however, the crucial fact is that some change in the patterns of tenure of the consulate took place around 290. Prior to that date multiple consulships were common; afterward persons were restricted to two turns at intervals ranging from one to twenty-three years until the crisis of 216, when multiple consulates appeared once again.[36] These ended after 208, and beginning with 200 a ten-year interval between consulates became the rule until 152, when M. Claudius Marcellus held his third only three years after his second. Shortly thereafter specific legislation debarred iteration altogether.[37] In unusual circumstances exceptions were made, but by and large the rule endured down to 81, when Sulla restored the status quo ante 151. In practical terms, from 366 (when consuls began to hold office regularly for the first time in the fourth century) through 291 B.C. between fifty-eight and sixty-one of the 144 consulates were iterations filled by men being reelected to that office, about 40–42 percent of the total.[38] From 290 through 217 that figure dropped by a factor of nearly one half, to 22–23 percent, and plunged to a mere 5 percent after 201 until 104, when Marius' succession of consulates disrupted the normal pattern.[39] Put somewhat differently, in the period from 366 through 291, men who held more than one consulate represented between 34 percent and 39.5 percent of all consuls who held offices in those years and accounted for between 61 percent and 64.5 percent of all consulates. From 290 through 217, iterators represent between 26.6 percent and 28.3 percent of all consuls and held between 41 percent and 42 percent of all consulates; from 200 through 105, 5 per-

---

35. For a survey, see Billows *Phoenix* 43 (1989): 112–33.

36. The sole exception is M'. Curius Dentatus, in 290, 275, and 274, if this is the same person in each case.

37. Livy *Per.* 56; Festus p. 282, 4, cf. *ORF*[4] p. 75; further sources and discussion of the ten-year rule are in Astin, *Latomus* 16 (1957): 602 n. 6, 606 n. 5 (= *Lex Annalis before Sulla* 19 n. 6, 23 n. 5); Calvert, *Ath.* 39 (1961): 19–23.

38. The variation is due to uncertainty over the identities of the consuls of 357, 354, and 328.

39. Between 290 and 217 B.C. thirty-four of 151 or thirty-five of 152 consulates were second consulates (omitting the supposed suffect consul of 265), the variation being due to uncertainty about whether a suffect consul was elected in 221; between 210 and 104 B.C. there were eleven iterations out of a total of 201 consulates.

cent accounted for 9.5 percent of all consulships.⁴⁰ In the first century B.C. second consulates accounted for an even more minuscule proportion of the total.⁴¹ Thus the tendency in the long run was both to attenuate the number of times that a single person could attain the consulate and to limit the overall number of men who gained reelection. The result was a steady increase in the total number of men able to hold that office.⁴² This seems to have been only the most common manifestation of a more general injunction against multiple tenure of the same magistracy. Repeating the praetorship appears to have been unusual under normal circumstances, and there is only one case of a second censorship.⁴³ In keeping with this trend, prorogation of a consul in his province during the second century was comparatively rare and generally did not extend beyond an additional year.⁴⁴

Yet what was necessary for the stability of the system of competition, for harmony and cooperation among the ruling class, and for the preservation of senatorial authority was fundamentally at odds with the Republic's practice of sending at least one army to war almost every year. Winning high office frequently brought with it the task of discharging the most serious military responsibilities—often at the praetorian level, and almost always for con-

---

40. In 366–291 B.C. between thirty and thirty-two consuls out of a total of between eighty-one and eighty-eight persons elected to that office held between eighty-eight and ninety-three of 144 consulates, counting their first and all subsequent consulates. In 290–217 B.C. between thirty-three and thirty-four consuls out of between 120 and 124 persons elected to that office held between sixty-two and sixty-four consulates (excluding five held previous to 290) out of a total number between 151 and 152; in 200–104 B.C. ten consuls out of 191 men elected held nineteen out of 201 consulates.

41. None between 99 and 89 B.C.; after 80 only three—Pompey and Crassus in 55 and Pompey again in 52.

42. Analysis of the reasons for these changes would carry the discussion far beyond the bounds of this study. See, e.g., Billows, *Phoenix* 43 (1989): 112–33.

43. *Praetores iterum* (aside from those during the early years of the Hannibalic War): C. Livius Salinator, 202 and 191; P. Manlius Vulso, 195 and 182; A. Atilius Serranus, 192 and 173; C. Cluvius Saxula, 178(?) and 173 (see *MRR* 1:397 n. 4 for discussion); M. Furius Crassipes, 187 and 173; Cn. Sicinius, 183 and 172; C. Hostilius Mancinus, 140(?) and at some point after 136 (see appendix 1.1, no. 41); M. Marius Gratidianus, 85 and 84(?); P. Cornelius Lentulus Sura, 74 and 63; P. Varinius, 73 and 65. On Marius, see *MRR* 2:59 n.1, 3:140; on Varinius, see appendix 1.1, no. 91. Note that most hold their second praetorships after a lapse of at least ten years. Why a cluster of these occurred in 173 and 172 is unclear. C. Marcius Rutilius was censor in 294 and 265. Thereafter second censorships were outlawed (Plut. *Cor.* 1.1, cf. Val. Max. 4.1.3; *De Vir. Ill.* 32.2).

44. Brunt, *Fall of the Roman Republic*, 44.

suls. War is a dangerous and uncertain enterprise in which experienced leadership is always an asset; yet the need to ensure that many different men held the chief magistracies led the Republic normally to deny itself this advantage. Once victory might seem to have proven a consul's aptitude for command, his opportunities to hold similar posts thereafter were highly restricted. Instead, the needs of the system dictated that competition for such positions be limited to men possibly without prior experience in command of an army or those whose earlier showings there had been mediocre at best. To be sure, praetors who had triumphed seem to have enjoyed a significant advantage over their competitors in rivalry for the consulate, and certainly on occasion the citizens turned to a leader of proven competence in a crisis.[45] But these instances only make it all the more surprising that the superior claims of consular *triumphatores* to further commands could be denied in the normal course of competition for office: as the Romans' conquests became more extensive and the stakes in their wars progressively greater, they became increasingly reluctant to return seasoned commanders to office to conduct these operations.

Naturally this state of affairs could lead to tensions. It is not easy for soldiers to march off to war lacking confidence in their leader, and any custom forbidding the repetition of consulates and praetorships would have become difficult to sustain if the public had come to perceive it as an impediment to military success. Hence it was imperative to have some means of instilling confidence when untried or unimpressive generals gained command in order to reconcile the demands of war with those of aristocratic competition and the political status quo. Several can be identified. Older, more experienced men might be sent along as *legati* to advise; an oath could be required of the soldiers that they would stand firm in the battle line. It is for this reason that many of the religious ceremonies associated with war-making cluster around a new consul's assumption of office and departure from the city—moments of maximum tension when a new and generally unproven leader was about to venture out on his own. In all these ways the Romans sought to accommodate the presence of uncertainty and risk in

---

45. See Harris, *War and Imperialism*, 31–33, on praetorian triumphs and the consulate.

combat and minimize their impact on the outcome, which undoubtedly had a bearing on how they viewed the wisdom of sending relatively green commanders abroad each year. Of inestimable importance too was the Republic's long record of victorious warfare, for it demonstrated that such measures, and indeed the system itself, had worked successfully in the past. But when it did not, and things on the battlefield went tragically wrong, it was also essential to prevent a general's role in causing the defeat from becoming an issue in subsequent rivalry.

Blaming a leader's inexperience or incompetence was in effect an argument for awarding such offices to those who had already demonstrated that they had what it took to win, and the implications threatened to allow the demands of Roman war-making to undermine the internal arrangements of the competitive system. Once criticism of a general's decisions became an issue in partisan strife, sooner or later the public was going to get the idea that some candidates were less qualified for the job than others and that placing the conduct of important military affairs in their hands could lead to very unhappy results. If all contenders were not equal in this regard, then the voters might well come to see it as vital to weigh demonstrated ability heavily when making their choice, particularly those who would go on to serve as soldiers under the winning candidate. No one could really gauge accurately ahead of time the ability of someone who had never before led an army to discharge the actual duties of command. Why take chances with an unknown? If no candidate had evinced any real aptitude for the job, then simple prudence dictated giving it to someone who had. In the long run this kind of thinking ultimately would have subverted the limit on iteration of office as voters repeatedly sought to award commands to men who had already manifested their competence in order to avoid defeat and enhance prospects of victory. Public reluctance to gamble on untested leaders in turn would have caused the distribution of honor and authority and political power within the upper class to become increasingly skewed.

The needs of the system thus demanded a myth of universal aristocratic competence: to award military commands to those whose principal qualifications might lie in such seemingly irrelevant assets as high birth, rhetorical talent, or knowledge of the law, it was imperative that the voters perceive all candidates as more or less equally able to undertake whatever tasks the office they were seeking entailed. This perception in turn required that in such contests the fact of having presided over a military defeat be denied any relevance to questions of fitness or capability. If what lost the Republic's battles was not an inept general but rather the poor state of its accord with the gods and a want of courage and discipline among its fighting men, then both senators and voters alike might elevate untried or untalented candidates or even *victi* once again to important military posts and yet still believe that in doing so they were not exposing Rome to serious risk. What held in rivalry for election to positions of command had to apply to nonmilitary offices like the censorship as well, for it is inconceivable that if contenders could gain an advantage against an opponent by making an issue of prior defeat here, the practice could be kept from spilling over into other contests where concern about a candidate's war record was far more appropriate. Although it is true that emergencies like the early stages of the Hannibalic war sometimes led to the demand for men of proven ability in command, what compels our attention is how such episodes could remain isolated events and never develop into a customary pattern among a people almost continuously at war. That was peculiarly Roman.

One feature of the *pax deorum* that deserves particular stress in this regard is its utter indifference to the matter of who was in command of an army. The gods really did not care. As long as the city fulfilled its obligations to the letter, they would continue to uphold their part of the agreement between them and Rome and lend their aid in battle. Failure did not occur because the gods were hostile to a particular leader or because he was just plain unlucky.[46] Preventing allegations to the contrary from gaining currency was essential because they carried the unavoidable implication that success demonstrated just the reverse—that the gods bestowed victory on those whom they especially favored. The prevalence of such a belief among the voters afforded strong grounds for arguing that these fortunate few had a stronger claim to office than others.[47]

---

46. Cicero did assert that the gods avenged the crimes of Piso on his soldiers in the form of an illness (*Pis.* 85), and Q. Servilius Caepio is said to have defended himself before the tribunes regarding the loss of his army on the grounds of *fortuna* (*Rhet. Her.* 1.24, cf. Cic. *Brut.* 135). But such notices are unusual.

47. Cicero, in fact, so argues for Pompey (*Leg. Man.* 46–47).

It was folly, therefore, to gamble on a man for whom the gods had not yet demonstrated any great regard when prior success indicated clearly whom they loved. Insisting that defeat was due to some error or omission in the city's religious duties helped avoid imputing to victory any significance other than that the flawless execution of the rituals and scrupulous attention to signs and the auspices had once again secured the continued participation of Rome's heavenly allies in the *pax deorum* and thereby produced the usual felicitous results. Certainty on that score, in turn, contributed much toward instilling confidence that as long as the requirements of cult were correctly discharged, any candidate might be elevated to command an army and enjoy the gods' support when he marched off to war.

On the mortal plane a conventional view that the soldiers' courage and discipline were the crucial factors in a battle also worked to give voters faith in untested leaders in ways that went beyond simply implying that a general's lack of talent or prior experience had little to do with causing defeat. Far more important was the subtle effect of a clear parallel between, on the one hand, the insistence of the aristocratic ethos that a *victus* display great personal courage in a crisis and an unbowed attitude in defeat and, on the other, the demand for similar qualities among the men he led—bravery in the line of battle and a determination not to flee when the tide began to run against them. Rome never developed anything like a formal military academy nor any other structure to identify promising young men and impart to them the technical skills required to fit them for the duties entailed by the offices they would eventually assume. To be sure, young aristocrats spent a decade or more at war before they ever sought election to positions that involved command of an army, but few of those years need have been spent actually leading troops into battle. Leadership in war, like much else, remained an amateur affair, for the principles of meritocracy are fundamentally opposed to those of an aristocracy in which birth, wealth, and honor formed the primary requisites for political success and an attendant military command.[48] What young aristocrats could and did do, however, was pursue *virtus* and *gloria*, particularly by striving to win a reputation for

---

48. Campbell, *JRS* 77 (1987): 20–22; Gruen, *Hellenistic World*, 203–49, esp. 247–49; *contra*, however, see Harris, *War and Imperialism*, 10–15.

courage, something positively vital for anyone intending to embark on a political career.[49] Hence the one thing voters could know about a candidate was his moral character. Being satisfied that a man measured up on this score thus bolstered confidence that even if he had little practical experience in command, he could still be entrusted with full responsibility for leading an army to war, for the one was directly relevant to the other: in a crisis his principal duty was to serve as a model of the bravery and steadfastness required in his men, on whom victory or defeat in turn depended. *Victi* who won praise for their stance in a crisis thus helped confirm the central importance of *virtus*, rather than any specific technical proficiency, in fitting someone for public office and enabling him to benefit the Republic.[50]

This confirmation was particularly critical for the noble *gentes*, the inner core of the senatorial class, comprising a handful of families in which generation after generation of offspring succeeded to the consulate. Their preeminence was always precarious: elevating sons to the highest magistracies of the state was necessary to maintain such exalted status, but no one could predict with what talents or aptitude these sons would be born. The very fact that offices circulated widely within the elite, coupled with their limited number and the fierce struggle to secure them, meant that families that had already made it into the highest stratum of honor could never take it for granted that they would continue to garner the electoral victories needed to stay there. However, one distinct advantage a noble *gens* enjoyed over most competitors was a tradition of *virtus* among its members and the reputation for moral superiority that came with it. The *imagines* of a clan's ancestors advertised that fact at the funerals of its members and at the same time placed its younger members under great pressure to measure up to the achievements of their forebears.[51] Focusing principally on a *victus'*

---

49. Poly. 31.29.1.
50. Earl, *Sallust*, 18–27; idem, *Moral and Political Tradition*, 20–36; Mitchell, *Hermathena* 136 (1984): 23.
51. See Poly. 6.52.11–54.4 on death masks as an advertisement of a family's *virtus* and the achievements of its ancestors. On the pressures placed on a young noble, see Sal. *Iug*. 4.5: *saepe ego audivi Q. Maximum, P. Scipionem, praeterea civitatis nostrae praeclaros viros solitos ita dicere, cum maiorum imagines intuerentur, vehementissime sibi animum ad virtutem accendi.* Cf. Poly. 31.23.8–12 for one well-known example; see further Earl, *Moral and Political Tradition*, 25–27; MacMullen, *Past and Present* 88 (1980): 3–16.

personal deportment in defeat could do much to help underwrite the entitlement of the nobility to the highest offices of the Republic. If courage and a tenacious adherence to the dictates of a code of honor were what mattered most in a general, then the voters could not go wrong in selecting the offspring of families noted for those very qualities in generations past.[52]

Furthermore, personal bravery represented a standard to which such men were particularly well equipped to measure up. Most of those steeped in such traditions should have been capable of remaining in sufficient control of themselves to do what honor demanded as the fight began to go against them, even if it meant dying. Meeting that expectation put it within their power to protect the one thing that really mattered to their own, and their families', standing within the political community: public perception of their moral character. The *gloria* of a splendid death could benefit sons and posterity and help ensure a family's political survival within a highly competitive elite. The result, in turn, worked to obviate some of the disruptive potential of defeat within the confines of the hereditary core of the aristocracy. Continuity was the central goal: families strove to preserve status across time. Yet the link between political advancement and military leadership implied the risk that the fortunes of war might destroy at one blow an eminence carefully nurtured over the course of several generations. When a *victus* could manifest his *virtus* even in defeat, failure in war per se no longer had to threaten political status. Thus a noble *gens* would not see one of its leading members' prospects for further office or those of its scions suddenly cut short as a result of a single defeat, or even many defeats. Given the effort and expenditure of resources that bringing a son to the praetorship or consulate required of any family, the impact of having it all suddenly vanish could be devastating. Such concerns were perhaps even more pressing for the lesser *gentes* and the families of new men. Their stature within the aristocracy was more tenuous, their resources more limited, and hence their ability to sustain a political disaster that much less. A moral standard of judgment that allowed *victi* to succeed despite their lost battles therefore amounted to a kind of insurance policy for all concerned, designed to safeguard

---

52. Cf. Campbell, *JRS* 78 (1988): 23.

a political investment against the possibility of catastrophic loss. In effect it preserved the existing hierarchy of status within the political class against the shocks of war.

That preservation had broader implications as well. The outcome of war is fundamentally irrational, and linking a general's failure on the battlefield to a deterioration of his political standing back home would have introduced that same irrationality into the competitive arena. Forces outside the aristocracy itself and hence beyond its collective ability to control would have come to shape the outcome of the rivalry within its ranks—a troubling prospect. Part of the power the aristocracy could exercise over its members derived from the fact that as a body it largely determined their access to high office. It was difficult for anyone to go it alone, to achieve political success by relying on popularity and the willingness of the people to act against the wishes of its upper class. To be sure, some did, but not many; for the independent power of the people was limited in many ways, and reverence for aristocratic authority was great.[53] Hence, generally speaking, a complex equation of *beneficia* and patronage, alliance and *inimicitia*, family background and personal achievement, coupled with many other factors, determined to a great extent who won positions of power and privilege. If military failure were to render all of this subtle calculus suddenly meaningless, then the aristocracy as a whole would suffer a diminution of its corporate authority over the competition taking place within its ranks.[54] Protecting defeated generals thus helped sustain the political autonomy of the elite and un-

---

53. The case for the power of the public at Rome during the Republic has been forcefully put by Millar, *JRS* 74 (1984): 1–19; idem, *JRS* 76 (1986): 1–11; and without a doubt the aristocracy took seriously the need to woo voters and curry favor with the public generally. But it nevertheless remains true that instances in which the voters defied the express wishes of the senate remain by far the exception rather than the rule. Regarding the limits on the theoretical sovereignty of the populace, see Brunt, *Fall of the Roman Republic*, 23–32, and especially the penetrating critique developed by North, op. cit. above, n. 1.

54. To be sure, military victory and a triumph might have a similar effect in dramatically changing someone's political prospects, but their impact was moderated in other ways. A triumph, for example, never achieved the status of an entitlement to office; other, purely political factors could and did come into play: note Q. Caecilius Metellus Macedonicus, whose splendid victory over Andriscus while praetor was followed by two defeats for the consulate, both at the hands of men with no apparent military laurels (Val. Max. 8.5.1; *De Vir. Ill.* 61.3, cf. Livy *Oxy. Per.* 52). Note too L. Mummius, who waited six years for a consulate after his triumph as praetor in 152.

derwrote all the usual factors controlling the course of political rivalry. Moreover, the relationships involved in this process bound the elite together, whether as allies, enemies, or simply interested participants. Cohesiveness was vital to perpetuating their joint rule, and the value of one's connections in aristocratic rivalry contributed much to enhancing this sense of unity. Allowing defeat to have an impact thus posed a danger on this score as well.

By helping to support the belief of the public in a universal aristocratic competence, keeping the issue of defeat out of subsequent competition for high office allowed that competition to take on a different character than would otherwise have been the case. Once the Romans considered all contestants more or less equally able to undertake whatever military tasks came within the purview of the offices they were seeking, attributes and characteristics marginally or even wholly unconnected with the actual job of running a war could become prominent in deciding the outcomes. Candidates could seek to distinguish themselves from their rivals on the basis of such things as birth, wealth, personal character, or accomplishments in the fields of religion, oratory, or law, as well as garner votes on the basis of more pragmatic assets such as *gratia* and *beneficia*. Together these resources made up a political currency far more complex than plain military ability and far more appropriate to the needs of a diverse elite in which membership was in large part a function of descent but to a significant degree also the product of personal achievement. The result was vigorous rivalry and diversity among members of the upper class. The fact that a variety of paths could lead to political success helped keep an aristocracy that spent much of its time at war from becoming nothing more than a narrow warrior elite.

Appendix 1

1.1: THE *IMPERATORES VICTI*

The following is an alphabetical list of all Roman magistrates, promagistrates, and legates who suffered defeats against foreign enemies, survived, and returned to Rome between 390 and 49 B.C. without having achieved a subsequent victory. All dates and offices are as given in Broughton, *Magistrates of the Roman Republic*, unless otherwise indicated. Several doubtful cases, indicated by a question mark, have been included in this reckoning to avoid undercounting. Those marked with an asterisk are considered to have suffered a serious defeat. Any differentiation in the relative severity of defeats must remain to some extent arbitrary since no ancient source gives any objective criteria by which the Romans themselves evaluated such losses. Nevertheless, some rough guidelines can be put forward by which to separate major defeats from minor reverses: defeats in which the loss of life, particularly Roman life, was heavy; cases where the army fled the field in confusion, lost its camp and baggage, or was compelled to surrender; reverses that led to a serious deterioration in the military situation for Rome; and losses after which Roman forces were incapable of offering further resistance to the enemy all will be considered major defeats. The rest will be considered minor, either because they fail to meet one of these criteria or because there is not enough information to make a determination.

Each listing is divided into three parts. In the first (a), the defeat itself is briefly described and all ancient sources for it are listed except in a few particularly well-known cases where the reader is referred to the appropriate entry in *MRR*. Any controversies over the events are noted, and reference is made to discussions in the scholarly literature whenever possible. The second part (b) includes a brief synopsis of the *victus'* subsequent career. Sources may be found in *MRR* under the appropriate year or years. Again, any problems are noted, and references to discussions elsewhere are given. The third part (c) lists, first, all known sons who held the consulate or praetorship and, next, other male siblings or descendants. In the case of consular or praetorian sons I have tried to adopt a fairly conservative approach so as to avoid overcounting and have restricted attributions to those persons who are identified as such elsewhere in the prosopographical literature or are obviously sons. My debt to Münzer will be clear throughout. Where doubt exists, it is noted. In the case of nonconsular and nonpraetorian sons and other relatives, links are often proposed that are somewhat more conjectural. I make no pretensions to completeness in my collection of persons who fall into this last category.

1. M'. Acilius M'. f. C. n. Glabrio, cos. suff. 154

a. Obseq. 17 mentions a defeat in Gaul in this year, although Livy *Per.* 47 omits it. Acilius' colleague was active against the Ligurians near Massilia, thus leaving Acilius the primary candidate for the defeated general in Gaul, although a praetor cannot be ruled out.

b. No further public office.

c. M'. Acilius Glabrio, tr. pl. or perhaps praetor between 121 and 111, is probably his son (Badian, *AJPh* 75 [1954]: 382–83; *MRR* 3:2).

2. P. Aelius Q. f. P. n. Paetus, cos. 201.*

a. Seven thousand men lost when his prefect C. Ampius failed to protect foragers adequately (Livy 31.2.5–11). Because a legate rather than the consul himself was in command, it might be thought that criticism of Aelius might be softened somewhat, but the example of Sp. Postumius Albinus, cos. 110 (below, no. 74), suggests otherwise: Spurius was condemned by the Mamilian *quaestio* for his legate's defeat.

b. Elected censor in 199 B.C.

c. His son was Q. Aelius P. f. Q. n. Paetus, consul in 167; Publius' brother Sextus Paetus Catus became curule aedile in 200, consul in 198, and censor in 194.

3. M. Aemilius M. f. M. n. Lepidus Porcina, procos. 136.*

a. Failed in an attempt to besiege Pallantia in Spain; heavy losses at the siege and during the retreat; recalled by the Senate

(App. *Iber.* 80–83; Livy *Per.* 56; Oros. 5.5.13–14). On the question of whether the recall constituted a formal abrogation, see Bauman, *RhM*, n.s., 111 (1968): 37–50 at 45–50.

b. Fined on his return (App. *Iber.* 83); subsequently brought before the censors of 125 and fined for renting a house for HS 6,000 (Vell. 2.10.1; cf. Val. Max. 8.1 damn. 7 and Gruen, *Roman Politics*, 40 n. 70). This financial ostentation indicates an effort to keep himself in the public eye and suggests continued political activity.

c. A son perhaps died young (Sumner, *Orators*, 64). Mam. Aemilius Lepidus Livianus, cos. 77, seems to have been a nephew (Münzer *Röm. Adelsparteien* 307, cf. Sumner, *Orators*, 164), although his filiation is not securely attested, and the possibility that he was Porcina's adoptive son cannot be ruled out.

4. C. Antonius M. f. M. n. (Hibrida), procos. 62–61.*

a. Defeated twice in Macedonia by the Dardani and Bastarni, losing his legionary standards to the latter (Dio 38.10.1–4, 51.26.5; Livy *Per.* 103; Obseq. 61a; cf. Caelius in Quint. *Inst.* 4.2.123–24 [=*ORF*⁴ 17]).

b. Prosecuted, condemned and exiled on his return. The precise charges brought against him are unclear: see Gruen, *Latomus* 32 (1973): 301–10, and above, chap. 4, pp. 144–45. Antonius later returned to Rome after the death of Caesar (Cic. *Phil.* 2.56; Strab. 10.2.13) and was subsequently made censor in 42.

c. No known sons; his nephews were M. Antonius the triumvir, cos. 44, 34, C. Antonius, q. 51, and L. Antonius, cos. 41.

5. Q. Arrius, propr.(?) 72.

a. Shared in the defeat of L. Gellius Poplicola, no. 39, by Spartacus (Livy *Per.* 96, cf. App. *BCiv.* 1.117).

b. Consular candidate in 59 (Cic. *Att.* 25 [2.5].2; 27 [2.7].3, cf. *MRR* 2:161, 3:25; Wiseman, *New Men*, 214).

c. No known descendants in office during the Republic.

6. C. Atilius M. f. M. n. Regulus, cos. 250.*

a. Failed with his colleague to take Lilybaeum (see below, no. 57); heavy losses in connection with the siege (Poly. 1.42.7–48.11; Diod. 24.1.1–4; Oros. 4.10.2; Zonar. 8.15).

b. No subsequent mention in the sources; Regulus had already been consul once before, in 257.

c. No known sons.

7. C. (or M. or L.) Aurelius Cotta, propr. 80.

  a. Lost a battle at sea off the coast of Spain against Sertorius (Plut. *Sert.* 12.3). On the identity of this man, see Spann, *CJ* 82 (1986–87): 306–9; Konrad, *CPh* 84 (1989): 119–29.

  b. C. Aurelius M. f. Cotta became consul in 75; M. Aurelius M. f. Cotta became consul in 74; L. Aurelius M. f. Cotta became consul in 65.

  c. If this man was M. Cotta, his son may have been praetor in 54 or 50 (Klebs *RE* 2 col. 2489, cf. Münzer *Röm. Adelsparteien* 327; *MRR* 2:222).

8. Cn. Baebius Q. f. Cn. n. Tamphilus, pr. 199.*

  a. Heavily defeated by the Insubrian Gauls; more than sixty-seven hundred men lost. The consul relieved him of command (Livy 32.7.5–7; Zonar. 9.15).

  b. III vir col. deduc. 186 (Livy 39.23.4); consular candidate for 184 and previously (Livy 39.32.8); elected consul for 182.

  c. Cn. Baebius Tamphilus, pr. 168, is probably his son; the career of M. Baebius Q. f. Cn. n. Tamphilus, brother of the praetor of 199, is also noteworthy in the wake of the latter's defeat: tr. pl. 194(?); III vir col. deduc. 194; pr. 191; cos. 181.

9. L. Bassus, legate 67.

  a. Defeated at sea by Ariston (Dio 36.19.1).

  b. Possibly Lucilius Bassus (Syme, *Historia* 13 [1964]: 161 [=Syme, *Roman Papers*, 2:610]; Wiseman, *New Men*, 280). Nothing further is known.

  c. No known descendants in office.

10. Q. Calpurnius C. f. C. n. Piso, cos. 135.

  a. Apparently defeated at Numantia (Obseq. 26; Simon, *Roms Kriege in Spanien*, 169; Astin, *Scipio Aemilianus*, 135, cf. App. *Iber.* 83).

  b. No further offices.

  c. No known sons in the consulate or praetorship; Q. Calpurnius, pr. c. 100 (*MRR* 1:577), may be a son; possibly C. Calpurnius Piso, cos. 67, is a grandson. For a general discussion of the descendants of nos. 10–13, see Syme, *JRS* 50 (1960): 12–20 (= Syme, *Roman Papers*, 2:496–509).

11. L. Calpurnius C. f. C. n. Piso Caesoninus, pr. 154.

  a. Defeated in Lusitania along with M'. Manilius, no. 52; heavy losses (App. *Iber.* 56).

b. Consul in 148 (below no. 12).

c. His son, L. Calpurnius L. f. C. n. Piso Caesoninus, was consul in 112; note also the praetor of 90 (*MRR* 3:47), probably a grandson, and the consul of 58, perhaps a great-grandson. Q. Calpurnius Piso (above, no. 10) is likely to be a brother.

12. L. Calpurnius C. f. C. n. Piso Caesoninus, cos. 148.

a. Suffered some minor reverses in fighting around Carthage (App. *Lib.* 110).

b. No further offices.

c. See above, no. 11.

13. L. Calpurnius L. f. C. n. Piso Frugi, pr. 136 (or 138).

a. Defeated by rebellious slaves in Sicily (Florus 2.7.7). On the date of his praetorship, see *MRR* 1:483 n. 1 (138) and Sumner, *Orators*, 59 (136).

b. Consul in 133 (Münzer, *RE* 3 col. 1392); Sumner, *Orators*, 59; censor in 120.

c. His son was praetor c. 113 (*RE* 3 col. 1395); Sumner, *Orators*, 72; *MRR* 3:48.

14. C. Cassius L. f. Longinus, procos. 72.*

a. Defeated with heavy losses by Spartacus (Livy *Per.* 96; Plut. *Crass.* 9.7; Florus 2.8.10; Oros. 5.24.4).

b. No further office.

c. Two sons: C. Cassius Longinus, pr. 44, and one of Caesar's murderers; Q. Cassius Longinus, q. c. 52, tr. pl. 49 (Sumner, *Orators* 50).

15. L. Cincius Alimentus, propr. 208.*

a. Ambushed by Hannibal while marching from Tarentum to Locri without adequate reconnaissance—two thousand soldiers were slain and fifteen hundred captured; the rest fled to Tarentum (Livy 27.26.3–6).

b. Possibly an envoy in 208.

c. No sons known to have reached high office.

16. Ap. Claudius Centho, legate 170.*

a. Failed to capture Phanote; significant losses in the retreat; lost control of the countryside to the enemy (Livy 43.21.4–5, 23.1–6, cf. 11.10).

b. Continued in command as a promagistrate, 169–168; served as an ambassador, 154.

c. No known sons in the consulate or praetorship. C. Claudius Centho, legate ambassador in 155, may be a brother or son.

17. C. Claudius Glaber, pr. 73.*

a. Put to flight with his army by Spartacus; his camp was captured (Plut. *Crass.* 9.3; Florus 2.7.4; Frontin. *Str.* 1.5.21; Oros. 5.24.1).

b. No further offices.

c. No known descendants.

18. M. Claudius M. f. M. n. Marcellus, procos. 209.*

a. Defeated by Hannibal; Marcellus' army fled the field (Livy 27.12.7–17; Plut. *Marc.* 25.4). Marcellus' second, and victorious, battle on the following day (Livy 27.25.5–26.4; Plut. *Marc.* 26.1–4) may be either invention (Münzer, *RE* 3 cols. 2752–53), or exaggeration (*MRR* 1:289 n. 5).

b. Marcellus' conduct was harshly criticized by C. Publicius Bibulus, tr. pl., and Marcellus was forced to come back to Rome and defend himself before an assembly. He refuted all charges made against him and was unanimously elected consul for the following year shortly thereafter (Livy 27.20.11–13, 21.1–5; Plut. *Marc.* 27.1–4).

c. His son, M. Claudius M. f. M. n. Marcellus, was consul in 196 (below, no. 19).

19. M. Claudius M. f. M. n. Marcellus, cos. 196.*

a. During his year in office suffered a serious defeat at the hands of the Boii and won a victory over the Ligurians. Livy's sources were discordant on which came first (Livy 33.36.4–15, cf. Val. Ant. frg. 34 P; Oros. 4.20.11). If the defeat followed the victory, then Marcellus belongs in this list. That he was subsequently awarded a triumph need not imply that the victory capped his campaign in view of D. Iunius Brutus, no. 42, L. Licinius Murena, no. 48, and cf. L. Postumius Megellus, no. 75.

b. Awarded a triumph on his return; elected censor in 189.

c. His son was M. Claudius M. f. M. n. Marcellus, cos. 166, 155, 152.

20. P. Claudius Ap. f. C. n. Pulcher, cos. 249.*

a. Suffered a major defeat at sea, allegedly after displaying contempt for the auspices (Poly. 1.51.1–52.3; Diod. 24.1.5; Cic. *Nat. D.* 2.7; *Div.* 1.29, 2.20, 2.71; Livy frg. 12 [= Serv. 6.198]; *Per.* 19, cf.

22.42.9; Val. Max. 1.4.3; Suet. *Tib.* 2.2; Florus 1.18.29; Eutrop. 2.26; *Schol. Bob.* 90 St).

b. Recalled and forced to name a dictator (Livy *Per.* 19; Suet. *Tib.* 2.2). Put on trial for *perduellio* on his return, but the proceedings were interrupted by a storm; tried a second time and fined heavily (Cic. *Nat. D.* 2.7; *Div.* 2.71; Val. Max. 8.1.4; *Schol. Bob.* 90 St; see also Bauman, *Crimen Maiestatis*, 27–29; Linderski, *ANRW* 2. 16.3 (1986):2176–77 nn. 110–11). He died soon thereafter (Livy *Per.* 19; Val. Max. 8.1. abs. 4; Suet. *Tib.* 2.3; Gell. *NA* 10.6.2); Münzer, *RE* 3 col. 2858, suggests he committed suicide.

c. His son, Ap. Claudius P. f. Ap. n. Pulcher, was consul in 212.

21. Claudius Unimanus, pr. 146 (or 145).*

a. Defeated with serious losses by Viriathus in Spain (Florus 1.33; *De Vir. Ill.* 71.1; Oros. 5.4.3–4). Date and rank uncertain: see discussion in Astin, *Scipio Aemilianus* 344, who opts for the arrangement of Mommsen, *History of Rome*, 3:223, followed here. U. Hackl, *Senat und Magistratur in Rom*, 83–84, would have it that the senate recalled Claudius before the expiration of his year in Spain, but this view depends on accepting a doubtful chronology that places Claudius' praetorship in 145 rather than 146 (Simon, *Roms Kriege in Spanien*, 77–80; Richardson, *Hispaniae*, 187–88).

b. Nothing further known about this man.

c. No known descendants.

22. L. Coelius, legate 170.*

a. Apparently he, rather than Ap. Claudius Centho, was in command of the army that tried and failed to storm Uscana (Livy 43.10.1–8, cf. 21.1; *MRR* 1:422).

b. No further offices.

c. No known sons in office; possibly the father of Coelius Antipater, the historian (Sumner, *Orators*, 57).

23. L. (or Cn.) Cornelius Lentulus, pr. 137.

a. Defeated by slaves in Sicily; his camp may have been captured as well (Florus 2.7.7). On the date, see *MRR* 1:481 n. 1, 3:159.

b. This praetor is probably to be identified as L. Lentulus, who was consul in 130 (Sumner, *Orators*, 143), although he may also be Cn. Lentulus, who held no further office (Münzer, *RE* 4 col. 1357).

c. If this praetor is L. Lentulus, his son is likely to be the L. Lentulus who became praetor, probably by 83 (Cic. *Arch.* 9; cf.

Sumner, *Orators*, 143); if he is Cn. Lentulus, then Cn. Cornelius Cn. f. Cn. n. Lentulus, consul in 97, may have been his son (Münzer *RE* 4 col. 1361, cf. 1357).

24. Cn. Cornelius Cn. f. Lentulus Clodianus, cos. 72.*

a. Defeated twice by Spartacus—once separately, once with his colleague Gellius, no. 39 (Sall. *Hist.* 3.106 Maur.; Livy *Per.* 96; Plut. *Crass.* 9.7; App. *BCiv.* 1.117; Florus 2.8.10; Eutrop. 6.7.2; Oros. 5.24.4).

b. The senate took control of the war out of the consuls' hands altogether (Plut. *Crass.* 9.7); Rubinsohn, *Historia* 19 (1970): 625–26 (followed by Ward, *Marcus Crassus*, 83–84 n. 2), argues that Plutarch does not say that the senate formally abrogated their commands, since it had no power to do this, but only "urged the consuls to refrain from [further military] action"; cf. Marshall, *Crassus*, 26. That analysis is rejected, however, by Gruen, *Last Generation*, 41 n. 126. Lentulus was elected censor in 70 and served as a legate to Pompey in 67.

c. His son Cn. Lentulus Clodianus was praetor in 59.

(L. Cornelius Cn. f. L. n. Lentulus Lupus, cos. 156.*)

a. According to Zippel, *Die römische Herrschaft in Illyrien*, 133ff., followed by De Sanctis, *Storia* 4.1²:424–25, the Cornelius defeated by the Pannonians mentioned in App. *Ill.* 14 refers to Lupus; cf. Poly. frg. 64 B-W. This identification, however, is persuasively refuted by Morgan, *Historia* 23 (1974): 184–89, who identifies this Cornelius as P. Nasica Serapio (below, no. 43).

b. Prosecuted and convicted of *repetundae*, probably in 154 (Val. Max. 6.9.10, cf. Festus 360L); elected censor in 147 and appointed *princeps senatus* in 131 *MRR* 1:501 n. 1.

c. No sons known to have reached high office.

25. P. Cornelius L. f. L. n. Scipio, cos. 218.*

a. Defeated by Hannibal at the Ticinus River (Poly. 3.65.1–11; Livy 21.46.1–10; other sources in *MRR* 1:238).

b. Sent to Spain in 217 following his year in office as proconsul to conduct the Roman war effort; remained there until his death in 211.

c. His sons were P. Cornelius Scipio Africanus, cos. 205 and 194, and L. Cornelius Scipio Asiaticus, cos. 190.

26. Cn. Cornelius L. f. Cn. n. Scipio Asina, cos. 260.*

a. Trapped by the Carthaginians at Lipara; either compelled to surrender or seized by them during negotiations (Poly. 1.21.4–9, 8.35.9; Livy *Per.* 17; Val. Max. 6.6.2, 6.9.11; Florus 1.18.11; App. *Lib.* 63; Oros. 4.7.9; Zonar. 8.10).

b. Returned to Rome at some point, possibly in an exchange of prisoners (Livy 22.23.6; Walbank, *Comm.* 1:76), and elected consul for the year 254.

c. His son P. Cornelius Scipio Asina was consul in 221.

27. L. Cornelius Cn. f. Scipio Barbatus, propr. 295.

a. During an emergency, he led his legion out of camp without scouts and was surrounded and defeated (Livy 10.26.7–12).

b. Subsequently he served as a legate to the consul at the battle of Sentium in the same year and again as a legate in 293; censor in 283 or 280 (*CIL* 1^2.2.7; *MRR* 1:192 n. 2).

c. His sons were Scipio Asina, cos. 260 (above, no. 26), and L. Cornelius L. f. Cn. n. Scipio, cos. 259; his grandsons were Cn. Scipio, cos. 222, and P. Scipio (above, no. 25).

(P. Cornelius P. f. P. n. Scipio Nasica Serapio, pr. 141: see below, no. 43).

28. P. Decius P. f. P. n. Mus, cos. 279.

a. Defeated by Pyrrhus, although Pyrrhus' losses were also heavy and the outcome indecisive (Dion. Hal. 20.1–3; Livy *Per.* 13; Eutrop. 2.13.4).

b. He may have been consul again in 265 (*MRR* 1:202 n. 2).

c. No known sons.

29. Sex. Digitius, pr. 194.*

a. Defeated several times in Spain with heavy losses (Livy 35.1.1–2, cf. 2–3; Oros. 4.20.16).

b. Legate in 190; ambassador in 174; charged with the purchase of grain in 172.

c. No son known to have held office.

30. C. Fabius N. f. M. n. Ambustus, cos. 358.*

a. Defeated by the Tarquinienses (Livy 7.15.9–11).

b. Interrex in 355.

c. No sons known to have held office. The descendants of his brother Marcus reached the consulate regularly in ensuing generations.

31. M. Fabius Hadrianus, legate 68.

a. Defeated in a minor skirmish by Mithridates (Plut. *Luc.* 35.1; App. *Mith.* 88, 112; Dio 36.9-10).

b. No further office held.

c. No known descendants.

32. Q. Fabius Q. Serviliani f. Q. n. Maximus (Eburnus?), q. 132.

a. Sent home from Sicily in disgrace by the consul P. Rupilius, his father-in-law, for losing Tauromenium (Val. Max. 2.7.3, cf. Diod. 34.2.20; Oros. 5.9.7). On the identification, see *MRR* 1:499 and the references given there.

b. Praetor, probably in 119; consul in 116; censor in 108.

c. No son known to have reached high office. Fabius put a son to death on charges of unchastity, for which he was prosecuted and exiled (Val. Max. 6.1.5; Ps. Quint. 3.17; Oros. 5.16.8).

33. Q. Fabius Q. f. Q. n. Maximus Servilianus, procos. 140.*

a. Defeated and trapped by Viriathus in Spain, he signed a treaty of peace with the enemy to extricate his army (Livy *Per.* 54, *Oxy. Per.* 54; Diod. 33.1.4; App. *Iber.* 67-69; Charax Perg. *FGrH* 2A no. 103 frgs. 26-27).

b. No further offices known.

c. His son was apparently the consul of 116 and censor of 108, Q. Fabius Maximus Eburnus (*RE* 6 col. 1796; above, no. 32).

34. L. Fufidius, propr. 80.*

a. Routed by Sertorius with heavy losses (Plut. *Sert.* 12; see also *MRR* 3:93).

b. No further offices held.

c. No sons known to have held office. On his family, see Wiseman, *New Men*, 232; Spann, *CJ* 82 (1986-87): 306-9; Konrad, *CP* (1989): 119-29.

35. Cn. Fulvius M. f. Q. n. Flaccus, pr. 212.*

a. His army was put to flight by Hannibal (Livy 25.21.1-10, cf. 26.1.9, 27.1.9; Oros. 4.16.17). The occurrence of the battle has been doubted by De Sanctis, *Storia*, 3.2²:459 n. 28, but his objections are answered by Crake, *Archival Material in Livy*, 187-88, 279, 332: see below, appendix 3, for additional discussion.

b. Prosecuted on his return, condemned, and exiled (Livy 26.2.7–3.12).

c. His son Q. Fulvius Cn. f. M. n. Flaccus was suffect consul in 180; his grandson C. Fulvius Q. f. Cn. n. Flaccus was consul in 134.

36. Q. Fulvius M. f. M. n. Nobilior, cos. 153.*

a. Beaten in a number of battles in Spain with significant losses (App. *Iber.* 45–47).

b. When he returned to Rome, he spread stories about the enemy's valor and the extent of his own losses in Spain (Poly. 35.4.2). He intervened in the attempt to try Ser. Sulpicius Galba in 149 (Livy *Per.* 49) and was elected censor in 136.

c. No son known to have held office.

37. L. Furius, legate 73.

a. Defeated by Spartacus (Plut. *Crass.* 9.4).

b. No further office held.

c. No descendants known to have held office.

38. L. Furius Sp. f. L. n. Medullinus, mil. tr. c. p. 381.

a. Defeated by the Praenestinians and Voscians (Livy 6.23.1–24.4, cf. 25.4–5; Plut. *Cam.* 37–38).

b. Furius was again mil. tr. c. p. in 370 and censor in 363.

c. No sons known to have held office.

39. L. Gellius L. f. L. n. Poplicola, cos. 72.*

a. Defeated twice by Spartacus—once with the praetor Arrius, no. 5, once with his colleague Lentulus Clodianus, no. 24 (Livy *Per.* 96; App. *BCiv.* 117; cf. Plut. *Crass.* 9.6–7).

b. The senate took control of the war out of the consuls' hands (above, no. 24); Gellius was elected censor in 70 and served as legate to Pompey in 67, commanding naval forces in the Etruscan Sea.

c. L. Gellius L. f. L. n. Poplicola, the consul of 36, was probably his son (Münzer, *RE* 7 col. 1003; Syme, *Augustan Aristocracy*, 28); Wiseman, *Cinna the Poet*, 122 argues for identifying the consul of 36 as a grandson but is not persuasive.

40. A. Hostilius L. f. A. n. Mancinus, cos. 170.

a. Defeated by Persius in an attempt to enter Macedon (Plut. *Aem.* 9.3; cf. Livy 43.11.9).

b. His command was prorogued for 169 until his successor arrived. No further offices known.

c. Two sons: A. Hostilius Mancinus, cur. aed. in 151(?), ambassador in 149; C. Hostilius Mancinus, cos. 137 (below, no. 41).

41. C. Hostilius A. f. L. n. Mancinus, cos. 137.*

a. Trapped while retreating from Numantia and compelled to surrender and swear to a treaty of peace (App. *Iber.* 80; Plut. *Ti. Gracch.* 5.1–4; other sources and discussion in Simon, *Roms Kriege in Spanien*, 150–54; Astin, *Scipio Aemilianus*, 132–133; Wikander, *Opuscula Romana* 11, no. 7 [1976]: 84–104).

b. Recalled to Rome and replaced by his colleague (App. *Iber.* 80). The senate rejected his treaty and arranged to have Mancinus handed over to the Numantines to nullify his treaty (Cic. *Rep.* 3.28, *Off.* 3.109; App. *Iber.* 83; Dio frg. 79; discussion in Rosenstein, *CA* 5 [1986]: 230–52). He returned to Rome and was later elected praetor for a second time (*Dig.* 50.7.17; *De Vir. Ill.* 59.4).

c. No sons known to have held public office.

42. D. Iunius M. f. M. n. Brutus Callaicus, procos. 136.*

a. Cooperated with M. Aemilius Lepidus Porcina in the siege of Pallantia and shared in the retreat, during which the losses were serious (sources above, no. 3).

b. Continued in command subsequently by the senate (Simon, *Roms Kriege in Spanien*, 169–71). Celebrated a triumph for his earlier victories (Plut. *Ti. Gracch.* 21.2; Eutrop. 4.19).

c. His son D. Iunius D. f. M. n. Brutus was consul in 77 (*RE* 10.1 col. 968).

43. D. Iunius Silanus / P. Cornelius P. f. P. n. Scipio Nasica Serapio, pr. 141.*

a. In 14 an unnamed praetor was defeated by the Scordisci in Thrace (Livy *Oxy. Per.* 54, cf. Obseq. 22 [misdated?]). *MRR* 1:477 suggests he is D. Iunius Silanus; Morgan, *Historia* 23 (1974): 208–15, argues for P. Scipio Serapio on the basis of App. *Ill.* 14; cf. *MRR* 3:113.

b. Iunius was later accused of accepting bribes, was tried before his father, and committed suicide (Cic. *Fin.* 24; Livy *Per.* 54); Serapio became consul in 138.

c. Silanus' son was almost certainly M. Iunius D. f. D. n. Silanus, cos. 109, no. 44 (Sumner, *Orators*, 78); Serapio's son was P. Cornelius P. f. P. n. Scipio Nasica Serapio, cos. 111.

44. M. Iunius D. f. D. n. Silanus, cos. 109.*

a. Lost a major battle against the Cimbri (Ascon. 68 C, 80 C; Livy *Per.* 65; Vell. 2.12.2; Florus 1.38.4; cf. Eutrop. 4.27.5; for the date, see Badian, *Mélange Piganiol* 913 n. 3.

b. Brought to trial in 104 by Cn. Domitius, tr. pl., for undertaking an unauthorized war and acquitted by a wide margin (Cic. *Div. Caec.* 67; Ascon. 80 C; Vell. 2.2.118).

c. D. Iunius M. f. Silanus, cos. 62, is likely to have been his son (Syme, *Augustan Aristocracy*, 189); M. Silanus, pr. 77, possibly was also a son: see *MRR* 3:114–15 on the problems surrounding the identity of this man, however.

45. P. Licinius M. f. P. n. Crassus, legate 90.

a. Suffered a minor defeat in which eight hundred men were killed: App. *BCiv.* 1.41.

b. Elected censor for 89; legate again in 87.

c. His son was M. Licinius Crassus, cos. 70 and 55.

46. L. Licinius L. f. Lucullus, propr. 103.

a. After defeating an army of slaves and driving them from the field, he besieged them unsuccessfully at Triocala and retired with losses (Diod. 36.8.3–5; Florus 2.7.11).

b. Brought to trial subsequently on charges of *peculatus* or *repetundae*, convicted, and exiled: Cic. 2 *Verr.* 4.147; *Acad.* 2.1; *Off.* 2.50; cf. *Prov. Cons.* 22; Diod. 36.8.5–9.2; Plut. *Luc.* 1.1; Quint. 12.7.4; cf. *De Vir. Ill.* 6.2.4.

c. His sons were L. Licinius Lucullus, cos. 74 (below no. 47), and M. Licinius Lucullus, cos. 73.

47. L. Licinius L. f. L. n. Lucullus, procos. 67.*

a. His legate, C. Valerius Triarius, was heavily defeated by Mithridates (Plut. *Luc.* 35.1–2; App. *Mith.* 89, cf. 112; Dio 36.12).

b. Lucullus was superceded in his command in 67, but this defeat apparently had little to do with his removal: Williams, *Phoenix* 38 (1984): 223, 226, 228, 231. He remained somewhat active in public life until his death (Plut. *Luc.* 42.4–43.3).

c. No sons known to have held public office.

48. L. Licinius Murena, propr. 82.*

a. Invaded Pontus without authorization and was seriously defeated by Mithridates (App. *Mith.* 64–66; Memnon *FGrH* 3B no. 434 frg. 26).

b. Murena secured a triumph on his return (Cic. *Leg. Man.* 8; *Mur.* 11, 15, 88; Gran. Licin. 36.5 C).

c. His son was L. Licinius Murena, cos. 62.

49. P. Licinius Nerva, pr. (or propr.) 104.*

a. A small force he dispatched under the command of M. Titinius (below no. 86) to deal with a slave revolt was defeated (Diod. 36.4.3). He later attacked the camp of the slaves and captured it, but his soldiers were put to flight by the enemy counterattack. Many of his soldiers lost their weapons or were captured (Diod. 36.4.6–8). Discussion of the events is in Rubinsohn, *Athenaeum*, n.s., 60 (1982): 436–51 at 448–49.

b. No further public office.

c. No sons known to have reached high office.

50. M. Livius Macatus, prefect 212.*

a. While in command at Tarentum, he was surprised by Hannibal, and most of the city was captured. Polybius indicates he was drunk at the time of the attack. Livius retained control of the citadel, however (Poly. 8.27.1–31.6; Livy 25.9–10; Plut. *Fab.* 23.3).

b. After the Romans recovered the city in 208, the senate debated whether to punish Livius or reward him for holding out for five years, but it is not clear whether any formal action was ever taken against him (Livy 27.25.3–5, cf. Cic. *Sen.* 11; *De Or.* 2.273; Plut. *Fab.* 23.3). No further offices known.

c. No descendants known to have held public office.

51. Cn. Mallius Cn. f. Maximus, cos. 105.*

a. After failing to secure the cooperation of the proconsul P. Servilius Caepio, no. 81, both lost major battles to the Cimbri and Teutones (Livy *Per.* 67; Florus 1.38.4; Gran. Licin. 33.6–11 C; Eutrop. 5.1.1; Dio frg. 91.1–4; Oros. 5.16.1–7 [= Val. Ant. frg. 63 P]; other sources in *MRR* 1:555).

b. Mallius went into exile in the following year (Gran. Licin. 33.24 C), probably voluntarily withdrawing, although perhaps after a trial and conviction: see chap. 4, n. 47, for discussion.

c. No sons known to have reached public office.

52. M'. Manilius P. f. P. n., pr. 155 (or 154).*

a. Defeated with his colleague L. Calpurnius Piso, no. 11, by the Lusitanians with heavy losses (App. *Iber.* 56; on the date and the rank of Manilius at the time, see Simon, *Roms Kriege in Spanien*, 13; Richardson, *Hispaniae*, 185).

  b. Manilius was consul in 149 (*RE* 14.1 col. 1135; below, no. 53).

  c. P. Manilius, the consul of 120, was either his son (Sumner, *Orators*, 62) or his nephew (*RE* 14.1 col. 1139).

53. M'. Manilius P. f. P. n., cos. 149.

  a. Suffered a number of reverses along with his colleague Marcius, no. 59, in their attempt to storm Carthage (App. *Lib.* 97–104, cf. Poly. 36.8.4; Diod. 32.8; Livy *Per.* 49–50; *Oxy. Per.* 49; Oros. 4.22.1–7; Zonar. 9.26–27).

  b. No further offices held; he may be the man mentioned in connection with Tiberius Gracchus' agrarian law in 133 (Plut. *Ti. Gracch.* 11.1; *RE* 14.1 col. 1138; doubted by Astin, *Scipio Aemilianus* 348). Cicero cast him as an interlocutor in the *De Republica*.

  c. On his descendants, see above, no. 52.

54. Cn. Manlius, pr. 72.

  a. Defeated together with the proconsul C. Cassius Longinus, no. 14, by Spartacus (Livy *Per.* 96; cf. *MRR* 3:135 on the date).

  b. No further offices held.

  c. No sons known to have reached public office.

55. L. Manlius, procos. 78.*

  a. Defeated in Spain by Sertorius' forces and again in Gaul (Caes. *BGall.* 3.20.1; Livy *Per.* 90; Oros. 5.23.4).

  b. Possibly the consul of 65, but this view is not generally accepted (*RE* 14.1 col. 1159; Sumner, *Orators*, 129).

  c. No sons known to have reached high office.

56. (A.?) Manlius (Torquatus?), pr. 138(?).

  a. Defeated by slaves in Sicily (Florus 2.7.7); on the date of his praetorship, see Sumner, *Orators*, 59.

  b. No further offices held.

  c. No sons known to have reached the consulate or praetorship.

57. L. Manlius A. f. P. n. Vulso, cos. 250.*

  a. Failed with his colleague C. Atilius Regulus, no. 6, to capture Lilybaeum by siege; suffered considerable losses. For sources, see above, no. 6.

  b. No further office held.

  c. His sons were L. Manlius Vulso, pr. 218, and P. Manlius

Vulso, pr. 210; his grandsons were L. Manlius Vulso, pr. 197, C. Manlius Cn. f. L. n. Vulso, cos. 189, and A. Manlius Cn. f. L. n. Vulso, cos. 178 (*RE* 14.1 col. 1215).

58. L. Manlius Vulso, pr. 218.*

a. Ambushed by the Boii and put to flight; later besieged (Poly. 3.40.11–14, Livy 21.25.8–14).

b. Candidate for the consulship of 216 (Livy 22.35.1; Münzer, *RE* 14.1 col. 1223). Münzer identifies him as one of the three envoys sent by Hannibal to Rome after Cannae to discuss ransom of the Roman prisoners. Following the refusal by the senate to negotiate, he and the other envoys returned to Hannibal and probably spent the remainder of the war as prisoners (Livy 22.61.5–7).

c. No sons known to have held public office; his three nephews won praetorships and consulships (see above, no. 57 c).

59. L. Marcius C. f. C. n. Censorinus, cos. 149.

a. Fought with little success against Carthage and sustained several small reverses (App. *Lib.* 97–99; sources cited for Manilius, no. 53).

b. Elected censor in 147.

c. No sons known to have reached the consulate or praetorship. Cn. Marcius Censorinus, tr. pl. in 122, may have been his son.

60. C. Marcius C. f. Q. n. Figulus, pr. 169.

a. Driven off while besieging Cassandreia and other cities (Livy 44.10–12).

b. Consul *vitio creatus* in 162; elected again in 156.

c. His son was C. Marcius Figulus, pr. ca. 130 (Val. Max. 9.3.2; Münzer *RE* 14 col. 1554).

61. Q. Marcius L. f. Q. n. Philippus, cos. 186.*

a. Ambushed and seriously defeated by the Ligurian Apuani with heavy loss of life; many legionary standards also fell into enemy hands (Livy 39.20.5–10; Oros. 4.20.26). Stayed away from Rome for the rest of the year (Livy 39.23.1).

b. Ambassador in 183; made a *decemvir s.f.* in 180; ambassador again in 173–172; consul for the second time in 169; censor in 164.

c. No sons known to have reached the praetorship or consulate. A son, Q. Marcius Philippus, was a legate in 169 and an ambassador in 163.

62. M. Minucius C. f. C. n. Rufus, dict. 217.

a. Trapped and nearly destroyed by Hannibal (Poly. 3.104.1–105.9; Nep. *Hann.* 5.3; Val. Max. 5.2.5; Livy 22.28.3–29.6; Plut. *Fab.* 11.1–12.4; Frontin. *Str.* 2.5.22; Sil. 7.494–50; App. *Han.* 13; *De Vir. Ill.* 43.3; Zonar. 8.26).

b. No further offices held; he died at Cannae (Livy 22.49.16).

c. M. Minucius Rufus, pr. 197, may conceivably have been a son, but since Münzer does not comment on his family, he will not be counted as such here. The consul of 197, Q. Minucius C. f. C. n. Rufus, was apparently his younger brother.

63. Mummius, legate 72.*

a. Fought a battle against Spartacus contrary to orders and was heavily defeated (Plut. *Crass.* 10.1–3).

b. No further offices held.

c. No descendants known to have held public office.

64. C. Nigidius, pr. (or legate) 145 (or 144).

a. Defeated by Viriathus in Spain (*De Vir. Ill.* 71.1). On the controversy over his rank, see Astin, *Scipio Aemilianus*, 344, and the works cited there. If he was a praetor, his command in Spain may have fallen in 144 (Simon, *Roms Kriege in Spanien*, 78–79; *MRR* 3:147; Richardson, *Hispaniae*, 187–88).

b. No further offices held.

c. No sons known to have reached high office; P. Nigidius Figulus, pr. 58, may be a descendant (Shackleton-Bailey, *CQ* 54 [1960]: 253–67 at 262; idem, *Cicero's Letters to Atticus*, 1:354).

65. Cn. Papirius C. f. Carbo, cos. 113.*

a. Attacked the Cimbri without provocation and sustained a massive defeat (Strabo 5.1.8; Livy *Per.* 63; Vell. 2.12.2; Plut. *Mar.* 16.5; App. *Gall.* 13).

b. Perhaps prosecuted on his return; if so, probably acquitted (Cic. *Fam.* 188 [9.21].3; Shackleton-Bailey, *Cicero: Epistulae ad Familiares*, 2:330; discussion above, p. 142). No further offices held.

c. His sons were Cn. Papirius Cn. f. C. n. Carbo, cos. 85, 84, and 82, and C. Papirius Carbo, pr. c. 81. The circumstances of these elections cannot be considered normal by Republican standards, but Gnaeus' election to a praetorship for 89 probably was; Gaius may also have won a tribunate for the same year.

66. C. Perperna, legate 90.*

a. Defeated by Italian forces; casualties were serious, and the weapons of many of the survivors were lost (App. *BCiv.* 1.41).

b. Deprived of his command by the consul P. Rutilius Lupus (App. *BCiv.* 1.41).

c. No sons known to have held elective office; his brother was censor in 86. Possibly M. Perperna Vento, pr. 82, is related.

67. C. Plautius Hypsaeus, pr. 146.*

a. Heavily defeated by Viriathus, he fled to a city and refused to venture out as the enemy overran the countryside (Livy *Per.* 52; App. *Iber.* 64; Oros. 5.4.3).

b. Prosecuted on his return, but the charge is unclear: Diodorus' language at 33.2 indicates *maiestas*, but it is not certain whether this crime existed at the time. Hence the charge may have been *perduellio* (cf. Bauman, *Crimen Maiestatis*, 22; Gruen, *Roman Politics*, 29 and n. 46); condemned and exiled (Diod. 33.2).

c. No sons in the consulate or praetorship. L. Plautius Hypsaeus, pr. 135 (below, no. 68), and M. Plautius Hypsaeus, cos. 125, are probably kinsmen (*RE* 21.1 col. 14).

68. L. Plautius Hypsaeus, pr. 139 (or 138 or 135).

a. Defeated by slaves in Sicily; his camp may have been captured (Florus 2.7.7; Diod. 34-35.2.18; cf. *MRR* 1:481 n. 1, 3:159; Green, *Past and Present* 20 [1960–61]: 10–29).

b. Hackl, *Senat und Magistratur*, 83, asserts that Plautius was prosecuted at the behest of the senate, but the sources offer no support for her contention. Plautius held no further offices.

c. See above, no. 67.

(Q. Pompeius A. f., pr. 143 [?]: see below, no. 76.)

69. Q. Pompeius A. f., cos. 141, procos. 140.*

a. Suffered a series of reverses at Numantia; opened negotiations with the enemy leading to a treaty of peace (App. *Iber.* 78–79; cf. Dio frg. 77).

b. Pompeius denied he had made a *foedus* when his successor arrived and continued to deny it when the senate investigated the matter on his return to Rome. The senate elected to continue the war (App. *Iber.* 79). At some point he stood trial for *repetundae* and was acquitted (Cic. *Font.* 23; Val. Max. 8.5.1). The prosecution is generally seen in the context of the political backlash of his defeat

(Gruen, *Roman Politics*, 36; Hackl, *Senat und Magistratur*, 81–82); that linkage has recently been doubted: see Richardson, *JRS* 77 (1987): 1–12, esp. 11–12, who suggests nevertheless that some sort of hearing regarding Pompeius' dealings with the Numantines took place in the senate. In 136 an attempt was made to hand Pompeius over to the Numantines in order to invalidate his treaty, but a bill to this effect was defeated (Cic. *Off.* 3.109; *Rep.* 3.28, cf. *Fin.* 2.54; Vell. 2.1.5; App. *Iber.* 83; discussion in Rosenstein, *CA* 5 [1986]: 248–50). Pompeius was elected censor in 131.

c. His son was Q. Pompeius Rufus, consul in 88 (*RE* 21.1 col. 2250; Sumner, *AJAH* 2 [1977]: 10–13).

70. M. Popillius M. f. P. n. Laenas, procos. 138.

a. Defeated and put to flight by the Numantines (Livy *Per.* 55, cf. *Oxy. Per.* 55; App. *Iber.* 79).

b. No further office held.

c. No sons known to have reached high office; but M. Popillius M. f. Laenas, legate propr. early in the first century, may be his son (*MRR* 3:168).

71. C. Porcius M. f. M. n. Cato, cos. 114.*

a. Seriously defeated by the Scordisci in Thrace (Livy *Per.* 63; Florus 1.39.4; Dio 26 frg. 88).

b. Cato was tried, convicted, and fined a trifling sum on charges of *repetundae* (Cic. *Verr.* 2.3.184, 4.22; Vell. 2.8.1; see above, p. 141, for discussion). He may have served subsequently as an ambassador to Numidia (Gruen, *Roman Politics*, 146) or as a legate during the Jugurthine war (*MRR* 1:544). He was later condemned and exiled by the Mamilian commission (Cic. *Brut.* 128; *Balb.* 28, 110).

c. No sons elected consul or praetor; his nephew was apparently M. Porcius Cato, pr. in an unknown year (*RE* 22.1 col. 165, cf. 105).

72. A. Postumius Albinus, legate 110.*

a. Left in command by his brother, the consul of 110 (below, no. 74), Aulus was lured into a trap by Jugurtha, surrounded, attacked, and compelled to surrender. He agreed to make a treaty with the king and pass under the yoke (Sall. *Iug.* 38; Livy *Per.* 64; Florus 1.36.9; Oros. 5.15.6).

b. Although his brother was prosecuted and condemned before the Mamilian commission, no action seems to have been taken against Aulus. He was probably elected consul for 99 (*Suppl. MRR* 50–51; *MRR* 3:173; Sumner, *Orators*, 82–84; Badian, *Chiron* 14 [1984]: 124–25). He was legate in 89 in command of a fleet and killed during a mutiny of his soldiers.

c. No sons known to have reached the consulate or praetorship.

73. Sp. Postumius Albinus, cos. 321.*

a. Trapped with his colleague T. Veturius Calvinus by Samnite forces at the Caudine Forks; compelled to surrender, agree to a treaty of peace, and pass under the yoke (Livy 9.1.1–6.2; Dion. Hal. 16.1.3; App. *Sam.* 4.2–6; Dio frg. 36.10; discussion in Nissen, *RhM* 25 [1870]: 1–65).

b. The senate ordered him and his colleague to appoint a dictator to hold elections, the new consuls from which were to enter office immediately; however, owing to *vitia* the elections took place under an interregnum (Livy 9.7.12–8.1, cf. App. *Sam.* 4.7; Zonar. 7.26). Postumius and Veturius were handed over to the Samnites by way of invalidating their treaty. Postumius himself urged this step. The Samnites refused to accept the generals, and Postumius returned to Rome (discussion in Nissen, *loc. cit.* and Crawford, *PBSR* 41 [1973]: 1–7). He held no further office, but enjoyed great fame (Cic. *Off.* 3.109; Livy 9.8.1–12.3; Gell. *NA* 17.21.36; Florus 1.11.11; Dio frg. 36.19–21; Zonar. 7.26).

c. No sons known to have reached the consulate or praetorship.

74. Sp. Postumius Albinus, cos. 110.*

a. Left his brother Aulus in command of his army while he returned to Rome to conduct elections. Aulus was trapped and forced to surrender (sources above, no. 72).

b. Returned to Africa with the intention of resuming prosecution of the war (Sall. *Iug.* 39.4–5). Prorogued until the arrival of his successor, Spurius was condemned by the Mamilian commission (Cic. *Brut.* 128; Sall. *Iug.* 44.1).

c. No sons known to have reached the consulate or praetorship.

75. L. Postumius L. f. Sp. n. Megellus, cos. 294.*

a. According to Claudius Quadrigarius (frg. 34 P = Livy 10.37.13), Postumius was defeated in Apulia, compelled to flee the field, and forced to take refuge in Luceria with a few men. However, the tradition as Livy found it was uncertain. Fabius Pictor, frg. 19 P (= Livy 10.37.14) wrote only of many deaths on both sides at Luceria, whereas other authors Livy drew on seem not to have mentioned a defeat at all (Livy 10.34.1–14, 37.1–5). In the dominant tradition it was his colleague Atilius who sustained an initial defeat and later won a victory after vowing to raise a temple to Jupiter Stator (Livy 10.32.3–33.7, 35.1–36.16).

b. Sought and celebrated a triumph, against the wishes of the senate (Livy 10.37.6–12). Indicted by a tribune of the plebs in the following year on unspecified charges but escaped prosecution through appointment as his successor's legate (Livy 10.46.16). Interrex in 291; elected consul in the same year; ambassador in 282.

c. His son was L. Postumius L. f. L. n. Megellus, cos. 262.

76. Quinctius, pr. 143.*

a. Defeated by Viriathus and retired early into winter quarters; lost control of the countryside (App. *Iber*. 66). His identification with Q. Pompeius, cos. 141 (above, no. 69), has been challenged (Simon, *Roms Kriege in Spanien*, 80–86; cf. Astin, *Historia* 13 [1964]: 251–52) but is now defended by Richardson, *Hispaniae*, 189–90.

b. If this person is Q. Pompeius, he became consul in 141; Quinctius is not known to have held any other office.

c. If Q. Pompeius, his son was Q. Pompeius Rufus, cos. 88 (above, no. 69). No sons of Quinctius are known.

77. L. Quinctius, legate 71.

a. Defeated with Tremellius Scrofa, no. 88, by Spartacus (Plut. *Crass*. 11.4); Frontin. *Str*. 2.4.34.

b. Praetor in 68. On his identity, see Syme, *Historia* 4 (1955): 52–71 at 67–68 (= Syme, *Roman Papers*, 1:287–88).

c. No sons known to have held public office.

78. Ti. Sempronius C. f. C. n. Longus, cos. 218.*

a. Defeated by Hannibal at the Trebia River (Poly. 3.70.1–75.8; Nep. *Hann*. 4; Livy 21.53.1–56.8; Frontin. *Str*. 2.5.23; Florus 1.22.12; App. *Hann*. 6–7; *De Vir. Ill*. 42.3; Oros. 4.14.7; Zonar. 8.24).

b. May have served as a legate in 215 (*MRR* 1:258 n. 7).

c. His son was Ti. Sempronius Ti. f. C. n. Longus, cos. 194.

79. C. Sentius, propr. 92–87.

a. After losing initially to the Thracians, he won several successes against them (Livy *Per*. 70; Oros. 5.18.30). He lost Macedon to the forces of Mithridates in 87 (App. *Mith*. 35); on his lengthy tenure of this province, see Badian, *Studies*, 73–74, who suggests he was allowed to stay on after his initial defeat to afford him a chance to redeem himself with a subsequent victory.

b. No further offices.

c. No sons known to have held public office. On his family, see Syme, *Historia* 13 (1964): 156–66 (= Syme, *Roman Papers*, 2:605–16).

80. C. Servilius, pr. 102.

a. Achieved nothing worthy of note, according to Diod. 36.9.1. Florus 2.7.11 reports he was defeated by the slaves in Sicily and driven from his camp, but Florus is highly untrustworthy as a source for events in Sicily during this period (Rubinsohn, *Athenaeum*, n.s., 60 [1982]: 439–40).

b. Prosecuted for his lack of success, convicted, and exiled: Diod. 36.9.1, cf. Cic. *Div. Caec.* 63; Ps. Asc. 203 St.; see also above, pp. 142–44.

c. No sons known to have held public office; P. Servilius Vatia Isauricus, cos. 79, may be his younger brother.

81. Q. Servilius Cn. f. Cn. n. Caepio, procos. 105.*

a. He and the consul Cn. Mallius Maximus each sustained a massive defeat at the hands of the Cimbri and Teutones (sources above, no. 51).

b. Caepio was prosecuted in connection with the disappearance of the treasure from a temple at Tolosa and acquitted or possibly fined (Cic. *Nat. D.* 3.74; Dio frg. 90; Oros. 5.15). His *imperium* was abrogated; he was removed from the senate, tried on charges stemming from the defeat, convicted, and exiled and his property confiscated (*Rhet. Her.* 1.24; Cic. *Balb.* 28; *Brut.* 135; Livy *Per.* 67; Strab. 4.1.13; Val. Max. 4.7.3, 6.9.13; Gran. Licin. 33.24 C; cf. Lengle, *Hermes* 66 [1931]: 302–16).

c. His son was Q. Servilius Caepio, q. 100, perhaps a praetor in 91 (*MRR* 2:24 n. 4; Sumner, *Orators*, 116–17; cf. Syme, *Augustan Aristocracy*, 158).

82. Ser. Sulpicius Ser. f. P. n. Galba, pr. 151.*

a. After routing the enemy, his forces suffered heavy losses in pursuit and fled the field (App. *Iber.* 58; Oros. 4.21.3).

b. Prorogued for 150. Following his return to Rome in 149, an attempt was made to try him in connection with his enslavement and murder of the Lusitanians who had surrendered to him in the previous year, but the bill to establish a court to hear the charges was defeated (Cic. *Brut.* 80, 89–90; *De Or.* 1.227–228; *Mur.* 59; cf. *Att.* 316 [12.5b]; Nep. *Cato* 3.4; Livy *Per.* 49 and *Oxy. Per.* 49, cf. 39.40.12; Val. Max. 8.1.2, 9.6.2; App. *Iber.* 59–60; Suet. *Galba* 3.2; Oros. 4.21.10; Ps. Asc. 203 St.). His crimes in Spain are discussed by Rubinsohn, *RSA* 11 (1981): 161–204 at 187–90. Elected consul for 144.

c. His son, Ser. Sulpicius Ser. f. Ser. n. Galba, was consul in 108.

83. Q. Sulpicius Longus, mil. tr. c. p. 390.*

a. Held command at the Allia when Roman forces were heavily defeated by the Gauls (Cass. Hem. frg. 20 P; Cn. Gellius frg. 25 P [both = Macrob. *Sat.* 1.16.21]; Livy 5.37.1–38.10; Diod. 14.114; Dion. Hal. 13.12; Plut. *Cam.* 18.4–7).

b. In command of the Capitol during the siege of the city (Livy 5.47.9, 48.8; Plut. *Cam.* 28.4). No further offices held.

c. No sons known to have reached high office. Possibly C. Sulpicius Ser. f. Q. n. Longus, cos. 337, was a grandson.

84. P. Sulpicius P. f. Ser. n. Saverrio, cos. 279.

a. Defeated by Pyrrhus in an indecisive battle together with his colleague P. Decius Mus (sources above, no. 28).

b. No further offices held.

c. No sons known to have reached high office; his grandsons were P. Sulpicius Galba, cos. 211 and 200; Ser. Sulpicius Galba, cur. aed. 209, pont. 203–199; and C. Sulpicius Galba, pont. 202–199 and possibly pr. 211.

85. C. Terentius C. f. M. n. Varro, cos. 216.*

a. Led Roman forces to a disastrous defeat against Hannibal at Cannae (Poly. 3.110.1–117.6; Livy 22.40.5–50.3; other sources in *MRR* 1:247).

b. Publicly thanked by the senate following the battle for "not having despaired of the state" (Livy 22.61.13–14; other sources in *MRR* 1:247). Promagistrate, 215–213 and 208–207; ambassador in 203 and 200; III vir col. deduc. in 200.

c. His son was A. Terentius Varro, pr. 184 (*RE* 5A col. 676).

86. M. Titinius, legate (or prefect) 104.

a. Given command of six hundred soldiers by P. Licinius Nerva (no. 49), the praetor governing Sicily, and sent to attack rebellious slaves at Mt. Caprianus; defeated and put to flight. Many of his men were killed; the rest threw away their arms to escape (Diod.

36.4.3). At some point he made a dedication of booty, apparently in connection with an earlier victory (Diod. 36.3.5, *Suppl. MRR* 63, *MRR* 3:106).

b. No further offices held.

c. No sons known to have reached public office.

87. C. Toranius, q. 73.

a. Defeated by Spartacus (Sall. *Hist.* 3.96 Maur.; Florus 2.85).

b. Probably plebeian aedile in 64 or 63; possibly praetor in 44 (*CIL* 1^2.1, p. 199; *MRR* 2:164 n. 3; *Suppl. MRR* 63–64; *MRR* 3:107).

c. No descendants known to have reached public office.

88. Cn. Tremellius Scrofa, q. 71.

a. Defeated by Spartacus along with L. Quinctius, no. 77 (Plut. *Crass.* 11.4).

b. Military tribune in 69; at some point apparently a praetor; promagistrate in 51–50 (Cic. *Att.* 115 [6.1].13; *MRR* 3:208).

c. No descendants known to have held public office.

89. P. Valerius Laevinus, cos. 280.*

a. Defeated by Pyrrhus with heavy losses (Livy *Per.* 13; Dion. Hal. 19.9–12; Frontin. *Str.* 4.1.24; Plut. *Pyrr.* 16.3–17.5; Florus 1.13.7–8; Just. 18.1.4–9; Zonar. 8.3, cf. Dio frg. 40.18–19, 21–24; other sources in *MRR* 1:191.

b. The question of deposing Laevinus from command was debated in the senate. No action against him was taken, however (Plut. *Pyrr.* 18.1, cf. Frontin. *Str.* 4.1.24). Degrassi, *Inscr. Ital.* 13.1: 113, suggests that the gap on the Capitoline Fasti between Laevinus' name and that of the dictator subsequently appointed to hold elections was due to a note on the stone that Laevinus had either died in office or abdicated. But so little remains of the stone itself that the suggestion can neither be proven nor refuted. He held no further offices.

c. No son is attested; his grandson was M. Valerius P. f. P. n. Laevinus, cos. 220(?) and 210.

90. C. Valerius Triarius, legate 67.*

a. Served under Lucullus; heavily defeated by Mithridates, he narrowly escaped lynching at the hands of his own soldiers (Plut. *Luc.* 35.1–2; App. *Mith.* 89; Dio 36.12).

b. No subsequent offices held.

c. No sons in the praetorship or consulate. He or a son may have been the C. Valerius Triarius, praef. class., for Pompey in 49.

91. P. Varinius, pr. 73.*

a. Defeated several times by Spartacus; his horse and lictors captured (Sall. *Hist.* 3.95-98 Maur.; Plut. *Crass.* 9.4-5; App. *BCiv.* 1.116; Florus 2.7.5).

b. Propraetor in Asia, 72 or 65; possibly praetor for the second time in 65 (*MRR* 2:108, 142 n. 9, 3:215).

c. No sons known to have reached public office.

92. T. Veturius Calvinus, cos. 321.*

a. Trapped with his colleague Sp. Postumius Albinus by the Samnites at the Caudine Forks; compelled to surrender, make a treaty, and lead their army under the yoke (sources above, no. 73).

b. Handed over to the enemy by the senate in order to invalidate the treaty. The Samnites refused to accept the generals, and Veturius returned to Rome (sources above, no. 73). Held no further offices.

c. No sons known to have reached high office.

1.2: CONSULARS KILLED IN DEFEATS

The following is a list of all consuls or men of consular rank in command of armies who were killed in defeats between 249 and 50 B.C. and who are not listed in appendix 1.1, together with their consular or praetorian sons, if any. The criteria for deciding who counts as a son are the same as those used in appendix 1.1.c. An asterisk denotes those who suffered serious defeats.

1. L. Aemilius M. f. M. n. Paullus, cos. 216.*
His son was L. Aemilius L. f. M. n. Paullus, cos. 182 and 168.

2. M. Aurelius Scaurus, legate 105.*
No consular or praetorian son is known.

3. M'. Aquillius, legate 88.*
No consular or praetorian son is known.

4. L. Cassius L. f. Longinus, cos. 107.*
His son was probably C. Cassius L. f. Longinus, cos. 73 (Münzer, *RE* 3 col. 1727; Sumner, *Orators*, 50-51).

5. Cn. Cornelius L. f. L. n. Scipio Calvus, procos. 211.*

His sons were P. Cornelius Cn. f. L. n. Scipio Nasica, cos. 191, and Cn. Cornelius Cn. f. L. n. Scipio Hispallus, cos. 176.

6. C. Flaminius C. f. L. n., cos. 217.*

His son was C. Flaminius C. f. C. n., cos. 187.

7. Cn. Fulvius Cn. f. Cn. n. Centumalus Maximus, procos. 210.*

His son was M. Fulvius Centumalus, pr. 192 (Münzer, *RE* 7 col. 232).

8. M. Licinius P. f. M. n. Crassus, procos. 53.*

No consular or praetorian son is known.

9. P. Licinius P. f. P. n. Crassus Dives Mucianus, procos. 130.*

No consular or praetorian son is known.

10. L. Porcius M. f. M. n. Cato, cos. 89.

His son may have been C. Porcius Cato, possibly praetor in 55 (*MRR* 3:169–70), but is not counted as such here.

11. L. Postumius A. f. A. n. Albinus, cos.-elect 216.*

His son was Sp. Postumius L. f. A. n. Albinus, cos. 186.

12. P. Rutilius L. f. L. n. Lupus, cos. 90.*

His son was probably P. Rutilius Lupus, pr. 49 (Münzer, *RE* 1A col. 1267).

Appendix 2: Auspicial Powers of Promagistrates

The auspical powers of promagistrates is a knotty problem. Cic. *Div.* 2.76–77 indicates that by the end of the Republic promagistrates conducting military operations had not possessed the auspices for some time: *Quam multi anni sunt, cum bella a proconsulibus et a propraetoribus administrantur, qui auspicia non habent*. Yet promagistrates in the late third and second centuries did have the auspices (Livy 29.27.2; *CIL* 1^2 2.2662). In such cases the power to take the auspices was probably carried over into a promagistracy from the magistracy in the year immediately preceding. Cicero, however, is probably thinking of persons given special commands apart from a regular magistracy—Pompey in Spain, for example, or those who, like himself, went to war after a long hiatus. Much turns on what is meant by *habere auspicia*. It seems inconceivable that the Romans sent those appointed to special commands into their provinces blind as regards the *pax deorum*. Hence provision for taking the auspices was probably included in the enabling legislation; cf. the *pullarius* furnished under the terms of the *lex Sempronia* (Cic. *Leg. Agr.* 2.31). *Auspicia non habent*, however, appears to refer to the fact that such special commands were not associated with the passage of a *lex curiata*, as in the case of a regular magistracy, in anticipation of which the auspices were taken. As a result of a favorable auspication here, a regular magistrate obtained a general sanction from the gods for the conduct of his whole magistracy and could therefore be said to *habere auspicia*. On the whole problem, see Valeton, *Mnemosyne*, n.s., 18 (1890): 221–32.

Appendix 3: Defeats against Hannibal

De Sanctis, *Storia*, 3.2²: 445 n. 28, argues that the two Roman defeats Livy records at Herdonia in 212 and 210—one of the praetor Cn. Fulvius Flaccus, the other of the proconsul Cn. Fulvius Centumalus, both against Hannibal—are in reality one and the same. He alleges that Livy, or the annalist he followed, found the battle dated to 212 in one source and to 210 in another and so mistakenly reported these as two distinct events. Crake challenged this view in his 1939 Ph.D. dissertation, "Archival Material in Livy," as did, independently, Toynbee, *Hannibal's Legacy*, 2:48. More recently, however, Brunt, *Italian Manpower*, 652, has accepted De Sanctis' arguments and rejected Flaccus' defeat in 212. This position is mistaken, however.

De Sanctis bases his case first of all on the fact that the commanders' *nomina* and *praenomina* are the same: Cn. Fulvius in each case. But as Toynbee points out, this resemblance is not so remarkable given the peculiarities of Roman nomenclature. Of greater weight is the fact that the far more distinctive *cognomina* are different—Flaccus and Centumalus—and securely attested as belonging to two different branches of the Fulvian *gens*. The fact that both battles took place at Herdonia, which De Sanctis likewise finds suspicious, Toynbee rightly explains by stressing the high military importance both sides attached to control of the region as well as the exposure of the legions to attack in open country that any attempt to seize the place entailed.

Crake (174, 187–88 n. 17) and Toynbee also emphasize the difference in the fates of the two commanders: Centumalus was killed; Flaccus survived to face trial on his return. De Sanctis regards the death of Centumalus as a fundamental point in favor of accepting the validity of his defeat and rejecting Flaccus', but, as

Crake argues convincingly, it is difficult to understand the charge against the latter apart from the defeat. De Sanctis assumes he was tried on other grounds and cites Val. Max. 8.4.3. But this source offers no support for the notion that Flaccus was not tried in connection with his defeat. In fact, this person may not even be the praetor of 212: he went into exile at Tarquinii to escape certain condemnation (Livy 26.3.12), whereas the Flaccus of Val. Max. 8.4.3 was found guilty of the charges against him. Crake (332 n. 26) also points out, in support of the reality of the defeat in 212, that it is difficult to account for Hannibal's ability to march on Rome in 211 if Flaccus' two legions had not been destroyed in the previous year.

Yet De Sanctis' strongest evidence for the alleged doublet is the parallels he finds between the details of the two events: in each the principal causes are negligence on the part of the commander and indiscipline among the soldiers; both involved rash decisions to attack Hannibal head-on; in both battles the left *ala* was placed in front together with a legion; and a cavalry envelopment in the Romans' rear decided each battle. But De Sanctis is largely mistaken, and closer examination turns up few such parallels. Only in 212 is the indiscipline of the soldiers a prominent cause of the defeat (Livy 25.20.6–7, 21.1–2, 21.5–8). On the contrary, in 210 the Roman soldiers fought steadfastly and with great determination (Livy 27.1.10–11), with no sign of indiscipline in the ranks. However, the carelessness and foolishness of Centumalus are highlighted in Livy's account of the causes of the disaster in 210 (27.1.4, 7), whereas Flaccus' faults largely center on his failure to enforce discipline and the fact that he corrupted his soldiers (Livy 25.20.7, 21.5, cf. 26.2.8, 11–16; but cf. 25.21.9, 26.2.15). The cavalry envelopment occurred only in 210 (Livy 27.1.8, 11); in 212 the Romans ran before they even made contact with the enemy (Livy 25.21.8, cf. 5; lightly armed soldiers previously hidden in ambush did attack the Romans from behind [Livy 25.21.10, cf. 3], but the role of the cavalry was to pursue the fugitives [Livy 25.21.4]). Both battles involved set-piece confrontations simply because it was normally how they were fought. Placing the left *ala* in the front lines hardly signifies much since there were only two to choose from. Note by way of contrast that the legionary numbers in each case were different—the first legion in 212; the fifth in 210 (Livy 25.21.6; 27.1.8). Altogether, the assertion of parallelism in the two accounts lacks substance, and each should be considered a distinct event.

Bibliography

Adcock, Frank E. *The Roman Art of War*. Cambridge, Mass., 1940.
Afzelius, A. "Zur Definition der römischen Nobilität vor der Zeit Ciceros." *Class. et Med.* 7 (1945): 150–200.
Alföldi, A. *Early Rome and the Latins*. Ann Arbor, Mich., 1963.
Astin, Alan E. "The *Lex Annalis* before Sulla." *Latomus* 16 (1957): 558–613, 17 (1958): 49–64. Also published as *The Lex Annalis before Sulla*. Brussels, 1958.
———. "The Roman Commander in Hispania Ulterior." *Historia* 13 (1964): 245–54.
———. *Scipio Aemilianus*. Oxford, 1967.
———. *Cato the Censor*. Oxford, 1978.
———. "Regimen Morum." *JRS* 78 (1988): 14–34.
Badian, Ernst. "Lex Acilia Repetundarum." *AJPh* 75 (1954): 374–84.
———. *Foreign Clientelae*. Oxford, 1958.
———. *Studies in Greek and Roman History*. Oxford, 1964.
———. "Notes on Provincia Gallia in the Late Republic." In *Mélanges Piganiol*, 3 vols., 901–18. Paris, 1966.
———. "Sulla's Augurate." *Arethusa* 1 (1968): 26–46.
———. *Titus Quinctius Flamininus: Philhellenism and Realpolitik*. Cincinnati, 1970.
———. *Roman Imperialism in the Late Republic*. 2d ed. Ithaca, N.Y., 1971.
———. "Tiberius Gracchus and the Beginning of the Roman Revolution." *ANRW* 1.1 (1972): 668–731.
———. "The Death of Saturninus." *Chiron* 14 (1984): 101–147.
Balsdon, J. P. V. D. "L. Cornelius Scipio: A Salvage Operation." *Historia* 21 (1972): 224–34.
Βασης, Σ. "ΖΗΤΗΜΑΤΑ ΡΩΜΑΙΚΑ." *ΑΘΗΝΑ* 7 (1895): 142–44.
Bates, Richard L. "*Rex in Senatu*: A Political Biography of M. Aemilius Scaurus." *PAPhS* 130 (1986): 251–88.
Bauman, Richard A. "The Abrogation of *Imperium*: Some Cases and a Principle." *RhM*, n.s., 111 (1968): 37–50.
———. *The Crimen Maiestatis in the Roman Republic and Augustan Principate*. Johannesburg, 1970.
Bayet, J. "Les malédictions du tribun C. Ateius Capito." In *Hommages à Georges Dumézil*, 31–45. Paris, 1960.
———. *Croyances et rites dans la Rome antique*. Paris, 1971.

Beard, Mary, and Michael Crawford. *Rome in the Late Republic: Problems and Interpretations*. London, 1985.
Billows, Richard. "Legal Fiction and Political Reform at Rome in the Early Second Century B.C." *Phoenix* 43 (1989): 112–33.
Broughton, T. Robert S. *Magistrates of the Roman Republic*. 3 vols. Chico, Calif., 1951–84.
Brunt, Peter A. Review of *Tiberius Gracchus*, by Donald Earl. *Gnomon* 37 (1965): 189–92.
———. *Italian Manpower, 225 B.C.–A.D. 14*. Oxford, 1971.
———. "Nobilitas and Novitas." *JRS* 72 (1982): 1–17.
———. *The Fall of the Roman Republic and Related Essays*. Oxford, 1988.
Caltabiano, M. "La morte del console Marcello nella tradizione storiografica." *CISA* 3 (1975): 65–81.
Calvert, R. L. "M. Claudius Marcellus, cos. II 155 B.C." *Ath.*, n.s. 39 (1961): 11–23.
Campbell, Brian. *The Emperor and the Roman Army, 31 B.C.–A.D. 235*. Oxford, 1984.
———. "Teach Yourself How to Be a General." *JRS* 77 (1987): 13–29.
Carney, Thomas Francis. *A Biography of C. Marius*. Assen, Neth., 1961.
———. "Prosopography: Payoffs and Pitfalls." *Phoenix* 27 (1973): 156–79.
Cichorius, C. *Römische Studien, historisches, epigraphisches, literargeschichtliches aus Vier Jahrhunderten Roms*. Leipzig, 1922.
Combès, Robert. *Imperator: Recherches sur l'emploi et la signification du titre d'imperator dans la Rome républicaine*. Paris, 1966.
Cornell, T. J. "Some Observations on the *Crimen Incesti*." In *Le délit religieux dans la cité antique*, 27–37. Rome, 1981.
———. Review of *Cleo's Cosmetics*, by T. P. Wiseman. *JRS* 72 (1982): 203–6.
Crake, J. E. A. *Archival Material in Livy*. Ph.D. diss., Johns Hopkins University, 1939.
Crawford, Michael. "Foedus and Sponsio." *PBSR* 41 (1973): 1–7.
———. *Roman Republican Coinage*. 2 vols. Cambridge, 1974.
———. *The Roman Republic*. Atlantic Highlands, N.J., 1978.
Culham, Phyllis. "Chance, Command, and Chaos in Ancient Military Engagements." *World Futures: The Journal of General Evolution* 27 (1989): 191–205.
Degrassi, A. *Inscriptiones Italicae*. Vol. 13, *Fasti et Elogia*. Rome, 1947.
Develin, R. *Patterns in Office-Holding, 366–49 B.C.* Brussels, 1979.
———. *The Practice of Politics at Rome, 366–167 B.C.* Brussels, 1985.
Dorey, T. A. "Scipio Africanus as a Party Leader." *Klio* 34 (1961): 191–98.
Duffy, Christopher. *The Military Experience in the Age of Reason*. London, 1987.
Dumézil, Georges. *Archaic Roman Religion*. Translated by P. Krapp. 2 vols. Chicago, 1970.
Dyson, Stephen L. *The Creation of the Roman Frontier*. Princeton, 1985.
Earl, Donald. *Tiberius Gracchus: A Study in Politics*. Brussels, 1963.
———. *The Political Thought of Sallust*. Amsterdam, 1966.

———. *The Moral and Political Tradition of Rome*. Ithaca, N.Y., 1967.
Eckstein, Arthur M. "T. Quinctius Flamininus and the Campaign against Philip in 198 B.C." *Phoenix* 30 (1976): 119–42.
———. "Human Sacrifice and Fear of Military Disaster in Republican Rome." *AJAH* 7 (1982): 69–95.
———. *Senate and General: Individual Decision-Making and Roman Foreign Relations, 264–194 B.C.* Berkeley and Los Angeles, 1987.
Eisenhut, Werner. *Virtus Romana: Ihre Stellung im römischen Wertsystem*. Munich, 1973.
Epstein, David F. *Personal Enmity in Roman Politics, 218–43 B.C.* London, 1987.
Erkell, Harry. *Augustus, Felicitas, Fortuna*. Göteborg, 1952.
Finley, M. I. *Politics in the Ancient World*. Cambridge, 1983.
Frank, T. "Two Historical Themes in Roman Literature." *CPh* 21 (1926): 311–17.
Fussell, Paul. *Wartime: Understanding and Behavior in the Second World War*. Oxford, 1989.
Gabba, E. "Ricerche su alcuni punti di storia mariana." *Ath.*, n.s. 29 (1951): 12–24.
———. *Republican Rome, The Army and the Allies*. Translated by P. J. Cuff, Berkeley and Los Angeles, 1976.
Garoufalias, Petros. *Pyrrhus, King of Epirus*. London, 1979.
Geer, R. M. "M. Aemilius Scaurus (Suetonius *Nero* ii.1 and Asconius on Cicero *Pro Scauro* 1)." *CPh* 24 (1929): 292–94.
Gelzer, M. "Römische Politik bei Fabius Pictor." *Hermes* 68 (1933): 129–66.
———. *Kleine Schriften*. 3 vols. Wiesbaden, 1962–64.
———. *The Roman Nobility*. Translated by R. Seager. Oxford, 1969.
Green, Peter. "The First Sicilian Slave Wars." *Past and Present* 20 (1961): 10–29.
Griffen, Jasper. "Propertius and Antony." *JRS* 67 (1977): 17–26.
Gruen, Erich S. "Political Prosecutions in the 90's B.C." *Historia* 15 (1966): 32–64.
———. *Roman Politics and the Criminal Courts, 149–78 B.C.* Cambridge, Mass., 1968.
———. "The Trial of C. Antonius." *Latomus* 32 (1973): 301–10.
———. *The Last Generation of the Roman Republic*. Berkeley and Los Angeles, 1974.
———. "The Consular Elections for 216 B.C. and the Veracity of Livy." *CSCA* 11 (1978): 61–74.
———. *The Hellenistic World and the Coming of Rome*. Berkeley and Los Angeles, 1984.
Hackl, Ursula. *Senat und Magistratur in Rom von der Mitte des 2. Jahrhunderts v. Chr. bis zur Diktatur Sullas*. Kallmünz, 1982.
Hallett, J. *Fathers and Daughters in Roman Society*. Princeton, N.J., 1984.
Hansen, Mogens Herman. *Eisangelia: The Sovereignty of the People's Court in Athens*. Odense, 1975.

Harmand, J. *L'armée et le soldat à Rome de 107 à 50 avant notre ère.* Paris, 1967.
Harris, William V. *War and Imperialism in Republican Rome, 327–70 B.C.* Oxford, 1979.
Hartfield, Mary. "The Roman Dictatorship: Its Character and Its Evolution." Ph.D. diss., University of California, Berkeley, 1982.
Holladay, A. J., and M. D. Goodman. "Religious Scruples in Ancient Warfare." *CQ* 36 (1986): 151–71.
Holleaux, M. "Στρατηγὸς ἀνθύπατος." *Rev. Arch.* 8, ser. 5 (1918): 221–38.
Hopkins, Keith. *Conquerors and Slaves.* Sociological Studies in Roman History, vol. 1. Cambridge, 1978.
———. *Death and Renewal.* Sociological Studies in Roman History, vol. 2. Cambridge, 1984.
Janssen, J. "De Fontibus Inter Se Contaminatis Apud Livium." *Mnemosyne* 54 (1926): 189–94.
Jocelyn, H. D. "The Roman Nobility and the Religion of the Republican State." *JRH* 4 (1966–67): 89–104.
———. "Varro's *Antiquitates Rerum Divinarum* and Religious Affairs in the Late Roman Republic." *Bull. J. Rylands Lib.* 65 (1982): 148–205.
Keaveney, Arthur. *Sulla: The Last Republican.* London, 1982.
———. "Sulla Augur." *AJAH* 7 (1982): 150–71.
———. "Sulla and the Gods." In *Studies in Latin Literature and Roman History*, 3:44–79. Brussels, 1983.
Keegan, John. *The Face of Battle.* London, 1976.
———. *The Mask of Command.* London, 1988.
Keppie, Lawrence. *The Making of the Roman Army from Republic to Empire.* London, 1984.
Klotz, A. "Über die Stellung des Cassius Dio unter die Quellen zur Geschichte des zweiten punischen Krieges. Eine Vorarbeit zur Quellenanalyse der dritten Dekade Livius." *RhM* 85 (1936): 68–116.
Konrad, C. F. "Cotta off Mellaria and the Identities of Fufidius." *CPh* 84 (1989): 119–29.
Kromayer, J., and G. Veith. *Heerwesen und Kriegsführung der Griechen und Römer.* Munich, 1928.
Latte, Kurt. *Römische Religionsgeschichte.* Munich, 1960.
Le Bonniec, H. "Aspects religieux de la guerre à Rome." In *Problèmes de la guerre à Rome*, ed. J. P. Brisson, 101–15. Paris, 1969.
Lefkowitz, Mary R. "Pyrrhus' Negotiations with the Romans, 280–278 B.C." *HSCPh* 64 (1959): 147–77.
Lengle, J. "Die Verurteilung der römischen Feldherrn von Arausio." *Hermes* 66 (1931): 302–16.
Liebeschuetz, John H. W. G. *Continuity and Change in Roman Religion.* Oxford, 1979.
Lind, L. R. "Concept, Action and Character: The Reasons for Rome's Greatness." *TAPhA* 103 (1972): 235–83.
Linderski, Jerzy. Review of *L'ordre équestre*, by Claude Nicolet, vol. 2. *CPh* 72 (1977): 55–60.

———. "Cicero and Roman Divination." *PP* 37 (1983): 12–38.
———. "Augural Law." *ANRW* 2.16.3 (1986): 2146–2312.
MacBain, Bruce. *Prodigy and Expiation: A Study in Religion and Politics in Republican Rome.* Brussels, 1982.
MacMullen, Ramsey. "Roman Elite Motivation: Three Questions." *Past and Present* 88 (1980): 3–16.
Malcovati, H. "Ad Cic. Fam. 9,21,3." In *Studi in onore di G. Funaioli*, 216–20. Rome, 1955.
Malcovati, H., ed. *Oratorum Romanorum Fragmenta Liberae Rei Publicae.* 2 vols. 4th ed. Turin, 1976.
Marshall, Bruce A. *Crassus: A Political Biography.* Amsterdam, 1976.
———. *A Historical Commentary on Asconius.* Columbia, Mo., 1985.
Michels, Agnes K. *The Calendar of the Roman Republic.* Princeton, N.J., 1967.
Millar, Fergus. "The Political Character of the Classical Roman Republic." *JRS* 74 (1984): 1–19.
———. "Politics, Persuasion, and the People before the Social War (150–90 B.C.)." *JRS* 76 (1986): 1–11.
Mitchell, T. N. "Cicero on the Moral Crisis of the Late Republic." *Hermathena* 136 (1984): 21–41.
Mommsen, Theodor. *Römisches Staatsrecht.* 3 vols. Leipzig, 1888.
———. *A History of Rome.* Translated by W. Dickson. New York, 1895.
———. *Römisches Strafrecht.* Reprint. Graz, 1955.
Morgan, M. Gwyn. "Polybius and the Date of the Battle of Panormus." *CQ* 22 (1972): 121–29.
———. "Cornelius and the Pannonians: Appian, *Illyrica* 14,41 and Roman History 143–138 B.C." *Historia* 23 (1974): 183–216.
Münzer, F. *Römische Adelsparteien und Adelsfamilien.* Stuttgart, 1920.
Niccolini, G. *I fasti dei tribuni della plebs.* Milan, 1954.
Nicolet, Claude. "Armée et société à Rome sous la république: à propos de l'ordre équestre." In *Problèmes de la guerre à Rome,* ed. J. P. Brisson, 117–56. Paris, 1969.
———. *The World of the Citizen in Republican Rome.* Translated by P. S. Falla. Berkeley and Los Angeles, 1980.
Nisbet, R. G. M., ed. *M. Tulli Ciceronis In L. Calpurnium Pisonem Oratio.* Oxford, 1961.
Nissen, H. "Der Caudinische Friede." *RhM* 25 (1870): 1–65.
North, John. "Conservatism and Change in Roman Religion." *PBSR* 44, n.s. 30 (1976): 1–12.
———. "The Development of Roman Imperialism." *JRS* 71 (1981): 1–9.
———. "Democratic Politics in Republican Rome." *Past and Present* 126 (1990), forthcoming.
———. "Power and Aristocracy in Republican Rome." *CPh* 85 (1990), 3–21.
Oakley, S. P. "Single Combat in the Roman Republic," *CQ* 35 (1985): 342–410.
Ogilvie, R. M. *A Commentary on Livy I–V.* Oxford, 1965.

Passerini, A. "Caio Mario come uomo politico." *Ath.*, n.s. 12 (1934): 10–44, 109–43, 257–97, 348–80.
Peter, H. *Historicorum Romanorum Reliquiae*. 2 vols. Reprint. Stuttgart, 1967.
Pritchett, W. Kendrick. *The Greek State at War*. 4 vols. Berkeley and Los Angeles, 1971–85.
Rawson, Elizabeth. "Scipio, Laelius, Furius, and the Ancestral Religion." *JRS* 63 (1973): 161–74.
———. "Religion and Politics in the Late Second Century B.C. at Rome." *Phoenix* 28 (1974): 193–212.
Rich, John W. *Declaring War in the Roman Republic in the Period of Transmarine Expansion*. Brussels, 1976.
———. "The Supposed Roman Manpower Shortage of the Later Second Century B.C." *Historia* 32 (1983): 287–331.
Richardson, J. S. *Hispaniae: Spain and the Development of Roman Imperialism, 218–82 B.C.* Cambridge, 1986.
———. "The Purpose of the *Lex Calpurnia de Repetundis*." *JRS* 77 (1987): 1–12.
Roberts, Jennifer Tolbert. *Accountability in Athenian Government*. Madison, Wisc., 1982.
Rosenstein, Nathan. "*Imperatores Victi*: The Case of C. Hostilius Mancinus." *Class. Ant.* 5 (1986): 230–52.
Rubinsohn, Zeev. "The Viriatic War and Its Roman Repercussions." *RSA* 11 (1981): 161–204.
———. "Some Remarks on the Causes and Repercussions of the So-Called 'Second Slave Revolt' in Sicily." *Ath.*, n.s. 60 (1982): 436–51.
Salmon, Edward T. *Samnium and the Samnites*. Ithaca, N.Y., 1967.
Sanctis, G. de. *Storia dei Romani*. 4 vols. 2d ed. Florence, 1956.
Scheid, John. "Le délit religieux dans la Rome tardo-républicaine." In *Le délit religieux dans la cité antique*, 117–71. Rome, 1981.
Schilling, Robert. "A propos des 'exta': L'extispicine etrusque et la 'litatio' romaine." In *Hommages à Albert Grenier*, 1371–78. Brussels, 1962.
Schleussner, Bernhard. *Die Legaten der römischen Republic*. Munich, 1978.
Schochat, Yanir. *Recruitment and the Programme of Tiberius Gracchus*. Brussels, 1980.
Scullard, H. H. *Roman Politics, 220–150 B.C.* 2d ed. Oxford, 1973.
Seager, Robin. "*Factio*: Some Observations." *JRS* 62 (1972): 53–58.
———. *Pompey: A Political Biography*. Oxford, 1979.
Shackleton-Bailey, D. R. "The Roman Nobility in the Second Civil War." *CQ* 54 (1960): 253–67.
Shackleton-Bailey, D. R., ed. *Cicero's Letters to Atticus*. 7 vols. Cambridge, 1965–70.
———. *Cicero: Epistulae Ad Familiares*. 2 vols. Cambridge, 1977.
Shatzman, I. "The Roman General's Authority over Booty." *Historia* 21 (1972): 177–205.
———. *Senatorial Wealth and Roman Politics*. Brussels, 1975.
Sherwin-White, A. N. "Violence in Roman Politics." *JRS* 46 (1956): 1–9.

Simon, Helmut. *Roms Kriege in Spanien*. Frankfurt, 1962.
Smith, R. E. *Service in the Post-Marian Army*. Manchester, 1958.
Spann, P. O. "C., L. or M. Cotta and the 'Unspeakable' Fufidius." *CJ* 82 (1986–87): 306–9.
Stambaugh, J. E. "The Functions of Roman Temples." *ANRW* 2.16.1 (1978): 554–608.
Stockton, David. "The First Consulship of Pompey." *Historia* 22 (1973): 205–18.
Strong, D. E. "The Administration of Public Building in Rome during the Late Republic and Early Empire." *BICS* 15 (1968): 97–109.
Sumner, G. V. *The Orators in Cicero's Brutus: Prosopography and Chronology*. Toronto, 1973.
———. "The Pompeii in their Families." *AJAH* 2 (1977): 8–25.
Suolahti, J. *Junior Officers of the Roman Army in the Republican Period*. Helsinki, 1955.
———. "*Claudia Insons*: Why Was a Fine Imposed on Claudia Ap.f. in 246 B.C.?" *Arctos* 11 (1977): 133–51.
Syme, Ronald. *The Roman Revolution*. Oxford, 1939.
———. "Missing Senators." *Historia* 4 (1955): 52–77.
———. "Piso Frugi and Cassius Frugi." *JRS* 50 (1960): 12–20.
———. *Sallust*. Berkeley and Los Angeles, 1964.
———. "The Stemma of the Sentii Saturnini." *Historia* 13 (1964): 156–66.
———. *Roman Papers*. 5 vols. Oxford, 1979–88.
Szemler, G. *The Priests of the Roman Republic*. Brussels, 1972.
Szidat, Joachim. *Caesars diplomatische Tätigkeit im gallischen Krieg*. Wiesbaden, 1970.
Taylor, Lily Ross. "New Light on the History of the Secular Games." *AJPh* 55 (1934): 101–20.
———. "The Opportunities for Dramatic Performances in the Time of Plautus and Terence." *TAPhA* 68 (1937): 284–304.
———. *Party Politics in the Age of Caesar*. Berkeley and Los Angeles, 1949.
———. *Roman Voting Assemblies from the Hannibalic War to the Dictatorship of Caesar*. Ann Arbor, Mich., 1966.
Toynbee, Arnold. *Hannibal's Legacy*. 2 vols. Oxford, 1965.
Tromp, S. P. C. *De Romanorum Piaculis*. Lugduni Batavorum, 1921.
Twyman, B. L. "The Consular Elections for 216 B.C. and the *Lex Maenia de Patrum Auctoritate*." *CPh* 79 (1984): 285–94.
Tyrell, R., and L. Pruser, eds. *The Correspondence of M. Tullius Cicero*. 7 vols. Dublin, 1879–1901.
Valeton, I. M. J. "De Modis Auspicandi Romanorum." *Mnemosyne*, n.s. 17 (1889): 275–325, 418–52; 18 (1890): 208–63, 406–56.
Van Doren, M. "*Peregrina Sacra*, Offizielle Kultübertragungen im alten Rom." *Historia* 3 (1954): 488–97.
Van Ooteghem, J. *L. Licinius Lucullus*. Brussels, 1954.
Versnel, H. *Triumphus: An Inquiry into the Origin, Development and Meaning of the Roman Triumph*. Leiden, 1970.

Vretska, Karl. *C. Sallustius Crispus, De Catilinae Coniuratione*. 2 vols. Heidelberg, 1976.
Walbank, Frank W. *A Historical Commentary on Polybius*. 3 vols. Oxford, 1957–79.
Ward, Allen M. *Marcus Crassus and the Late Roman Republic*. Columbia, Mo., 1977.
Wardman, Alan. *Religion and Statecraft among the Romans*. London, 1982.
Weinstock, S. "Pax and the Ara Pacis." *JRS* 50 (1960): 44–58.
———. *Divus Julius*. Oxford, 1971.
Wiedemann, T. "The Fetiales: A Reconsideration." *CQ* 36 (1986): 478–90.
Wikander, O. "Caius Hostilius Mancinus and the *Foedus Numantium*." *Opuscula Romana* vol. 11, no. 7 (1976): 84–104.
Will, W. "Imperatores Victi: Zum Bild besiegter römischer Consuln bei Livius." *Historia* 32 (1983): 173–82.
Willems, Pierre. *Le sénat de la république romaine, sa composition et ses attributions*. 2 vols. Louvain, 1878–85.
Williams, Richard. "The Appointment of Glabrio (cos. 67) to the Eastern Command." *Phoenix* 38 (1984): 221–34.
Wiseman, T. P. *New Men in the Roman Senate, 139 B.C.–A.D. 14*. Oxford, 1971.
———. *Cinna the Poet, and Other Roman Essays*. Leicester, 1974.
———. *Cleo's Cosmetics*. Leicester, 1979.
Wiseman, T. P., ed. *Roman Political Life, 90 B.C.–A.D. 69*. Exeter, 1985.
Wissowa, Georg. *Religion und Kultus der Römer*. 2d ed. Munich, 1912.
Wistrand, E. *Felicitas Imperatoria*. Göteborg, 1987.
Zieske, Lothar. *Felicitas: Eine Wortuntersuchung*. Hamburg, 1972.
Zippel, G. *Die römische Herrschaft in Illyrien bis auf Augustus*. Leipzig, 1877.

Index

Acilius Glabrio, M'. (cos. suff. 154, app. 1.1 no. 1), 45n
Aediles, 4, 131; religious duties of, 60
Aelius Paetus, P. (cos. 201, app. 1.1 no. 2), 15n; election to censorship, 25
Aemilius Lepidus Porcina, M. (cos. 137, app. 1.1 no. 3), 3n, 14n, 21, 38, 39, 40, 151n, 159; recall of, 38, 42
Aemilius Paullus, L. (cos. 219, app. 1.2 no. 1), 12n, 30, 98, 118n, 122, 140; death of, 123
Aemilius Paullus, L. (cos. 182), 30, 138n
Aemilius Paullus, M. (cos. 255), 42n
Aemilius Scaurus, M. (cos. 115), 61–62, 63n, 128n; prosecution of, 161
Alexander the Great, 130n
Allia, battle of, 73, 84, 158
Ambition, personal: repression of, 5
Amicitia (friendship), 51, 155
Anicius Gallus, L. (cos. 160), 26
Antonius, M. (cos. 99), 125–27, 128
Antonius Hibrida, C. (cos. 63, app. 1.1 no. 4), 11, 15n; cowardice of, 145; prosecution of, 144–45, 151
Apuani (Ligurian tribe), 28
Aquinius, L. (*haruspex*), 73–74
Arausio, battle of, 12, 38, 47–48, 62n, 125; political aftermath of, 49, 161; and religious causes for defeat, 61
Aristocracy: authority of, 177; cohesiveness of, 178; control over religious matters, 62n, 63; expansion of, 167; maintenance of status of, 153, 175–76; myth of competency of, 172–73; in Roman army, 109–11, 174
Aristocratic competition, xi, 2, 6, 10, 46, 48, 91, 148; under Augustus, 164; limitations on, 114, 156–57
Aristocratic ethos, 114–15, 128, 130–31; consequences of violation, 148; and defeated generals, 138, 140, 150–52, 153, 160–61; definition of, 116; in late Republic, 131–32; and views on death, 136
Aristonicus (pretender), 122
Aristotle, 166–67
Armilustrium (festival), 54n
Army, Carthaginian, 99
Army, Roman: composition of, 109–10; cowardice in, 100–102; drilling of, 98–99, 112–13; and negotiations with the enemy, 133–35; proletarianization of, 50; slaves in, 102; tactical formations in, 95–96
Arrius, Q. (propr.? 72, app. 1.1 no. 5), 17, 22n
Ateius Capito, C. (tr. pl. 55), 71
Athens, 9; military failures at, 164–67
Atilius Caiatinus, A. (cos. 258), 36
Atilius Regulus, C. (cos. 225), 118n
Atilius Regulus, M. (cos. 256), 121
Atilius Serranus, A. (pr. 192), 170n
Atinius, C. (pr. 188), 118n
Auctoritas (authority), 2, 5, 40; and voters, 155
Augurs, 61, 66, 73, 74; regulations governing, 64n
Augustus, 119, 132, 164
Aurelius Cotta, L. (cos. 144), 31–32
Aurelius Cotta, M. (cos. 74, app. 1.1 no. 7?), 3n, 29n, 33n, 138n
Aurelius Scaurus, M. (cos. 108, app. 1.2 no. 2), 118n, 122, 135n
Aurunculeius Cotta, L. (legate 54), 118n
Auspices, 54, 57n, 59, 64–65, 162; at battle of Cannae, 85; and military actions, 60

Baebius Tamphilius, Cn. (cos. 182, app. 1.1 no. 8), 16, 24–25, 41; consulship of, 29
Bastarnae (Thracian tribe), 145
Boii (Gallic tribe), 11, 17

218   Index

Caecilius Metellus Macedonicus, Q. (cos. 143), 14, 26
Caecilius Metellus Numidicus, Q. (cos. 109), 124
Caecilius Metellus Pius, Q. (cos. 80, 33, 138n
Caelius Rufus, M. (pr. 48), 93, 117, 145
Calpurnius Piso, C. (cos. 180), 138n
Calpurnius Piso, Q. (cos. 135, app. 1.1 no. 10), 21
Calpurnius Piso Caesoninus, L. (cos. 148, app. 1.1 no. 12), 16, 18; as censor, 20; election to consulship, 29
Calpurnius Piso Caesoninus, L. (cos. 58), 15n, 30, 52–53
Calpurnius Piso Frugi, L. (cos. 133, app. 1.1 no. 13), 15n; election to consulship, 29
Calpurnius Piso Frugi, L. (pr. 112), 118n
Candidates, spending of, 2
Cannae, battle of, 30, 35, 41, 122–23; aftermath of, 102–4, 139, 164; losses at, 32; political consequences of, 49; preparations for, 98; and religious transgressions, 68–70, 74, 85
Carrhae, battle of, 71, 72n, 162
Carthage, military failure at, 9
Cassius Longinus, C. (cos. 73, app. 1.1 no. 14), 3n, 21
Cassius Longinus, L. (cos. 107, app. 1.2 no. 4), 118n, 137
Caudine Forks, battle of, 43, 70
Celtiberians, 14
Censorship (office), 4, 15, 20, 168, 170, 173; election to, 50, 154; and military failure, 13
Centenius, C. (propr. 217), 34
Centenius Paenula, M., 11n, 118n, 122nn
Centuriate assembly. See *Comitia centuriata*
Centurions, role of in army, 109
Chickens (as auspices), 81, 85
Cicero: advice to Lentulus Spinther, 78–79; and consulship of Cornelius Scipio, 32n; criticism of Calpurnius Piso, 11n, 15n, 52–53, 173n; and defeat of Crassus, 72n, 123n; as governor of Cilicia, 93, 117, 132; on influence of soldiery, 10n; and prosecution of Caepio, 125–28; and prosecution of Carbo, 142; and religious causes of victory, 161; struggle with Clodius, 123–24; and taking of auspices, 205; and war against Mithridates, 101
Cimbri (Germanic tribe), 127, 141
Cincius Alimentus, L. (historian), 99n
Cinnae dominatio, 23
Civil war, 5; between Pompey and Caesar, 13
Claudius Caecus, Ap. (cos. 307), 24, 165
Claudius Centho, Ap. (pr. 175, app. 1.1 no. 16), 11n, 24, 33
Claudius Glaber, C. (pr. 73, app. 1.1 no. 17), 18, 23
Claudius Marcellus, M. (cos. 222, app. 1.1 no. 18), 12, 25, 29n, 36n, 38n, 79n, 118n, 131, 139; as *augur optimus*, 81; defeat by Hannibal, 104, 105n, 138; and discipline of soldiers, 109n
Claudius Marcellus, M. (cos. 196, app. 1.1 no. 19), 15n, 45n, 138n; triumph of, 42
Claudius Marcellus, M. (cos. 166), 169
Claudius Pulcher, Ap. (cos. 212), 43
Claudius Pulcher, Ap. (cos. 143), 20–21, 72n, 88, 138n
Claudius Pulcher, P. (cos. 249, app. 1.1 no. 20), 35, 36, 39, 40, 106n; defeat at Drepana, 79; impiety of, 43, 80, 84–85, 90, 151, 158; public opinion on, 11; sons of, 46
Claudius Sabinus, Ap. (cos. 471), 157, 158n
Claudius Unimanus (pr. 146, app. 1.1 no. 21), 23
Clients, 155; in elections, 51
Cluvius Saxula, C. (pr. 178?), 170n
Coelius, L. (legate 170, app. 1.1 no. 22), 11n
Comitia centuriata (centuriate assembly), 7, 10, 37, 50, 115, 164; structure of, 153–56
Comitia curiata, 70
Consuls, sons of, 44–46
Consulship: election to, 50, 154; privileges of, 2; prorogation of, 170; tenure of, 168–70, 171
Contio (public meeting), 155
Cornelius Lentulus Clodianus, Cn. (cos. 72, app. 1.1 no. 24), 14, 15n, 38, 40, 41; abrogation of, 39; election to censorship, 25
Cornelius Lentulus Lupus, L. (cos. 156, app. 1.1 no. 24), 12n, 13, 15n, 18n, 45n
Cornelius Lentulus Spinther, P. (cos. 57), 78–79

Index 219

Cornelius Lentulus Sura, P. (cos. 71), 170n
Cornelius Merula, L. (cos. 193), 11, 105n
Cornelius Rufinus, P. (cos. 290), 11n, 138n
Cornelius Scipio, Cn. (cos. 222, app. 1.2 no. 5), 118n
Cornelius Scipio, P. (cos. 218, app. 1.1 no. 25), 32, 118n; defeat on the Ticinus, 105, 119n
Cornelius Scipio Aemilianus, P. (cos. 147), 30, 100–101
Cornelius Scipio Africanus, P. (cos. 205), 30, 82, 108, 119
Cornelius Scipio Asiaticus, L. (cos. 190), 32, 41, 82
Cornelius Scipio Asina, Cn. (cos. 260, app. 1.1 no. 26), 18, 30; second consulship of, 29; surrender of, 16, 121
Cornelius Scipio Barbatus, L. (cos. 298, app. 1.1 no. 27), 15n
Cornelius Scipio Nasica Serapio, P. (cos. 138, app. 1.1 no. 43), 14n, 26
Cornelius Sulla Felix, L. (cos. 88), 23, 109n, 138; conduct as general, 118, 120
Cosinius, L. (pr. 73), 118n
Courts, composition of, 3
Cowardice: in battle, 22; and prosecution of defeated generals, 145–46
Cremera, battle of, 70, 73, 157
Crucifixion, of Carthaginian generals, 9
Cult, 160; deliberate violation of, 77–78; execution of, 58; formal requirements of, 66; functioning of, 55, 113; ritual errors in, 61, 63, 73–74, 77, 86, 92, 162, 174. *See also* Rituals, execution of
Cunctatio (strategy), 36
Curius Dentatus, M'. (cos. 290), 169n
Cursus honorum, 16, 18, 24, 25, 43; and military defeat, 20
Curule offices, 1n

Decemviri Sacris Faciundis, 60–61, 66; and Lake Trasimene, 58; and prodigies, 75
Decius Mus, P. (cos. 312), 118n
Decius Mus, P. (cos. 279, app. 1.1 no. 28), 118n
Defeat. *See* Military failure
Deities, Roman, 61, 75; access to, 87; belief in, 88–89; characteristics of, 56
Dictators, 33–37
Didius, T. (cos. 98), 118n

Dies atri (unlucky days), 73n, 81–82, 84, 85; at battle of Cannae, 85–86
Dies religiosi, 67–68, 82
Digitius, Sex. (pr. 194 app. 1.1 no. 29), 22n, 41
Dignitas (dignity), 1, 40; and public office, 2
Dio Cassius, 144–45
Diodorus Siculus, 143
Divine will, 110–11, 112, 114, 130, 153; and outcome of battles, 31, 36, 54, 92
Domitius Ahenobarbus, Cn. (cos. 96), 62n, 161
Domitius Calvinus, M. (pr. 80), 118n
Drepana, battle of, 11, 87n, 158

Equestrian centuries, 50, 154, 155n, 163
Equiria (festival), 54n
Extortion, trials for, 140–52

Fabius Ambustus, C. (cos. 358, app. 1.1 no. 30), 34, 41
Fabius Buteo, M. (cos. 245), 131
Fabius Hadrianus, M. (legate 68, app. 1.1 no. 31), 18
Fabius Maximus Gurges, Q. (cos. 292), 138n
Fabius Maximus Gurges, Q. (cos. 265), 11n, 40n, 118n
Fabius Maximus Servilianus, Q. (cos. 142, app. 1.1 no. 33), 20, 137n
Fabius Maximus Verrucosus, Q. (cos. 233), 34, 35, 38, 78n, 166
Fabius Pictor, Q. (historian), 98, 99n
Fabricius, C. (cos. 282), 106
Fama (reputation), in political contests, 7
Fetial priests, 54
First-class centuries, 50, 154, 155n, 163
Flamines (priests), 61
Flaminius, C. (cos. 223, app. 1.2 no. 6), 11n, 80, 82–83; death of, 34, 79, 116–17, 118n; religious transgressions of, 58, 77–78, 90
Flight from the enemy, 103, 104, 106–8, 109, 111, 129, 159
Foedus Caudinum, 35
Fortuna (of generals), 161–62
Fufidius, L. (pr. 81, app. 1.1 no. 34), 22n
Fulvius Centumalus, Cn. (cos. 211, app. 1.2, no. 7), 11n, 103n, 118n, 121n, 207, 208
Fulvius Flaccus, Cn. (pr. 212, app. 1.1 no. 35), 22, 103n, 132, 207; cowardice of, 129, 151; descendants of, 44, 46;

220   Index

Fulvius Flaccus, Cn. (*continued*)
  flight of, 127n, 128–29; prosecution
  of, 106–8, 120, 146
Fulvius Flaccus, Q. (cos. 237), 44, 129
Fulvius Nobilior, Q. (cos. 153, app. 1.1
  no. 36), 13–14, 18, 20, 88, 100n; as
  censor, 21; explanations for defeat,
  92
Fulvius Nobilior, ser. (cos. 255), naval
  triumph of, 42n
Furius Camillus, M. (dict. 390), 34
Furius Crassipes, M. (pr. 187), 170n
Furius Medullinus, L. (mil. tr. c. p.
  381, app. 1.1 no. 38), 11n, 15n
Furius Philus, L. (cos. 136), 14n

Games, public, 4, 60; repetition of, 59n
Gellius Poplicola, L. (cos. 72, app. 1.1
  no. 39), 14, 15n, 38, 40, 41; abrogation of, 39; election to censorship, 25
Generals: expectations of Romans for,
  117–21, 126, 130; selection of, 28–30
Generals, defeated: accountability of,
  112–13; and aristocratic ethos, 114–
  16, 130–31, 160; as censors, 21; conduct of in defeat, 148; cowardice of,
  145–46; deaths of, 122–23; and divine
  opposition, 72–73; election to consulship, 22–27; and execution of rituals,
  59, 63; and flight of soldiers, 107;
  and negotiations with the enemy,
  133–37; political careers of, 6–7, 13,
  18–19, 40–41, 46–47, 92–93, 114, 150,
  153, 177–78; religious obligations of,
  87; religious transgressions of, 78–
  81; sons of, 6, 43–46; survival of,
  121–22, 124; trials of, 47–48, 52, 124–
  30, 159–60; and *virtus*, 130–31, 132.
  See also Military failure
Genucius Aventinensis, L. (cos. 365),
  79n
Gescon (Carthaginian), 9n
Gloria (glory), 1, 122, 159, 168; in
  death, 176; and political careers, 7,
  174

Hamilcar, 9n
Hannibal: ambush of Claudius Marcellus, 79n; at battle of Cannae, 30, 35,
  70, 85, 99; at battle of Herdonia, 104;
  defeat of Claudius Marcellus, 12; defeat of Sempronius Longus, 32n, 92;
  defeats of Fulvius Flaccus and Fulvius Centumalus against, 207–8; at
  Lake Trasimene, 34, 96; march on
  Rome, 208; at Ticinus, 11

Hannibalic war, 131, 170n, 173
Heracleia, battle of, 106
Herdonia, battle of, 104, 120, 207
Hostilius Mancinus, A. (cos. 170, app.
  1.1 no. 40), 139n
Hostilius Mancinus, C. (cos. 137, app.
  1.1 no. 41), 12, 40, 46, 61, 87n, 139n,
  146, 160–61, 165, 170n; descendants
  of, 43; handed over to the enemy,
  148–50, 159; surrender to Numantines, 38, 39, 68, 100–101, 136–37,
  138, 148
Hostilius Mancinus, L., 121

Imagines (funeral masks), 175
Imperium: abrogation of, 39; prestige
  of, 33
Inimicitia (political enmity), 49, 115,
  127, 139, 177
Insubrian Gauls, 16
Istrians, 12
Iulius Caesar, C. (cos. 59), 17, 89n,
  101, 122, 135; conduct of as general,
  118, 120; defeat of at Dyrrachium, 92
Iulius Caesar, L. (cos. 90), 138n
Iunius Brutus, M. (tyrannicide), 119
Iunius Brutus Callaicus, D. (cos. 138,
  app. 1.1 no. 42), 33n, 39
Iunius Bubulcus Brutus, C. (cos. 291),
  11n, 138n
Iunius Pera, M. (cos. 230), 36n
Iunius Silanus, D. (pr. 141, app. 1.1
  no. 43), 22
Iunius Silanus, M. (cos. 109, app. 1.1
  no. 44), 21; prosecution of, 47–48,
  128, 159
Iuventius Thalna, P. (pr. 149), 118n

Jugurtha (king of Numidia), 17, 97,
  135, 138
Jugurthine War, 124
Juno, 68–69
Jupiter, 54, 60, 69n
Juries, composition of, 125n

Labienus, T. (pr. 59?), 101n
Lake Trasimene, battle of, 34, 78, 83,
  116–17; religious aspects of, 58
Latin Festival, 59
Legates, 110–11; role of in army, 109
Legiones Cannenses, 102–3, 107
Lex Claudia, 117n
Lex Genucia, 168
Lex Sempronia, 205
Licinius Crassus, M. (cos. 70, app. 1.2,
  no. 8), 15, 170n; religious transgres-

sions of, 71–72, 79, 162; and war with Spartacus, 38
Licinius Crassus, P. (cos. 171), 133, 134n, 147
Licinius Crassus Dives Mucianus, P. (cos. 131, app. 1.2 no. 9), 12, 118n
Licinius Lucullus, L. (pr. 104, app. 1.1 no. 46), 22; prosecution of, 49, 142–44, 159
Licinius Lucullus, L. (cos. 74, app. 1.1, no. 47), 11, 17, 101; religious transgressions of, 81–82
Licinius Murena, L. (pr. 88, app. 1.1 no. 48), 22, 42, 138n
Licinius Nerva, P. (pr. 104, app. 1.1 no. 49), 22
Ligurians, 15
Livius Macatus, M. (pref. 212, app. 1.1 no. 50), 11n
Livius Salinator, C. (cos. 188), 170n
Livy, 157, 158; account of Flaminius, 116–17, 120; and battles of Herdonia, 207; and trial of Flaccus, 129–30
Lucretius Gallus, C. (pr. 171), 3n
Lutatius Catulus, Q. (cos. 102), 33, 138n

Macedonian War, Second, 58n
Macedonian War, Third, 16
Magistracies, 2, 167–68; composition of, 3
Magistrates: competence of, 27; election of, 1; religious duties of, 56, 64, 65–66, 75n; restrictions on re-election of, 168–69
Mallius Maximus, Cn. (cos. 105, app. 1.1 no. 51), 39, 126n, 127, 159
Manilius, M'. (cos. 149, app. 1.1 no. 53), 16, 26, 156; as censor, 20; election to consulship, 28–29
Manlii (family), 22–23
Manlius Vulso, A. (cos. 178), 12, 33n, 138n; rout of, 38, 120
Manlius Vulso, L. (pr. 218, app. 1.1 no. 58), 17; defeat for consulship, 25; election to praetorship, 23
Manlius Vulso, P. (pr. 195), 170n
Marcius Censorinus L. (cos. 149, app. 1.1 no. 59), 15n, 20n; election to consulship, 25
Marcius Figulus, C. (cos. 162, app. 1.1 no. 60), 26, 29n
Marcius Philippus, Q. (cos. 186, app. 1.1 no. 61), 12, 15n, 18, 41; defeat of, 15–16, 28, 30; re-election to consulship, 28; political career of, 16

Marcius Rutilus, C. (cos. 357), 34
Marius, C. (cos. 107), 30n, 50, 128n, 169
Marius Gratidianus, M. (pr. 85), 170n
Menenius Lanatus, T. (cos. 477), 157
Metilius, M. (tr. pl. 217), 38
Military ethos, 105, 107, 111
Military failure: and abrogation of power, 37–39; changing attitudes toward, 157–58; characteristics of, 111–13; collective responsibility for, 110–11; consequences of, 9–10; danger of to state, 52; domestic consequences of, 165–66; effect of on elections, 30; extenuating circumstances in, 48–49, 93; in Greece, 9; moral aspects of, 115–16; political consequences of, 6–7, 18–19, 172–73; and promagistracy, 33; religious aspects of, 55, 57, 62, 66–67, 76, 92, 159; trials resulting from, 10. See also Generals, defeated
Minucius Rufus, M. (cos. 221, app. 1.1 no. 62), 11, 41, 105n
Mithridates (king of Pontus), 101, 161–62; defeat of Sothimus, 33n; defeat of Triarius, 11
Mucius Scaevola, Q. (cos. 95), 81n
Mummius, L. (cos. 146), 20, 26, 138n

Nearer Spain, campaigns in, 99, 147, 160–61
Nicias (Athenian general), 165, 166n
Nigidius, C. (pr. 145, app. 1.1 no. 64), 22n
Nobilitas (nobility), 1
Norbanus, C. (cos. 83), 125–26
Novi homines, 22, 24
Numantines, 14, 136, 146; negotiations of Mancinus with, 148–49

Octavius, Cn. (cos. 87), 123n
Omens, 90; definition of, 71. See also Prodigies (signs indicating crises)

Papirius Carbo, Cn. (cos. 113, app. 1.1 no. 65), 21; prosecution of, 141–42, 159
Papirius Cursor, L. (cos. 326), 34, 70–71, 80n
Patronage, 177; in elections, 51
Pax deorum, 54, 160, 161–62; belief in, 91; and blood sacrifice, 64–65; breakdowns in, 68–69, 72, 77, 86, 92, 94, 165; as limit to aristocratic competition, 56, 93; maintenance of, 55, 110–12; and military defeat, 173–74;

and religious transgressions, 72; respect of generals for, 85; rites governing, 81; role of ritual in, 60; and success in war, 163; and taking of auspices, 76
Penates, 59, 62n
Peperna, C. (legate 90, app. 1.1 no. 66), 23–24
Peperna, M. (cos. 130), 23
Perseus (king of Macedonia), 133
Petilius Spurinus, Q. (cos. 176), 89, 118n, 119n, 120, 138
Philippi, second battle of, 119
Plautius Hypsaeus, C. (pr. 146, app. 1.1 no. 67), 22, 44, 139, 144, 151, 159
Plautius Hypsaeus, L. (pr. 139, app. 1.1 no. 68), 22
Plautius Hypsaeus, M. (cos. 125), 44
Pleminius, Q. (legate 205), 108
Plutarch, 104, 106
Polybius, 133; account of Aemilius Paullus, 98–99; account of Flaminius, 116–17
Pompeius, Q. (cos. 141, app. 1.1 no. 69), 12, 14, 68, 100, 156, 161, 165; prosecution of, 146–48, 159
Pompeius, Sex. (pr. 119), 118n
Pompeius Magnus, Cn. (cos. 70), 15, 17, 33, 42, 138n, 170n; campaign against Mithridates, 161–63
Pontifex maximus, 65–66
Pontifices, 61, 74
Popillius Laenas, C. (legate 107), 137–38, 159
Popillius Laenas, M. (cos. 139, app. 1.1 no. 70), 21, 100
Porcius Cato, C. (cos. 114, app. 1.1 no. 71), 42; prosecution of, 141, 159
Porcius Cato, L. (cos. 89, app. 1.2 no. 10), 118n
Portents. *See* Prodigies (signs indicating crises)
Postumius, L. (pr. 90), 118n
Postumius Albinus, A. (cos. 99, app. 1.1 no. 72), 12, 17, 18, 41n, 135–36, 138, 165; surrender of, 97
Postumius Albinus, L. (cos.-elect 216, app. 1.2 no. 11), 118n, 121
Postumius Albinus, Sp. (cos. 321, app. 1.1 no. 73), 11n, 35, 36, 39
Postumius Albinus, Sp. (cos. 110, app. 1.1 no. 74), 135, 138, 159
Postumius Albinus Regillensis, M. (tr. mil. c. p. 426), 157–58
Praetorship: and election to consulship, 26; military duties of, 171; religious duties of, 60; tenure of, 170, 171
Principate, 164; soldiers in, 163
Prodigies (signs indicating crises), 69n, 70–71, 163; at battle of Cannae, 86; explanation of, 74, 75. *See also* Omens
Promagistrates, 47; auspicial powers of, 205; creation of, 32–33; religious duties of, 60
Provinces, consular: selection of, 30, 31
Ptolemy (king of Egypt), 78–79
Punicus (Lusitanian commander), 28
Punic Wars, 16, 35, 111
Pyrrhus (king of Epirus), 102n, 164–65; at Heraclea, 106

Quaestio Mamiliana (court), 136
Quaestors, 110, 131
Quinctius Cincinnatus Poenus, T. (tr. mil. c. p. 426), 157–58
Quinctius Crispinus, L. (pr. 186), 138n
Quinctius Crispinus, T. (cos. 208), 79n, 118n
Quinctius Flamininus, T. (cos. 198), 116, 117, 133
Quinctius (pr. 143, app. 1.1 no. 76), 23

Religion, Roman, xi, 54, 56–57; characteristics of, 74–75; and warfare, 54–57
Religious festivals, 3–4, 54
Repetundis. *See* Extortion, trials for
De Republica (Cicero), 42
Res publica (the state or public affairs), 2, 33, 166; and religious matters, 62; support of the gods for, 75
Rituals, execution of, 56–57, 63–64, 112. *See also* Cult
River Allia, battle of, 67
Roman Republic: development of, 157; entry into the aristocracy of, 1; factional politics in, 51–52; political culture of, 7, 48, 155, 156; political failure in, 4; political hierarchy of, 60; political history of, 5; regulation of government in, 4–6, 7–8
Rome: public buildings at, 2, 4; sack of by Gauls, 13, 67, 158
Rutilius Lupus, P. (cos. 90, app. 1.2 no. 12), 23, 79, 101n, 118n

Sacrifices, blood, 63–65
Salassi (Alpine tribe), 88
Salii (priests), 61, 82n
Sallust, 97, 121, 124

Scordisci (Thracian tribe), 141
Scribonius Curio, C. (propr. 49), 118n, 119, 122
Sempronius Atratinus, C. (cos. 423), 157–58
Sempronius Blaesus, C. (cos. 253), 42n
Sempronius Gracchus, Ti. (cos. 215), 80n, 118n
Sempronius Gracchus, Ti. (cos. 177), 4n
Sempronius Gracchus, Ti. (cos. 137), 136
Sempronius Longus, Ti. (cos. 218, app. 1.1 no. 78), 11–12, 21, 32n, 41, 106n; explanations of failure, 92
Sempronius Tuditanus, P. (cos. 204), 138n
Senate, 168; appointment of dictators, 33–37; authority of, 87, 160, 170; and battle of Cannae, 102–4; composition of, 1, 3; moral authority of, 128n; religious authority of, 62, 76; and selection of consular provinces, 31; and selection of military commanders, 31–37
Senatorial class, 154, 164, 175; military ambitions of, 49
Sentius, C. (pr. 94, app. 1.1 no. 79), 33n, 138n
Sergius Catilina, L. (pr. 68), 4, 97, 121, 167
Sergius Fidenus, M'. (tr. mil. c. p. 402), 158
Servilius, C. (pr. 102, app. 1.1 no. 80), 22, 49n, 160; prosecution of, 142–44
Servilius Caepio, Cn. (cos. 141), 3n, 14n
Servilius Caepio, Q. (cos. 106, app. 1.1 no. 81), 12, 39, 40, 106n, 132; abrogation of, 38; cowardice of, 126; exile of, 124, 126n; prosecution of, 49n, 124–28, 151, 159, 173n
Servilius Caepio, Q. (procos. 90), 118n
Servilius Geminus, Cn. (cos. 217), 34, 35, 98
Servilius Pulex Geminus, M. (cos. 202), 132n
Servilius Structus, Sp. (cos. 476), 157
Sibylline books, 60, 66, 69n, 88; and battle of Cannae, 70n; and Lake Trasimene, 58
Sicinius, Cn. (pr. 183), 170n
Slaves, in Roman army, 102
Social war, 101, 161
Soldiers, Roman, 114; at battle of Cannae, 102–3, 107; cowardice of, 104; discipline of, 96, 100–102, 106–9, 110, 112, 129, 153, 174; donatives to, 2; influence of in elections, 9–10; quality of, 94, 165; recruitment of, 108, 163
Sothimus (king of the Thracians), 33n
Spartacus, 14, 15n, 17; defeat of Gellius Poplicola, 25, 38, 39; and elections of 70 B.C., 21; threat of to Italy, 52
Standard-bearers, role of in army, 109
Status, preservation of, 114
Struggle of the Orders, 158
Sullan reforms, 1n
Sulpicius Galba, Ser. (cos. 144, app. 1.1 no. 82), 16, 26, 33n; defeat of, 31–32; as orator, 156
Sulpicius Longus, Q. (mil. tr. c. p. 390, app. 1.1 no. 83), 34
Sulpicius Peticus, C. (cos. 364), 34
Sulpicius Saverrio, P. (cos. 279, app. 1.1 no. 84), 18, 21
Surrender, 36; Roman view of, 121

Terentius Varro, C. (cos. 216, app. 1.1 no. 85), 11n, 32, 40, 41, 85, 103, 123; and aftermath of Cannae, 139–40; promagistracy of, 33, 35, 105n; religious transgressions of, 68–69, 84–85
Thorius Balbus, L. (legate 79), 118n
Thucydides, 9
Tigranes (king of Armenia), 82
Tigrini (Gallic tribe), 137
Titurius Sabinus, Q. (legate 54), 11n
Tribunes, military, 108–9, 110
Tribunes of the plebs, 131, 158
Tullius Cicero, Q. (pr. 62), 134, 147
Turpilius Silanus, T. (prefect 109), 124

Valerius Laevinus, P. (cos. 280, app. 1.1 no. 89), 11n, 106, 119n
Valerius Triarius, C. (legate 67, app. 1.1 no. 90), 11; defeat by Mithridates, 42
Varinius, P. (pr. 73, app. 1.1 no. 91), 22n, 170n
Veii, siege of, 158
Verginius Esquilinus, L. (tr. mil. c. p. 402), 158
Vesta, 59, 61–62
Vestal virgins, 61; entombment of, 80n; unchastity of, 69–70, 70n, 74
Vetilius, C. (pr. 147), 118n
Veturius Calvinus, T. (cos. 321, app. 1.1 no. 92), 11n, 35, 36, 39, 40; descendants of, 43
Victi. See Generals, defeated

Victory, ideology of, 54–55, 89, 92, 94, 161–62; religious basis for, 8, 162
Viriathus (Lusitanian general), 20, 21n, 31, 139
Virtus (courage), 1, 2n, 131, 133, 160; and aristocratic status, 154; importance of to defeated generals, 130–31, 175–76; and political careers, 7, 174; role of in defeat, 115; of soldiers, 94–98, 105n
Vitia (errors in ritual), 57, 59, 89n; and military defeat, 67–69. *See also* Cult; Rituals, execution of
Volcanalia (festival), 88
Volusci, 34
Vows, 60

Warfare: and personal glory, 3; religious aspects of, 54–57, 162, 171; and Roman political system, 9, 171–73; strategy in, 95–96, 105

Compositor: Wilsted & Taylor
Text: 10/13 Palatino
Display: Palatino

www.ingramcontent.com/pod-product-compliance
Lightning Source LLC
Chambersburg PA
CBHW021705230426
43668CB00008B/724